Doing Things for Reasons

Doing Things for Reasons

RÜDIGER BITTNER

OXFORD

UNIVERSITY PRESS

2001

OXFORD

UNIVERSITY PRESS

Oxford   New York

Athens   Auckland   Bangkok   Bogotá   Buenos Aires   Cape Town
Chennai   Dar es Salaam   Delhi   Florence   Hong Kong   Istanbul   Karachi
Kolkata   Kuala Lumpur   Madrid   Melbourne   Mexico City   Mumbai   Nairobi
Paris   São Paulo   Shanghai   Singapore   Taipei   Tokyo   Toronto   Warsaw

and associated companies in
Berlin   Ibadan

Copyright © 2001 by Rüdiger Bittner

Published by Oxford University Press, Inc.
198 Madison Avenue, New York, New York 10016

Oxford is a registered trademark of Oxford University Press.

Library of Congress Cataloging-in-Publication Data
Bittner, Rüdiger, 1945–
Doing things for reasons / by Rüdiger Bittner.
p.   cm.
Includes bibliographical references and index.
ISBN 0-19-514364-7
1. Act (Philosophy)   I. Title.
B105.A35 B55 2000
128'.4—dc21   00-058440

1 3 5 7 9 8 6 4 2

Printed in the United States of America
on acid-free paper

Acknowledgments

I gratefully acknowledge the support by institutions that made the present work possible. In particular, sabbaticals granted by Yale University and the University of Bielefeld as well as a full year of research in the School of Economic and Social Studies at the University of East Anglia gave me the necessary time for writing. Oxford University Press (U.K.) gave me permission to reuse, in chapter 10 of this book, material contained in my article "Stronger Reasons," to be published in the volume *Rights, Culture and the Law: Essays after Joseph Raz,* edited by L. Meyer, S. Paulson, and T. Pogge, copyright © 2001 by Oxford University Press.

I have received a great deal of help and encouragement from many people in the course of writing this book. Gitta Schmidt turned the initial text and countless revisions into a finished manuscript. Diana Abad, Sarah Buss, Jonathan Dancy, Christoph Fehige, Harry Frankfurt, David Gauthier, Marco Iorio, Sam Kerstein, Margret Kohlenbach, Jens Kulenkampff, Georg Mols, Thomas Pogge, Amélie O. Rorty, Angus Ross, Nancy Schauber, Susan Sugarman, Jay Wallace, Marcus Willaschek, and three anonymous reviewers for Cambridge and Oxford University Presses read earlier versions of the text, in part or in full, and offered numerous critical comments, suggestions for improvement, or simply further thoughts on the matter; and while I tried to make use of all these as best I could, it is clear that I have not been able fully to do justice to them. But then how could one do justice to all one receives. In any case, it is largely thanks to the care and effort of all these, and perhaps of others still whose cooperation I no longer remember, that this work of mine has become what it is. I am grateful.

The one who helped most, however, is Martin Hollis, who died in February 1998. He was the moving force behind the University of East

Anglia's decision to invite me for a year of research in the School of Economic and Social Studies, in which year the core of this work was written; and during that time and later he accompanied me and my writing with illuminating and incisive criticism and also with a warm solidarity, in spite of the fact that much of what I was up to, and in particular the naturalist line I am pursuing, could not really appeal to him. The present book will not display anything like the grace, versatility, and wit of his writings. By its existence, though, it bears witness to this man's generosity, kindness, and critical spirit.

Contents

Introduction

People do things for reasons. The question of this book is: what are these reasons for which people do things, and how are they related to the actions? And it proposes the answer: a reason is something that is the case in the world, some state of affairs; and what is done for that reason is a response to that state of affairs. There is a broad consensus in the literature that reasons are items, or configurations of items, in the mind. This tenet is rejected here. This book tries to retrieve a thoroughly worldly understanding of reasons and acting for reasons.

The argument runs as follows. The first chapter presents the account of reasons for which people do things that has dominated the literature in recent decades, the account in terms of the agent's desires and beliefs. The chapter argues that this account is not supported by good reasons. In fact, closer inspection raises doubts about its very coherence.

To show that the standard account's dominant position is merely owed to tradition, the second chapter pursues it to its historical source, which is Plato's theory of action. There already the difficulties arise that beset the modern version, but there also the origins of such an understanding of doing things for reasons become apparent, origins, though, from which we may distance ourselves.

The third chapter turns to another, less popular conception of reasons for which one does something, that in terms of principles for action, a conception whose classical protagonist is Kant. Owing to the obscurity, however, of its basic terms, "holding a maxim" and "acting according to a maxim," this conception does not provide a viable understanding of reasons for which people do things.

The constructive part of the argument starts with chapter 4, which presents the basic idea of the conception proposed here: that a reason for which one does something is a state of affairs to which the action is a response.

This idea raises various questions, and the remaining chapters take up these questions one by one. Chapter 5 inquires how reference to a reason, understood as proposed here, can explain an action, since actually we do explain actions by reference to reasons for which they were done. The answer is that reason explanations of actions are historical explanations; and an account of historical explanations is offered to substantiate this answer.

The question of chapter 6 is whether the range of things that are eligible for being a reason for which something was done is limited. The answer is that there is no such limit. The opposing view, that actions and reasons are tied to local systems of meaning, can only be defended by recourse to the notion of a constitutive rule, whereas in fact, it is argued, there are no constitutive rules.

Chapter 7 is intended to explain in what way reasons for which people do things are relative to agents. It is argued that, while reasons for which people do things are normally not qualities of the agent, it does depend on qualities of the agent whether some state of affairs is or is not a reason for which that agent does something.

Chapter 8 proposes an account of reasons people have for doing something, parallel to the account defended here of reasons for which people do something. This account, it is argued, also makes good sense of our practices of deliberation and advice.

Two important objections to this understanding of reasons people have are the topic of chapter 9, that raised by internalists on the one hand, and that raised by defenders of the normativity of reasons on the other. Both objections are unfounded, it is argued. Reasons for doing things need not be tied in any way to appropriate motivation, and they need not be regarded as normative.

Chapter 10 suggests that the various qualities we commonly ascribe to reasons people have mark differences on just one dimension, which is that of strength; and this chapter proposes to understand what it is for one reason to be stronger than another in terms of the states of affairs or events in question being more or less important to the agent.

Chapter 11 considers two kinds of cases where the proposed account of reasons for which people do things seems to fail, namely, cases of doing things for a purpose and cases of doing things just for fun; and argues that, appearances notwithstanding, the account proposed can accommodate these.

Chapter 12, finally, draws the broader picture of rational agents, that is, creatures sometimes doing things for reasons, that emerges from this conception of reasons. It is no doubt a radically impoverished picture compared to how ordinarily, or traditionally, we describe rational agency. Yet it is not an unacceptable picture, a picture in which we cannot recognize ourselves. Or so at least the argument concludes.

The restricted scope of the inquiry should be kept in mind. Doing things for reasons is its central subject matter. True, not its exclusive one: having reasons for doing something and good reasons are considered, as adjacent phenomena, in chapters 8 and 10, and a broader view of a creature doing things for reasons is offered in chapter 12. Still, nothing is included here that should not help, directly or indirectly, to satisfy one who asks those initial questions: what is a reason for which one does something, and how is the reason related to the action? And no more than that should be included here. Thus it is taken for granted that we know what a case of somebody doing something is; and the concept of action in particular is nowhere discussed. Nor is any argument offered in defense of the very first statement that people do things for reasons: that this is so is just assumed. To be sure, with these as with other matters left unconsidered here it may be disputed whether their discussion is not needed to satisfy the questioner, and matters taken up may in turn be deemed superfluous. However that may be, the attempt of the argument just outlined is to stick to a fairly tight regimen of materials considered.

Individual chapters should by and large be separately intelligible, and readers can select a menu according to taste. The criticism of existing views in chapters 1–3 can easily be skipped if one is eager to get to the positive solution advocated in chapter 4. Lack of interest in the historical background of the currently dominant view makes chapter 2 in particular dispensable. The questions or objections discussed in chapters 5 through 11 will strike different readers with different urgency, and may be selected accordingly. The concluding chapter may, finally, be a good place to begin. This is so because the idea of doing things for reasons that emerges little by little in the course of the argument is likely to strike readers as rather unorthodox, and thus it may be helpful to see right from the start to what lengths of unorthodoxy the account presented here is prepared to go.

Translations are mine, except where a translator is mentioned.

Doing Things for Reasons

ONE

Desire and Belief

WHAT is a reason for which somebody does something, and how is the ⟨1⟩
reason related to the action? Alternatively, by reference to what do reason
explanations of actions explain, and how do they succeed in explaining?

THE ANSWER commonly given to these questions is in rough outline this. ⟨2⟩
A reason for which somebody does something is a combination of a desire
and a belief of the agent. Desire and belief are related to the action in
that the belief is one to the effect that the action contributes to the realization of what is desired. You want to drink a beer, and you believe that
going to the refrigerator will contribute to your actually drinking a beer:
your wanting the former and believing the latter may together constitute
the reason for which you go to the refrigerator, if you do. A full reason
explanation of an action therefore specifies a relevant desire of the agent
and the relevant belief about the action's contribution to the realization
of that desire.[1]

THERE are a number of difficulties about this answer. The first is about how ⟨3⟩
broadly to construe the term "desire." Various writers have insisted that,
with "desire" understood narrowly as something like lust or yearning, it is
not true that every reason for which somebody does something involves a
desire.[2] Most of what is done for moral reasons, but also what is done reluc-
tantly for prudential reasons, like going to the dentist, is not longed for by
any means. Nowell-Smith therefore introduced the broader term 'pro-
attitude',[3] and Davidson took up this term, which for him comprises

> desires, wantings, urges, promptings, and a great variety of moral views,
> aesthetic principles, economic prejudices, social conventions, and public

and private goals and values in so far as these can be interpreted as attitudes of an agent directed towards actions of a certain kind.[4]

Others recommend the term 'want' instead of the artificial 'pro-attitude', claiming that it has a sufficiently broad meaning.[5] This claim is widely accepted,[6] but other writers warn that extending the meaning of the term so far makes vacuous the account that uses it.[7] Considering Davidson's list just quoted, one would not want to reject such doubts out of hand. Here, though, they shall be disregarded: the assumption will be that "desire" can be specified so narrowly as to save the desire/belief thesis (§ 2) from vacuity and so broadly as to save it from obvious falsity—whatever that specification may actually be.

4 A SECOND difficulty arises from the fact that we practically never give reason explanations of actions in the terms prescribed by this answer. We do not say that you went to the refrigerator because you wanted to drink a beer and believed that going to the refrigerator would contribute to your drinking one. Often we only say that you went to the refrigerator because you wanted a beer. In other cases, conversely, we omit to mention a desire and only indicate a relevant belief: "I went via Salisbury because I thought it was shorter." In fact, this is a minor difficulty. The standard reply has been to plead elliptical usage, and this is a plausible suggestion. Given one of the two, a desire or a belief, we can very often figure out the other as a matter of course, and that is why we do not mention it explicitly.

5 IN FACT, however, not only do we often just mention one of the two, desire or belief, we often mention neither in explaining people's actions by their reasons. All sorts of things other than the agent's desires and beliefs are admitted in the position of a reason for which somebody does something. Here are a few examples showing the variety of what we ordinarily consider reasons:

- Jonathan takes out the garbage because it is Wednesday.
- I pulled over because the police ordered me to.[8]
- Reggie opened the window to get a breath of fresh air.[9]
- I took a cab, I could not have made it otherwise.
- David was in high spirits, so I stayed much longer.
- Thank you, I do not eat meat.
- I returned to John. It is not right to leave somebody in the lurch like that.

All these may be perfectly satisfactory explanations of what the agent in question does or did, and doubtless they all are reason explanations, but none of them refers to the agent's states, be it desire or belief or anything of the sort.

THE STANDARD reply here has been again to construe such an explanation   6
as tacitly relying on another one that does refer to states of the agent. Davidson called the pair of relevant desire and relevant belief "the primary reason why the agent performed the action,"[10] thereby implicitly admitting that some perfectly acceptable reason explanations of actions, those that are not primary, do not refer to the agent's desires or beliefs.[11] However, he insisted that what he calls primary reasons, the ones consisting of a desire and a belief of the agent, are indeed primary, in this sense: to understand how any reason explains an action, it is necessary and sufficient to see, at least in essential outline, how to construct a primary reason.[12] So nonprimary reasons do explain, but to see their explanatory force we need to have an idea of a primary reason. In Jonathan's case a primary reason might be the desire to get rid of the garbage, or the desire to appear a reliable housemate, together with the belief that, given that it is Wednesday and the garbage collectors come early Thursday morning, taking out the garbage tonight will contribute to satisfying one or the other of these desires. Some story of this sort we need to have in mind, on Davidson's view, in order to understand how its being Wednesday is a reason for Jonathan's doing what he does; and similarly for the other examples.

THE QUESTION now is why this should be so; why it should be the case   7
that a desire and a belief of the agent are, in this sense, primary reasons of actions. As just indicated, the mere observation of our practice of reason explanations does not establish the primacy of desires and beliefs. There is too much variety in what we commonly put forward as reasons for which people do things. Nor do we generally consider reason explanations elliptical whenever something other than a desire and belief of the agent is offered as a reason, as it is in Jonathan's case. A sentence like "Caesar built a bridge across the Rhine" is elliptical. At least, some of us will want to say that strictly speaking not Caesar, but his army built the bridge, or that Caesar did not actually build it, but had it built. Few of us, by contrast, feel a need to say that Jonathan took out the garbage not, strictly speaking, because it is Wednesday, but rather because of a certain desire and belief of his. So the thesis that a desire and a belief are primary reasons, in the sense indicated, does not register an obvious feature of our explanatory practice; it claims that, unobviously, this practice needs to be understood and construed in a certain way. To say this about the thesis is

not an objection, to be sure. It is just grounds for requesting an argument for it.

8 As THIS is the question to be pursued now, namely, why an agent's desire and belief should be considered a primary reason, a further problem about the desire/belief account of reasons can be shelved for the time being. This is the problem whether reasons for which people do things, specified as a desire and a belief combined, are also causes of the action; whether reason explanations in terms of desire and belief are causal explanations. This problem led to an extended if, on the whole, inconclusive discussion. It can be shelved here, because much of its interest depends on the truth of the primacy thesis, that is, the thesis that all reason explanations of actions depend, in the sense given, on explanations of actions in terms of suitable desires and beliefs. If primacy does not hold; if explanations of actions in terms of desires and beliefs are just one kind of reason explanation, alongside the others rather than underlying them, then the causality thesis tells us only that reasons of one kind are causes; and while this will be news for those who argued on conceptual grounds that a reason cannot be a cause,[13] it is not particularly breathtaking for the rest of us. That *some* reasons are causes is not the interesting thesis we were promised. The interesting thesis is that all reasons are. That thesis, however, is not within argumentative reach if there is not something like a standard normal form of reasons, as the primacy thesis holds that there is; if we are left with the garden variety of what our ordinary understanding admits as reasons. Davidson in his 1963 article, at any rate, clearly distinguishes between the primacy and the causality theses, and primacy comes first both in the exposition and in the argument, which suggests that it is the basis for the latter.[14] As long as primacy is not established, then, there is no need to worry about causality. The present question is whether primacy can be established.

9 PRIMACY is a bold claim. If you maintain that the primary reason for any action lies in, let us say, a feeling of anxiety and a perceptual memory, people will find it difficult to believe you. Some explanations no doubt use such a pair, you will be told, but to convince us that all are based on such a pattern will take quite a bit of argument. Things would seem to be similar with respect to the desire/belief thesis. Nobody will deny that explanations using this pair are sometimes offered, but argument is needed to show that all have to be based on an explanation of this form. It is not evident that explaining Jonathan's taking out the garbage by the fact that it is Wednesday is based, in the way indicated, (§ 6) on explaining his

taking out the garbage in terms of his desires and beliefs. Yet while argument is needed here, those who favor some version of the desire/belief thesis spend remarkably little time explicitly defending it.

DAVIDSON's essay "Actions, Reasons, and Causes" of 1963 is a case in point.   10
Support for the claim that one's desires and beliefs constitute the primary reason for which one does something is initially promised,[15] but actually never delivered. Here is what may seem to be an argument:

> 'I want that gold watch in the window' is not a primary reason and explains why I went into the store only because it suggests a primary reason—for example, that I wanted to buy the watch.[16]

That "I want that gold watch in the window" is not a primary reason, nor, to be more precise, the expression of the desire part of a primary reason, follows from Davidson's definition of a primary reason. A primary reason involves a pro attitude toward an action of a certain kind, with the agent believing that his or her action is of that kind; and the gold watch in the window is not a kind of action. Nevertheless, "I want that gold watch in the window" does explain, according to this passage, the agent's going into the store. So Davidson does recognize successful explanations of actions by nonprimary reasons, as suggested earlier (§ 6). Presumably, such nonprimary reasons need not even involve a state of the agent, as "I want that gold watch in the window" does. "There is a splendid gold watch in the window" should do just as well as an explanation of the action by a nonprimary reason. However, the explanatory force of nonprimary reasons is owed, Davidson tells us, to the fact that indicating them suggests another reason that *is* primary. Yet why this should be so we are not told. We do not learn why "I want that gold watch in the window" or "There is a splendid gold watch in the window" cannot stand on their own feet as explanations. Thus in fact there is no argument for the primacy thesis given here. The thesis is just reasserted for the particular case at hand.

THIS, it may be objected, is an uncharitable reading. Yes, Davidson does   11
not state explicitly why nonprimary reasons owe their explanatory force to their suggesting an explanation in terms of primary reasons. He does not, however, because it is so easy to see why. "I want that gold watch in the window" or again "There is a splendid gold watch in the window" do not explain specifically the agent's walking into the store and buying the watch. They could explain as well the agent's going home and making plans for breaking into the store at night. "I want to buy the watch," by

contrast, is specific. It explains what the agent did and nothing else. Hence this is the explanation that really explains what happened, and it is only by suggesting this explanation that the nonprimary reasons in turn explain.

12   HOWEVER, this defense does not accord with Davidson's explicit doctrine. A few lines before the passage just quoted he insists:

> Any one of an indefinitely large number of actions would satisfy the want and can be considered equally eligible as its object.

Hence, equally, any one of an indefinitely large number of actions could be explained by reference to that want. So it is not true that "I want to buy the watch" explains what the agent did and nothing else. Had the agent entered the store with the left foot first rather than with the right one, as in fact he did, that action would have been explained by the agent's wanting to buy the watch just as well. Thus the alleged difference between "I want that gold watch in the window" and "I want to buy the watch" disappears. Each of the two explains what the agent actually did, but each of the two also could explain an indefinitely large range of other things the agent might have done. Explanation by primary reasons, then, is not privileged by specificity; and so we still have not heard grounds for thinking that the explanatory force of nonprimary reasons is borrowed from the primary reasons suggested by them. To be sure, none of this is to deny that, as Davidson writes in an earlier passage,

> whenever someone does something for a reason . . . he can be character-ized as (a) having some sort of pro attitude toward actions of a certain kind, and (b) believing (or knowing, perceiving, noticing, remembering) that his action is of that kind.[17]

Very well, suppose that an agent *can* be so characterized. This does nothing to show that so to characterize agents makes us see, let alone is indispensable to make us see, why they do what they do. It does nothing to establish the truth of the primacy thesis.

13   OTHER authors are as short on argument on this point as Davidson is. Indeed, unlike Davidson, many even fail to realize that argument is needed here. Colin McGinn rather disarmingly asserts that a reason by which we explain an action

> is best conceived as a desire and belief in a certain sort of combination.[18]

Why it should best be conceived in this way we are not told. Nor do we learn the reasons for Martha Nussbaum's emphatic statement that it is of the nature of action that it is determined by a desire and a belief.[19]

People working in neighboring fields like philosophy of mind similarly rely on this assumption:

It seems essential to our concept of action that our bodies are moved in appropriate ways by our wants and beliefs.[20]

The point is taken as obvious, but in fact it is not, given the variety of what we ordinarily admit as reasons for which people do things (§ 5).

MICHAEL Smith is one writer who, recognizing the need for argument here, set himself the task of giving explicit grounds for saying that reasons for which people do things always consist of a desire and a belief.[21] Actually, Smith wishes to prove an even stronger result, namely, that motivating reasons, as he calls them, not just reasons for which people do things, consist of desires and beliefs; the difference being that a motivating reason for Smith is only potentially explanatory, which is to say that it need not in effect lead to appropriate action, for example when it is overridden.[22] This broader concept of motivating reasons, however, carries with it problems of its own that need not be considered here, and to avoid these the argument may better be restricted to reasons for which people really act. So recast, it runs in outline like this: 14

1. Having a reason for which one does something is among other things having a goal.
2. Having a goal is being in a state with which the world must fit.
3. Being in a state with which the world must fit is desiring.
4. Hence, having a reason for which one does something is among other things desiring.[23]

ACTUALLY, this is less than we were promised, indeed less on two counts. 15
For one thing, the conclusion only states that having a reason for which one does something involves desiring, whereas the argument was meant to show that it involves both desiring and believing. It might be replied that this is not an important difference. Once it is settled, one might say, that having a reason for which one does something always involves among other things having a desire, the rest of the way toward the full desire/belief thesis will be easy. Actually this is not so. The desire/belief thesis says that a reason for which somebody does something is a combination of a desire and a belief suitably related (§ 2). The thesis presupposes, therefore, that desires and beliefs are different things. That is to say, it presupposes that there is nothing that is both a belief and a desire, and it may fairly be taken to presuppose as well that having a belief never entails

having a desire; for otherwise talk of a combination, or of a pair,[24] of desire and belief would be misleading to the point of falsity. However, these assumptions have been called into question in recent debates. It has been argued that to do justice to the experience of moral agents we have to admit states of mind that are cognitive, in that the agent has a conception of what the circumstances are, but also involve a desire to take appropriate action.[25] To be sure, Smith rejects this idea,[26] but, contrary to his suggestion,[27] he does not reject it on the strength of the argument outlined in the last paragraph; he needs to put forward additional considerations. This emerges clearly from a recent critical article by Margaret Little.[28] Defending, against Smith, the idea that some beliefs of moral agents are, or entail, desires, she nevertheless finds no difficulty in accepting Smith's account of desiring, as contained in the argument just presented.[29] So even if that argument succeeds, the desire/belief thesis is not thereby saved as well, as Smith intended it to be, for the very difference between beliefs and desires may still be doubted.

16 SECOND, however, even if that argument already showed the desire/belief thesis to be correct, this would not suffice, contrary again to Smith's suggestion,[30] to establish a Humean theory of motivation, which says that reasoning "is not by itself capable of giving rise to a motivation to act."[31] Reinterpreting Thomas Nagel's distinction between motivated and unmotivated desires,[32] Jay Wallace has shown that the rationalist opponent of the Humean theory can accept the desire/belief thesis without jeopardizing the substance of the rationalist idea.[33] Smith's argument was to prove that any reason for which somebody does something involves a desire, but as long as that desire itself sometimes admits of an explanation purely in terms of rational principles, the rationalist has got all the ground he needs to build on his case.[34] The following discussion, however, will disregard these further problems that obstruct, first, the path from statement 4 (§ 14) to the full desire/belief thesis and, second, from the desire/belief thesis to the Humean theory of motivation. The question to be considered is only whether Smith's argument does establish statement 4.

17 IT DOES not: all the premises 1–3 appear doubtful. As for the first, Smith claims that it has the status of a conceptual truth. He claims that we understand what it is for someone to do something for a reason precisely by thinking of that person as having some goal.[35] This claim is unsupported. Viewing the large variety of things we refer to as reasons for which people do something (§ 5), it is not evident by any means that the agent's having some goal is what these cases have in common, let alone that it is

that by reference to which we understand all these different things to be reasons. A goal is a state of affairs such that somebody does something, or would do something given suitable circumstances, in order to bring it about. In Aristotelian language, a goal is a 'for the sake of which'. To explain metaphor by metaphor, a goal is what an agent shoots for in action. One of the examples given earlier (§ 5) clearly displays the relationship in question. There is the state of affairs of Reggie's getting a breath of fresh air, and there is his action of opening a window, and they are related in that Reggie does the latter in order to bring about the former. Other examples, however, are difficult to construe on this pattern. What might be the goal of the person returning to John for the reason that it is not right to leave somebody in the lurch like that? That John's situation be improved? In that case the person could have said just that: "I returned to John so as to make him better off," and mention of what is right and not right to do would have been otiose. Or that there be one more right action in the world? That seems to be a strained interpretation, alien to what people normally have in mind who speak like that. It would appear more natural to say that this person did what she did just for the reason that it was the right thing to do, and that there was no state of affairs she aimed to bring about thereby. Much the same holds for the case of the person pulling over because the police ordered her to. True, sometimes such a person may have a goal in pulling over, like giving the appearance of a law-abiding citizen or avoiding police violence. Sometimes, though, she may not. She may notice that the police are signaling to her, and simply for that reason she may pull over and stop. She does so intentionally, no doubt; she is not reacting to police signals the way people blink in strong light. Yet there is no state of affairs she is shooting for in doing what she does. She does it for a reason, true, but not for the sake of anything. In view of such examples, where an interpretation in terms of goals of the agent does not come naturally, Smith's claim that to have a reason for which one does something is among other things to have a goal would need explicit argument, and that has not been given. (More on goals and reasons in chapter 11, §§ 278–282.)

Smith might reply as follows: 18

> I will grant, if only for the argument's sake, that the two agents just considered do not have a *further* goal in doing what they do. Even so they have a goal. Their goal is their action itself. What they are shooting for is a situation in which, in the first case, the speaker returns to John, and in which, in the second case, the speaker pulls over her car. And something of this sort will hold whenever one is doing something for a reason: at least the action itself one aims to bring about. So it is true

after all that having a reason for which one does something involves having a goal.

This is only true if the term "goal" is given a broader meaning than it ordinarily has. In the ordinary sense one does something in order to reach a goal, and so the goal is not the action, but what results from the action, if all goes well. A goal after all is primarily the terminal point of a race: hence it could not be the race. Take that person again who returned to John for the reason that one must not leave someone in the lurch like that: it would sound like a lame joke to say of her that in returning for that reason she had a goal, namely, to return. Similarly for the driver stopped by the police: one just would not say, except as a joke, that, in pulling over because the police ordered her to, she yet had a goal, namely, to pull over. To be sure, Smith may stipulate the term "goal" to mean whatever it takes to render statement 1 of his argument true, or indeed conceptually true, but clearly such an empty victory is not what he is after, for then statement 1 would not accomplish any material step in the argument. Taking words in their ordinary meaning, however, it does not seem correct to say that having a reason for which one does something involves having a goal.

19 THE SECOND premise, that to have a goal is to be in a state with which the world must fit, derives from an idea of G. E. M. Anscombe.[36] She contrasted the shopping list a man receives from his wife with a detective's record of the man's purchases: if there is a discrepancy between the shopping list and what the man actually buys, the mistake is in the man's performance (barring cases in which items on the list are unavailable, or the man changes his mind, etc.), whereas if there is a discrepancy between the detective's record and what the man buys, the mistake is in the detective's list. For Smith there is a corresponding contrast between two kinds of mental states: those that like the detective's list must fit the world, beliefs being the prime example, and those like the shopping list with which the world must fit. As Smith readily admits, this is a metaphorical way of speaking: he explains it as follows. A mental state that must fit the world is a state that, in the presence of a perception that the intentional object of that state is not a fact, tends to go out of existence, whereas a state with which the world must fit is a state that, in the presence of such a perception, tends to endure, disposing the subject in that state to bring it about that the intentional object of the state becomes a fact.[37] What the second premise claims, then, is that having a goal is a state of the latter sort. If you have the goal of drinking a pint of beer, then you are in a state that tends to endure in the face of your perception that actually you

are not drinking a pint of beer and disposes you to bring it about that you *are* drinking a pint of beer.

ONE PROBLEM with this explanation lies in the term "perception." A perception, one would think, is a seeing or hearing or the like, but for many goals of people there is no perceiving, in this ordinary sense, of the fact that the state of affairs aimed at does not actually hold. I do not perceive, in this ordinary sense of the word, I just know, that I have not written the best book in philosophy of the century, while I might well have the goal to do so. I. L. Humberstone, in a discussion of Smith's earlier version of his idea,[38] therefore proposed to read Smith's "perception" more broadly to mean a coming to believe or coming to know.[39] As Humberstone pointed out, however, this reading leads into trouble as well.[40] We wanted to know how states that must fit the world and states with which the world must fit differ. The answer now refers to states, that is, believing or knowing, that themselves are supposed to have one direction of fit, namely, the former. This makes the answer uninformative. The explanation now amounts to this: states that must fit the world are sensitive to other states that must fit the world, but states with which the world must fit are not sensitive to those states that must fit the world. (Crudely, beliefs are sensitive to other beliefs, while desires are not sensitive to beliefs.) That does not give us any grip on what it is for a state to be such that it must fit the world or to be such that the world must fit with it.

WAIVE this objection and take as sufficient our vague understanding of what it is for a state to be one the world must fit: it is still questionable whether having a goal actually is one of those states. If the world refuses to fit, if for instance you are still sitting there without your pint of beer, who is going to call the world to task? For one thing, Smith says, your having that goal tends to endure in the face of things being otherwise. Actually, it may not endure. There are those who, frustrated, give up their goals. True, they may be taken care of by Smith's saying that the state of having a goal not endures, but tends to endure. Yet to say that the state tends to endure, but often doesn't is too weak to capture the idea, however vaguely understood, of a state being such that the world must fit with it. One would think that a state with which the world must fit should definitely not go out of existence in the face of things being otherwise, as the state of having a goal sometimes does. In the second place, Smith says, your having the goal disposes you to realize it. Again, though, it may not: your forces may not suffice, you may have better things to do, and so on. True, that is again taken care of by Smith's saying not that having a goal makes you realize it, but that it disposes you to do so. Yet then little

20

21

remains again of the idea that the world must fit your state of having that goal. If you are an unsuccessful goal-pursuer, the world actually does not fit your state of having that goal, and so it is false to say that it must. What may be true is only this: having a goal is a state that, more often than not, is followed by people realizing that goal. It is certainly doubtful that even that is true, but even if true, it is too weak for building anything on. In particular, it is too weak to support premise 3. If being in a state with which the world must fit amounts to no more than being in a state that has a tendency to be followed by a certain kind of action, then being in a state with which the world must fit is not desiring, contrary to what premise 3 claims. It might be, after all, that mere thinking of the Sahara desert has a tendency to be followed by people grabbing a bottle of beer. If that is so, mere thinking of the Sahara qualifies, on the weak reading that remained, as a state with which the world must fit, but in fact it is not a desire.

22   IT MAY be said in defense of Smith's premise 2 that this is to read "must fit" in an uncharitably narrow sense. What is meant, clearly, is not that one's having a goal is followed, by necessity, by one's realizing it, but that somebody's having a goal ought to be followed by realization. However, this is again not true in general. Not all the goals people have ought to be followed by realization.[41] Some ought, some ought not, it depends on the goal. To be sure, judging from the point of view of the particular goal, it ought to be realized, but that is a reading so charitable as to drain premise 2 of any content. "Having a goal is a state that, from the point of view of that goal, ought to be followed by realization" is to say no more than "Having a goal is to be aiming for its realization," and nothing of interest will follow from a tautology like that.

23   To TURN to premise 3 of Smith's argument, then, which says that being in a state with which the world must fit is desiring; suppose, for the sake of the argument, that there is an intelligible idea of a state with which the world must fit, and that it yields a reading of premise 2 strong enough to give premise 3 a chance of being true. (§ 20 was to show that the former, while §§ 21–22 were to show that the latter is false.) Now the basis on which Smith rests premise 3 is a dispositional conception of desire. According to this conception, to desire something is to have a set of dispositions, a disposition to do one thing under one kind of circumstances, another thing under another kind of circumstances, and so on, where circumstances will include, among other things, beliefs of the agent as to how things can be done, and also other desires.[42] For instance, to desire to drink a pint of beer is, on this conception, to be disposed to go to the

refrigerator if one thinks that this is the way to get one, and to be disposed to go to the basement if one sees that as the way to do it, and to be disposed to go to the pub, unless one hates the walk, if that is what one thinks will work, and so on. Smith's claim now is: being in a state with which the world must fit amounts to having such a set of dispositions. This can be seen, Smith suggests, by considering the alternative, a phenomenological conception of desire, as he calls it.[43] On this conception, desires are just a kind of feeling. Whatever the merits and demerits of this view, it is clear that such a feeling does not, explaining metaphor by metaphor once again, wait for the world to play its part. Such a feeling just occurs; and if the thing desired also occurs, this is only a further event, not something through which the world fits a state of the agent. On the dispositional view, by contrast, the agent is disposed to bring it about, one way or another depending on the circumstances, that the desired thing occurs, so its occurring is a fulfillment of the agent's state of desire: it is a case of the world fitting such a state.

THIS reasoning is unconvincing. Granted for the moment the dispositional conception of desire: that does not turn the occurrence of the desired event into a fulfillment of the agent's state, into an instance of the world fitting with it. As long as I merely desire that pint of beer, then on the present account of desiring there is this fact about me: I am such as, among other things, to go to the refrigerator in case I think that is the best way to get a pint of beer. Then, when I do get going, there is this fact about me: I both think this is the best way to get a pint of beer, and I do go to the refrigerator. So first a conditional is true of me, then both its antecedent and consequent are. However, there is no reason for saying that with the latter state the world fits the former. A true conditional in no sense is waiting for its antecedent and consequent to become true. It does not care. Less metaphorically, my state of being such that, if I think the best way to get a pint of beer is to go to the refrigerator, then I do go to the refrigerator, and my state of both thinking the former and doing the latter, are just different states, distinct existences in Hume's terminology, the same way desire and realization of the state desired were distinct existences on the phenomenological conception. So the dispositional conception of desire does not do any better than the phenomenological conception in making sense of the idea that desiring is a state with which the world must fit. The dispositional conception of desire, therefore, does not help Smith in establishing premise 3.

AND THE dispositional conception of desire is dubious in itself. It may be true, on the one hand, that whenever I have a desire, then I am disposed

24

25

to do certain things in case I hold certain opinions on what is the best means for what. It may be true, that is, that when I desire that pint of beer, I am disposed to go to the refrigerator in case I think that is the best way to get it. However, there are cases where this holds true only vacuously, for lack of suitable opinions. Very young people, for instance, clearly desire things, or indeed one thing, namely, to be fed, but they do not have any beliefs as to how to bring it about. The point is not that they do not have any beliefs. Perhaps they do believe that milk tastes fine, perhaps they don't, that is hard to tell. The point is that they do not have beliefs as to the ways and means to get milk. They cry because they are hungry, but they do not employ their crying for the purpose of getting somebody to feed them. Thus G. E. M. Anscombe's famous line, quoted again and again in the literature: "The primitive sign of wanting is trying to get,"[44] seems remarkably mistaken. Trying to get is precisely not a primitive sign of wanting, but a fairly sophisticated one. To show that sign, you already have to be in the business of doing one thing so as to get some other thing, and that is an accomplishment. It might be argued against this that babies do not desire to be fed after all, that they only cry because of the pain they feel when they lack food.[45] In fact, though, people find it perfectly natural to speak of a baby who cries as wanting something, and, for that matter, of a baby who falls asleep after feeding as satisfied. Nor are people conscious of any metaphorical twist in speaking this way, the way they *are* conscious of twisting language when they complain about the stubbornness of their computer. People by and large take it to be literally true that babies want to be fed. So the burden of proof would lie with those who deny that this is so, and it is difficult to see what argument they could give. Allowing, then, desires of babies, it will indeed be true to say that, when they desire to be fed, they normally cry in case they think that is the best way to get fed, but it will be true only vacuously, since they think no such thing. Now it is hard to believe that what is described by a conditional holding only vacuously in their case should *be* their desire. One would think there is more to their desire than the fact that, if they were to think, as they do not, that crying is the best way to get what they want, they would cry. And if in their case there is more to the desire than the truth of such a conditional, so there is in our case, since their desires and ours are the same sort of thing.

26   It is not true, on the other hand, that whenever one has a set of dispositions of the kind indicated, then one has a desire. Think of the man in Kant's example[46] who is decided to take away his life once continuing it promises more hardship than pleasure. Of that man it may well be true to say that right now he is disposed to poison himself if he thinks that is

the best way to kill himself, and if some other conditions hold of him, for instance, that he thinks his prospects are irrevocably bleak; and it may also be true to say that right now he is disposed to hang himself if he thinks that is the best way to kill himself, and some other conditions hold of him; and so on. This man has the dispositions required in the dispositional conception of desire, but for all that he may not, right now, desire to kill himself. He is only prepared to do it under certain conditions, and prepared to do it in a certain way if he thinks that is the best way, but that is clearly a far cry from desiring it.

Concluding the critique of Smith's argument, then: to have a set of dis-   27
positions of the kind indicated is not sufficient for having the appropriate desire (§ 26); and there are further reasons for thinking that a desire does not consist in a set of such dispositions (§ 25). Even if a desire does consist in them, though, premise 3 is no better off: the dispositional conception of desire does not support the idea that being in a state with which the world must fit is desiring (§ 24). Premise 2, in turn, is unclear, because we are not told what it is to be in a state with which the world must fit (§ 20). Staying with our vague initial understanding of the phrase, the premise is false: it is not the case that the world must fit with our having goals (§§ 21–22). Premise 1, finally, is unsupported: there is no good ground to suppose that all reason explanations of actions are teleological (§§ 17–18).

There are two further arguments, offered by David Lewis and John Col-   28
lins,[47] for holding that a reason for action includes a desire of the agent. The assumption that reasons could be just beliefs is incompatible, according to Lewis, with standard Bayesian decision theory, and it is incompatible, according to Collins, with a nonquantitative decision theory as well. These arguments do not need to be considered here.[48] The decision theories to which these arguments appeal are already cast in terms of desires and beliefs,[49] and whether a conception in terms of desires and beliefs can account for action is precisely what is at issue here. To claim that "surely decision theory is fundamentally right," as Lewis does,[50] is to beg the question in theory of action.

The question was (§ 7) why desire and belief should be primary reasons   29
of action, and the result of this survey is that, for all we learn in the literature, we do not know why. No good philosophical arguments have been offered for this thesis, even though it does not reflect our explanatory practice (§ 5). Neither did people support it by psychological, let alone neurological research. The idea seems to be just common opinion, with

nobody really knowing any grounds for it. Under these circumstances, the only way to reach a reasoned decision about its accuracy seems to be to complete the story. After all, the thesis that a desire and a belief form the primary reason for which somebody does something belongs to a whole picture of agency. Unfolding that picture in some more detail should provide the suitable basis for an assessment of the idea.

30   THE NATURAL question to ask here is this: why should it take just these two, desire and belief, to make a primary reason for which somebody does something? What is the specific function of each that would justify the privilege of that pair to constitute an agent's reason? To this question there is a standard answer in the literature. Robert Audi writes,

> an action for a reason is grounded in a guiding belief and a motivating want,[51]

and according to G. H. von Wright,

> want is what *moves* and understanding (of causal connections) is what *steers* the movement.[52]

So motivation and guidance are the respective tasks of desire and belief. Motivation is etymologically linked to moving: a motive, presumably, is what moves an agent to act.[53] It is what Kant calls a "Triebfeder,"[54] literally a driving spring, of action. Guidance, on the other hand, is what makes some moving thing take the right way: the pilot guides a ship into port. So the picture of agency emerging here seems to be this. I come to desire, never mind why, to have dinner. The desire for dinner is what sets me into motion. In this case it is what sets me going to slice onions. However, desire could not move me to do this without belief's guidance. The belief in this case is one to the effect that, under the circumstances, slicing onions is the best, or the only, or the most effective way to the state of my having dinner. This belief guides me, or my desire, toward onion slicing. Desire unsupported by belief leaves me longing for dinner, but helpless to reach it. This is why the belief is also called a connecting belief in the literature.[55] There is the desired dinner and here I am desiring it, but the two of us will not come together without belief stepping in and telling me that slicing onions is the way to reach dinner. (At least, the two of us will not normally come together without such a belief: occasionally, we reach what we desire by banging around mindlessly.) With another image that is frequently invoked, people do what they do "in the light of their beliefs."[56] As without light you are unlikely to find the watch for which you are searching at night, so without your belief you are unlikely to get the dinner you are after: with light you grab the watch from behind the book, and with the belief you start slicing onions.

YET THIS is not a coherent story.[57] Desire moves one to act, it says. It also says that desire on its own does not reach action. These two things do not go together. If desire by itself is a helpless longing for the goal, then it is not true that it moves one to act. What moves one to act, moves one to this or that action, and so it does reach action. Or is the idea that, not desire on its own, but only desire accompanied by belief, moves one to act? Then we are back where we started (§ 30), without an answer to the question what desire and belief specifically contribute to action. Or is the idea that desire by itself does move one to act, that it does reach action, but not, barring extraordinary luck, the right one that leads to the goal? That would mean that my desire for dinner might as well move me to do the laundry if belief did not step in and tell me that slicing onions is more promising. Then, however, it is not clear in what sense this moving force would be a desire for dinner. It would rather be a readiness to do anything. True, sometimes our desire for something, and in particular our desire to eat, gets us into a state of restlessness where we are ready to do more or less anything. In this sense it does happen that through a desire for dinner one comes to do the laundry. Still, desire *is not* such a readiness to do anything, it is only sometimes accompanied by it. Desire has a specific target, like dinner. Once we take it as mere energy, indeterminate as to which sort of action it sets off, we no longer have desire in mind.

THE INCOHERENCE of the story shows in the incompatible roles it gives to desire. In the first role, desire "sets the goal," as Audi puts it.[58] Thus, anyone who desires something is thereby one who has a goal. Of desire so conceived it may well be said that by itself it does not reach action. People frequently have the goal of getting dinner, while for one reason or another they do not take action that has, or is thought to have, this result.[59] In the second role desire is what moves the person who does take action. Of desire so conceived, however, it cannot be said that by itself it does not reach action. Reaching action is precisely its role. Yet desire so conceived does not do such a thing as set a goal. It is just a motor, a motor for onion-slicing in the present example. Getting dinner, the goal that the slicing of onions is supposed to serve, is immaterial for desire so conceived. This desire just consists in setting the cook moving.

No DOUBT it will be replied that so to separate the two conceptions is to miss the nature of desiring, which does not either set a goal or move the

31

32

33

agent, but by setting a goal moves the agent. However, this is to explain what is unclear by what is downright obscure. We do not understand how marking out a certain state of affairs, for instance that of my having dinner, as my goal, as a thing to be brought about by me, is also to move me to action, under certain circumstances. As long as we do not understand that, to declare that desire fills both roles is to hide behind a word. The following sentences by Alfred Mele display the obscurity in question:

> The functional connection between wanting and action has at least two dimensions. First, the representational content of an agent's want to A identifies a practical goal (or subgoal), the agent's A-ing, so that "action-wants" provide some practical direction, as it were. Second, wants have an inclinational or conative dimension. They incline agents to act on them.[60]

Never mind that Mele is speaking of wanting here, not of desiring. The important point is that, while he describes wanting in these two "dimensions" that correspond to the two conceptions of desire just distinguished, he fails to give any hint as to how these two things are linked. Traditionally they are indeed supposed to be linked. Yet without an account of how they are we are no better off with this story than with the fairy tale that also fails to tell us how it is that the dead brother *is* the bird singing so beautifully.[61]

34 THE INCOHERENCE of the story shows also in the incompatible roles it gives to belief. The duality of roles is hidden here in an ambiguity of the notion of a "guiding" belief. On the one hand, you can guide me to the post office with a leash, adjusting my movements in such a way that they eventually bring me to the post office. This is how one guides a horse and indeed, recalling von Wright's metaphor (§ 30), how one steers a boat. To understand belief's guiding role in this way accords well with the idea that suitable action occurs only thanks to such a determining influence: without it the agent is a boat adrift. What one fails to understand is how belief could perform this function. To believe is to hold true: how could my holding something true be such as to channel my movements into an action suitable under the circumstances? If I am convinced that slicing onions is the best way to get myself something for dinner tonight, how could my being so convinced also steer me into slicing onions? The conviction and the steering are different things, and in the absence of an account of their connection it is again just fairy tale to have belief fulfill both functions.

ALTERNATIVELY, you can guide me to the post office by telling me where   35
to go. This understanding gives the fact its due that it is belief that is
invoked here to guide action. Belief can, with good metaphorical sense,
be said to tell me that slicing onions is the way to get dinner, just as,
literally, you tell me that such and such is the way to the post office.
However, on this understanding in turn the determining influence ascribed to belief remains unintelligible. What I learn from you is only that
this is the way to the post office, and that piece of information makes me
more knowledgeable, it does not set me going there. To be sure, thanks
to what you tell me I do in fact turn my steps in that direction, but that
is because I am myself an agent acting for reasons; and that fact must not
be used to elucidate the role of belief in action, or else we will be going
in a circle, or will keep putting homunculi inside homunculi. After all,
what it is to be such an agent was precisely the question.

THE METAPHOR of "acting in the light of one's beliefs" throws the difficulty   36
into relief. It makes good metaphorical sense to speak of a belief as casting
light on features of the agent's situation. There, for instance, is the fact
that slicing onions is the best way for me to get something to eat tonight,
and while this is a fact whether I think it is or not, my believing that it
is puts it into the light of the stage where the action is. Yet light does not
guide. I see that slicing onions is the way to dinner, but that, so far, has
nothing to do with action: I am enlightened, but not guided. To be sure,
using this piece of knowledge I can guide myself to suitable action, but
this phrase is just what we wanted to understand. So the problem about
"guiding belief" is that where there is guidance, there is no reason to
ascribe it to belief, and where there is belief, there is no reason to think
of it as guiding.

THE GUIDING belief has been taken in this argument to guide the person.   37
It may be hoped that better sense can be made of this notion if what is
guided is taken to be, not the person, but the person's desire. Here the
guidance would take place only inside the person. The idea would be that
a desire for something to eat generates, under the influence of the belief
that slicing onions is the best way to get something to eat, the desire to
slice onions, and that desire then moves the person actually to slice onions.[62] Strictly speaking, this would not be an account of reasons for which
people do things in terms of desires and beliefs, but in terms of desires
alone, since the agent in the example slices onions for the reason that he
desires to do so. Still, that he has this desire is due to his desire for
something to eat together with the belief that slicing onions is the best

way to get something to eat, and so it is more illuminating to mention these two when indicating the reason for which this agent does what he does. Indeed, while strictly true, it could be misleading to refer only to the agent's desire for slicing onions when indicating his reason. It could well suggest that it is an underived desire of the agent, some particular fancy of his, to be slicing onions, and that would look like a rather strange state of mind. That is not his case, though. He has formed the desire for slicing onions from the desire to have something to eat under the guidance of the belief that this is the best way to get something to eat.

38 ONE MAY well wonder how reliable this mechanism is supposed to be. After all, there are those who, eager to eat and knowing full well that slicing onions is the way, are yet reluctant to do it, which would imply, on an ordinary understanding of these terms, that they do not desire to do it. Yet the real trouble with this version of the idea is that it does not improve matters. The question about belief guiding the person was why her being informed about the best way toward her goal should also move her in that direction. The question about belief guiding desire is, similarly, why the person's being informed about the best way toward her goal should also lead her to form a desire for going that way. As before, belief is asked to do two jobs here, providing information and altering one's desire profile, and an intelligible link between these two would have to be shown to make such a story acceptable.

39 THE IDEA of belief providing guidance, then, does not in the end make sense; and as the idea of motivation by desire similarly fell apart, with desire's setting a goal being one thing and its moving the agent another (§ 32), it seems fair to conclude that the picture of agency underlying the desire/belief thesis is incoherent (§ 31). That picture needed unfolding because the desire/belief thesis itself, in spite of its popularity (§ 2), has not received adequate justification. Most writers merely assert it to be true (§ 13), and the only sustained argument for it that has been offered, Michael Smith's, appears unsuccessful (§§ 14–27). It would seem, then, that the dominant view on what reasons are for which people do things does not stand up.

TWO

Sources of the Desire/Belief Thesis

40 It is not to be expected that these considerations will prevail against the mass of philosophical orthodoxy backing the desire/belief thesis. So that mass itself needs to be addressed: why is it that the conception of reasons for which people do things as consisting of a desire and a belief enjoys such broad support, given that the preceding arguments at least show the idea to be dubious? It may be suspected that this is in part because the idea is traditional; that contemporary philosophical orthodoxy backs it in part because it is the received view. This chapter elaborates on this suspicion, not in order to prove it, as that would require extensive historical research, but at least to give it some plausibility. The task is to delineate in some more detail the tradition that may be taken to lie behind the dominant view on reasons for which people do things and in particular to illuminate the origins of that tradition. Doing so may help to loosen the grip of that view on our understanding.

41 It is generally agreed that David Hume's work is the source from which modern accounts of reasons as pairs of desire and belief derive. Indeed, Hume devotes one section of the *Treatise* to proving

> *first*, that reason alone can never be a motive to any action of the will; and *secondly*, that it can never oppose passion in the direction of the will;[1]

and the moral theory offered in book 3 of the *Treatise* is built on, and explicitly refers to (457, 458), this doctrine. The connection between Hume's two theses just quoted and an account of reasons as pairs of desire and belief can be traced as follows. First, disregard the second of the two theses, since it is a mere consequence of the first, as Hume plausibly argues

(414–415). Second, take "motive" to refer to a reason for which somebody does something, since "motive" in a broad sense may cover anything that could be referred to in an appropriate answer to the question why an agent did something. Third, replace the word "reason" by "belief," for though Hume declares that "reason is the discovery of truth or falshood" (458), his examples (416–417) show that he intends his theory to account for cases in which the agent does not discover truth or falsehood, but acts on mistaken assumptions. Fourth, read Hume's denial that belief *alone* is ever a reason for an action as his affirmation that belief together with desire is. This last bit of interpretation is borne out by his statement

> that the impulse arises not from reason, but is only directed by it; (414)[2]

for what the impulse does arise from is desire or, as he puts it in the same paragraph, "aversion or propensity." So by desire we are carried to take that action that belief directs us to take: this is in different words the story of motivating desire and guiding belief considered earlier (§ 30).

42   HUME's famous statement,

> Reason is and ought only to be the slave of the passions, and can never pretend to any other office than to serve and obey them, (415)

needs to be understood in the light of this doctrine. Commentators tend to take this statement as the epitome of Hume's conception of reason, but in fact it tells us very little. It informs us about reason's subordinate status, but above all we want to know which job reason does. Slaves work, after all, and sometimes their work is indispensable to the running of the business. So the statement does not mean that reason takes no part in determining action. Reason does take part in determining action, since it directs the impulse of desire to suitable, or supposedly suitable, action. More controversially, perhaps, the statement does not mean either that reason, in its specific contribution to the determination of action, is only carrying out desire's orders. Desire cannot order reason, as far as reason's specific contribution to the determination of action is concerned, namely, directing the impulse. Desire is itself only that which provides the impulse and thus lacks any idea of how the impulse could or should be directed. Nobody tells reason to do what it does, as little as anybody tells desire to do what it does. Both just do their specific thing, impelling the one, directing the other. The point of the image of slavery is chiefly rhetorical, to turn upside down the traditional image of reason as a dictator to whose decrees the virtuous conform their actions (413). After all, the claim that reason ought to be, and not just is, the slave of the passions is, similarly, both needless and groundless here, and Hume adds it just for the sake of some *épater les rationalistes.* This reading is supported, not contradicted, by the pretended innocence with which Hume concedes in the next sentence that

> this opinion may appear somewhat extraordinary, (415)

only the more to infuriate his opponents who think that this opinion is positively outrageous. The substantial point in the slavery image is only a negative one. It is that reason is not a self-sufficient producer of action. Reason works, as far as action is concerned, in a cooperative, or if you prefer, on an assembly line: it needs the impulse provided by desire to work upon; and it works by giving that impulse direction. Thus reason is cooperating, it is not its own master. So the slavery image says no more than what the word "alone" conveys in Hume's programmatic statement "that reason alone can never be a motive to any action of the will" (§ 41). Reason is called a slave here because it does not by itself originate the person's action, it only contributes to it. Reason is called a slave here in spite of the fact that its contribution, the direction of desire's impulse, is certainly unslavish in character.

HUME does not argue for the full desire/belief thesis. Similar to Michael Smith (§ 15), he argues only against the idea that a mere belief could be somebody's reason for doing something. So what his argument, if successful, establishes is not: the primary reason for which one does something is a desire plus a belief of the agent. At best it establishes: if the primary reason for which somebody does something comprises a belief, it comprises a desire, too; which leaves open the possibility that it comprises neither. As before (§ 16), though, it will better serve the present discussion to disregard this difference. Hume's argument, then, for a desire/belief-thesis, by contrast to a mere-belief-thesis, is this:

43

> Reason is the discovery of truth or falshood. Truth or falshood consists in an agreement or disagreement either to the *real* relations of ideas, or to *real* existence and matter of fact. Whatever, therefore, is not susceptible of this agreement or disagreement, is incapable of being true or false, and can never be an object of our reason. Now 'tis evident our passions, volitions, and actions, are not susceptible of any such agreement or disagreement; being original facts and realities, compleat in themselves, and implying no reference to other passions, volitions, and actions. 'Tis impossible, therefore, they can be pronounced either true or false, and be either contrary or conformable to reason. (458)[3]

This argument shows, in Hume's view,

> that reason is perfectly inert, and can never either prevent or produce any action or affection. (458)

The natural way to read this passage seems to be as follows. An object of reason must be capable of being true or false, since truth and falsity are the qualities that reason discovers. Thus actions, incapable of being true or false, are not objects of reason. Hence they are not contrary or conformable to reason, either. Now in order to prevent or produce an action reason would have to judge correctly that the action is contrary or conformable to reason. Since all such judgments are false, reason cannot prevent or produce an action.

44   If that is the argument, it fails. The phrase "objects of reason" is ambiguous. In the first premise it means something like "the sort of thing that figures in deliberations of reason"; the currency of reason's reckonings, as it were. The phrase must mean that, for on this reading alone is the claim of the first premise plausible. It is only plausible to say that nothing but what is true or false figures as an item in the deliberations of reason. Thus "objects of reason" here does not mean what in other contexts it would be naturally taken to mean, namely, "things considered by reason," "what reason's judgments, themselves being true or false, are about." After all, what reason judges about are all sorts of things that are not true or false, like tomorrow's weather. So what can be inferred from these premises is only that actions are not themselves items figuring in the deliberations of reason. Reason is carrying on its business exclusively in the currency of judgments (or statements, or propositions). It cannot be inferred from the premises that actions are not among the things reason's judgments are about. In particular, it cannot be inferred that actions are not among the things such of reason's judgments are about as may have the form 'x is good' or 'x is bad'. Since just these actions would be contrary or conformable to reason, it cannot be inferred from the premises that there are no actions contrary or conformable to reason. As reason's inertia was proclaimed on the ground of there being no actions contrary or conformable to reason, reason's inertia cannot be inferred from the premises given, either.[4]

45   There is, however, another line of argument hinted at in the quoted passage, and it may be wondered whether that line is not more promising. The hint comes from Hume's italics for the two occurrences of the word "real" in this paragraph. This emphasis has no function within the argument from actions' lack of truth-values. That argument is based on excluding actions from the range of things agreeing or disagreeing to relations of ideas or matters of fact, and whether the things agreed or disagreed to are real or not is irrelevant. Thus the emphasis on the reality of the latter suggests another argument, which would run like this. It

must be a matter of the real relations of ideas or of real existence and matter of fact that an action has the quality by virtue of which it is contrary or conformable to reason. This is so because reason is the discovery of truth or falsehood, and there is nothing for true or false statements to be about but real relations of ideas and real existence or matter of fact. On the other hand it cannot be a matter of the real relations of ideas or of real existence and matter of fact that an action has the quality by virtue of which it is contrary or conformable to reason. This is so because the examination of any action by reason fails to make out such a quality. Thus the assumption that actions are contrary or conformable to reason leads to a contradiction and is false. Therefore, as in the previous argument (§ 43), reason cannot prevent or produce an action, since to do that it would have to judge correctly that the action is contrary or conformable to reason, and such a judgment is never correct.

THE CRUCIAL step in this argument is the claim that reason fails to discover   46
those qualities in actions that would make them contrary or conformable to reason. Unargued for here, this claim would need to be based on a defense of the sort Hume offers a couple of pages further down:

> But can there be any difficulty in proving, that vice and virtue are not matters of fact, whose existence we can infer by reason? Take any action allow'd to be vicious: Wilful murder, for instance. Examine it in all lights, and see if you can find that matter of fact, or real existence, which you call *vice*. In which-ever way you take it, you find only certain passions, motives, volitions and thoughts. There is no matter of fact in the case. The vice entirely escapes you, as long as you consider the object. (468)

Taking viciousness as a fair example of a quality that would make an action contrary to reason, the present argument would show that reason is unable to discern any such quality in actions. It is difficult to see, however, how this argument could impress Hume's rationalist opponent. Let that opponent take no exception to the proposed reasoning by analogy. Let her accept, that is, that if reason cannot discern viciousness in willful murder, it cannot discern any quality in actions that makes them contrary or conformable to reason. Yet why, she will ask, should reason be unable to discern the viciousness in willful murder? Why should not the viciousness of the murder be as much a matter of fact, discoverable by reason, as its time, say? It is true, you figure out in different ways the time of the murder and its viciousness, but you also figure out in different ways the time of the murder and the weapon used. It is also true, people sometimes have a hard time justifying their claims that willful murder, or that this particular instance of willful murder, is vicious, and perhaps all in all a harder time than justifying claims about times and weapons. This, however, is no good ground to exclude such claims from the province of reason. That province would become small indeed if only judgments were admitted the justification of which is not in dispute. It seems merely dogmatic, then, to hold "that vice and virtue are not matters of fact, whose existence we can infer by reason." More generally, it seems merely dogmatic to hold that reason cannot discern the qualities of actions by virtue of which the actions are contrary or conformable to reason. And with that claim gone, the second line of argument hinted at in the passage quoted earlier (§ 43) collapses as well.

47   THESE passages contain all the positive argument Hume offers for saying that reason is perfectly inert and that it takes desire to produce action. They contain all of Hume's positive argument for the desire/belief thesis. He does counter his opponent's case by trying to show that the phenomena on which that case is based admit of an explanation in accordance with a desire/belief-thesis. In this vein he argues that when we appear to be moved to action by empirical information, it could in fact be a prior impulse of desire, which is only directed by the information, that moves us (414). Furthermore, where such a desire cannot actually be discerned because its normal sign, some turmoil in the soul, is absent, a calm passion may still be supposed to be at work (417–418). However, these considerations, even if convincing, do not show the desire/belief-thesis to be true. They only show that certain arguments purporting to show that it is false do not succeed. So while it may be that Hume is the father of the modern tradition of understanding reasons for action in terms of desires and beliefs (§ 41), what justifies adopting this model does not become any clearer from his writing. In fact, speaking of persuasiveness rather than soundness now, it is difficult to imagine that the arguments just discussed could lead anyone to accept the desire/belief-thesis, if he had not believed it before. The reasoning from actions' lack of truth-values is just too contrived, and so is, if to a somewhat lesser degree, the argument from reason's incapacity to discover the qualities of actions that make them contrary or conformable to reason. The question raised earlier (§ 40) thus returns with renewed force for Hume: why is he convinced of an account in terms of desire and belief, since that can hardly be the effect of the arguments he puts forward? And the suspicion returns as well (§ 40) that this is to some extent due to philosophical habit; that Hume endorses such an account of reasons in part because, for him already, it is traditional. Which also renews the question: what tradition is that, and how did it become convincing?

THE DOCTRINE that the impulse for action does not arise from reason, but   48
is only directed by it serves Hume, as he tells us, to rebut "the greatest
part of moral philosophy, antient and modern" (413), which is founded
on the idea of a combat between reason and passion. This idea is undermined because, if reason of its own does not provide an impulse for action,
desire, which does provide it, lacks an opponent, and fighting is over. So
Hume himself sees his argument related, if only polemically, to a powerful
philosophical tradition, dominant in learned and popular moral discourse
alike (413).[5] This is fundamentally a Platonist tradition: it is in Plato's
Phaedrus that the idea of a violent fight between reason and desire first
appears. Hume's anti-Platonist polemic, however, may nevertheless be
wedded to Platonist assumptions. Rejecting the Platonist idea of a combat
between reason and passion by degrading reason to the status of a mere
slave, Hume could still be employing a conception that derives from the
same tradition. After all, it is in Plato's *Phaedrus*, too, that the doctrine of
reason directing desire first appears. To be sure, the account of reasons
for action in terms of agents' desires and beliefs owes its dominant role
in the philosophical tradition to Aristotle's unrivaled authority. Yet that
crucial element of this account, the idea of desire providing the impulse
and reason guiding it, is already Platonic. To understand, then, what made
this idea initially plausible one has to turn to Plato.

SOCRATES' second speech in the *Phaedrus* contains a discussion of the soul.   49
The soul resembles, we are told, "the united force of both a winged pair
of horses and a charioteer" (246a6–7).[6] Whereas in divine souls both horses
and the charioteer are good, in our souls one horse is good and one horse
bad (246a–b, 253a–e). However, this is incomplete information about the
soul so far. Just to be told that the soul is like a pair of horses plus
charioteer leaves one baffled, the way those jokes do that just tell you, for
example, "love is like an elevator": unless you are very clever or know
the joke already, you need to be told in what ways it is like an elevator.
(Don't pore over this one, I made it up.) Similarly we need to know in
what ways the soul is like a pair of horses with a charioteer. That is to
say, we need some story in terms of horses and charioteer that sheds light
on phenomena of the soul with which we are familiar.

SOCRATES' speech provides a number of such stories. One undergirds   50
knowledge. We do have knowledge, but it is flawed in various ways,
and flawed in different people to a different degree. The story in terms
of horses and charioteer accounts for this fact. When the souls once
were in the position to see what truly is, they were disturbed in their
sight by the horses, and also the chariots got into one another's way,

causing much confusion and quarrel, so that every soul saw less than it wished, and some souls saw less than others (248a–b). In this story, incidentally, the wings of the horses play a role, too. Important for the present purpose, however, is another story. The description of our soul as consisting of horses and charioteer serves to explain what sometimes happens when we act or omit action. With Socrates' example, it serves to explain what sometimes happens when a man, on seeing the boy with whom he is in love, does or does not approach him for sexual intercourse (253e–254e).

51 THIS is the story. On seeing the boy, the charioteer is filled with longing, and so, apparently, is the good horse, but both have qualms, too, as to whether it is right to go ahead. The bad horse, by contrast, is all eagerness to get going. So there is conflict: the bad horse pulls forward, the charioteer and the good horse resist. The bad horse finally gets the other two to agree to move forward, and they approach the boy. However, when they see the boy's face, the charioteer remembers the nature of beauty and sees again beauty and moderation in their holy place. Filled with fear and reverence, he falls backward and cannot help pulling back the bridles so violently that the horses come to sit on their buttocks. The good horse is deeply ashamed, whereas the bad horse is fuming with anger. This happens repeatedly, with violence rising to the point where the bad horse is bleeding under the charioteer's treatment. In the end the bad horse is tamed: it obeys the charioteer and perishes with anxiety once it sees the beautiful boy. In this way a state is reached in which the lover's soul follows the boy in fear and respect.

52 AT THREE points in particular this story of horses and charioteer purports to illuminate our ordinary experience. First, we have, or claim to have, the experience of a conflict within ourselves. As the expression is, we feel torn. According to the story, sometimes we are torn: the bad horse pulls this way, the good horse and the charioteer the other way. Second, we claim to have the experience of people not doing what they would very much like to do, even though they could do it, and know that they could. The story accounts for some of these cases. For all the bad horse's pulling, certain considerations or, perhaps one should say, certain contemplations have such a marked effect on the charioteer that he can get the better of the horse. Third, we have the experience of people leaving behind even strong desires. The story explains how sometimes this happens. Afflicted with pain repeatedly, the bad horse learns to change its ways. That is after all how animals are trained.

CENTRAL here is the second phenomenon, action contrary to what one 53 would like to do. Habituation, the third, is effected through repeated action contrary to what one would like to do, whereas internal conflict, the first, is not specific enough to warrant introducing horses and charioteer, since to account for that a duality of mere forces would suffice. The characters specifically of horses and charioteer are introduced to understand action contrary to what one would like to do, for such action is held to be sometimes taken by virtue of, and in accordance with, insight. Thus this is not just a case of two forces clashing and one of them getting the better of the other. What prevails is sight. In terms of the simile, it takes a charioteer to pull back the horses when they all are close to the boy, for he pulls them back by virtue of remembering beauty in its true nature and seeing it together with moderation in their holy place (254b). That is something only a charioteer can do. Only a charioteer can remember the nature of beauty because only he saw it, and so only he can see it again. Horses do not have eyes for such things. The text explicitly says that what truly is can only be seen by reason ('nous'), the helmsman of the soul (247c7–8), and this helmsman is, under a different metaphor, the charioteer. Accordingly, in the souls' procession round the things that are, the most godlike of the mortal souls are eager to raise the head of the charioteer up high (248a2–3), obviously in order to give him a good view on what is, whereas the point for the horses is to get most of the grass growing up there, since it is the best food for souls (248b7–c1). The charioteer's special position with regard to the horses can easily be overlooked, because the good horse is described as being constantly on his side, so that the main divide can appear to lie between the two of them and the bad horse. In fact the main divide lies, as the terms of the simile indicate, between charioteer and horses, for he can, and they cannot, see the truth, and so he can, by virtue of seeing the truth, determine the course of the chariot, as he does in the story two paragraphs back. Thus it is natural to interpret the charioteer in the soul as the agency procuring insight that may determine action, and to interpret the horses in the soul as the agency providing the impulse for action. The horses after all are what moves a chariot. For all his insight, the charioteer will not get anywhere without horses, good or bad. That is to say, without horses no action will be taken.

So THE charioteer in the soul is reason. What the horses in the soul are 54 is not made explicit in the text, but it can be gathered. The bad horse behaves like somebody who vehemently desires to embrace the boy. It is jumping forward with force, (254a4), tries to argue its companions into coming along, (254a4–5), is really annoying them (254b2). When the first time round they chicken out, or so at least the bad horse sees it, it is angry to the extreme and scolds them (254c7). The next time it pulls "shamelessly," bites the bit, and erects the tail (254d7), or indeed the penis, the Greek word meaning both. Depicted as violently desiring the boy, the bad horse is thus most plausibly taken *to be* the desire of a person, whether it be a desire for boys or for anything else.[7] Interpreting the horse in the soul as desire is natural anyway, given how frequently people describe their desires, especially their sexual desires, as something wild, incalculable, animal-like. The good horse, then, being a horse, too, will also be desire, but desire that is tame, governable, and, in this sense, reasonable.

55   HERE, then, is the answer, at least as far as action is concerned, to the question (§ 49) why the soul is like a pair of horses and a charioteer. It is because the soul, through desire, can set the person moving, the way horses can move a chariot. It is because the soul, through reason, can see the truth, the way a charioteer can see what is around the chariot. And it is because the soul can, again through reason, determine the person's movement to accord with the truth seen, the way a charioteer can steer a chariot in accordance with what he sees.

56   THE ACCOUNT of the soul in book 4 of Plato's *Republic* is quite similar.[8] Here as well the soul consists of three kinds of things, that which is calculating, that which is desiring, and that which is spirited (440e–441a). The latter two, initially appearing to be of the same nature (439e4), are separated on the grounds that the spirited part, unlike the desiring part, ordinarily joins forces with the calculating part (441a). Thus desiring part and spirited part can be identified with the bad and the good horse in *Phaedrus*: both are desire, but one is desire difficult to govern, the other is desire easy to govern. (This assimilation of desiring and spirited part is supported by the manifest etymological link between the Greek words translated as "desiring" and "spirited.") On the other hand, since it takes reason to calculate things, the calculating part in the *Republic* may be identified with the charioteer in *Phaedrus*. The relation between reason and desire is, as before, domination: reason is the lord of the soul (439c7, 441e4–6). The phenomena the account is intended to illuminate are again internal conflict (440b, e) and action against desire (439c), whereas habituation is not considered here. Action against desire is explained, as earlier, by reason thwarting the impulse of desire with force (439c–d), where desire is again "that which drives and pulls" (439d1). The *Republic* is only less explicit about the kind of sight that prompts reason to subdue desire. In *Phaedrus* it is on seeing beauty and moderation on their holy ground that reason pulls back the bridles, but what the calculating part is calcu-

lating in the *Republic* we are not told expressly. So while the *Phaedrus* account appears to be the more revealing of the two, basically the doctrine is the same.

It is Hume's doctrine. "The impulse does not arise from reason, but is only directed by it," Hume's essential thesis (§ 41), is an exact description of Plato's chariot. Here indeed the impulse that moves it does not come from the charioteer; he only determines in what way the impulse moves it. The very word Hume uses to describe what reason does, "to direct," would be perfectly suitable to describe what the charioteer does to his horses. "Reason is perfectly inert," Hume says,[9] and so does Plato, for if reason by itself could set the person moving, horses would be unnecessary, the charioteer himself could take on the harness, and the simile would be off. To be sure, reason is not inert either in Plato or in Hume in the sense that it does not accomplish anything in matters of reasoning. For Hume, "reason is the discovery of truth or falshood,"[10] and so such discovery is an accomplishment of reason. For Plato as well, discovery of truth or falsehood is the work of the charioteer, for on seeing the boy's face he comes to remember what beauty truly is, and such remembrance is an achievement, one of which the horses are incapable (§ 53). So reason does get reason-work done. Inert it is in that it does not move the person. What moves the person both in Plato and in Hume is desire.

To assimilate Plato's and Hume's doctrines in this way may appear misguided because Hume plainly denies, and Plato as plainly asserts, that there is sometimes conflict between reason and desire. Yet the fact that Hume explicitly denies such a conflict does not decide the matter. The question is whether he can stick to his denial while advancing his positive doctrine that reason directs the impulse of desire. Indeed he cannot. There is no directing where forces never diverge. There is no directing where there is harmony preestablished. You direct the ball into the corner of your opponent's field because balls do not do that automatically. You direct a child to the toilet because she does not find it by herself. You direct your thoughts to some question because left to themselves they tend to wander off. Thus reason directs desire because desire on its own goes astray. Desire on its own might lead the person to do all sorts of things, from going into a frenzy down to doing nothing, but it has no particular tendency toward the reasonable thing. Therefore reason has to take desire by the hand, as it were. Once that much is admitted, however, and Hume cannot fail to admit it if his talk of reason's directing the impulse of desire is to retain sense, then Plato has got all he needs. Hume is bound to accept the following description of the example: desire on its own may rush the person toward the boy, but if reason directs desire, it will sometimes direct it in such a way that the person does not approach him; and what this statement describes *is* the conflict between the two that Hume appeared to deny.

59   THERE may be conflict here, it will be replied, but if so, it is a conflict between two desires, not between reason and desire, as is required for assimilating Hume to Plato. Let us give our lover a more Humean cast of mind. Let him refrain from approaching the boy, not because he sees beauty and moderation as they really are, but because he fears for his reputation if discovered. (Plato's theory is intended to apply to such more mundane cases as well; witness the example in *Republic* 439c of the thirsty person who refrains from drinking—presumably for the sake of fitness, health, or the like.) Now this agent, it will be said, is only torn between his sexual desire and his eagerness to keep up his reputation. Reason is no party to the conflict.

60   YES, IT is. Between the mere desires there is no conflict. You may be lusting for the boy and caring for your reputation one beside the other. And that may be so no matter what you do. Perhaps you will madly pursue the boy at one time and worry desperately about your reputation at another. As long as you are at each time an unthinking desirer, you are not torn within yourself. You may be unhappy if at one time or another you do not get what you want; and with your unsteadiness this is quite likely to happen. Still, within your heart there is no quarrel. Quarrel arises only when you realize that going for the boy involves risking your reputation, and saving your reputation involves leaving alone the boy. It takes reason to realize that. Reason shows you that foregoing the sexual pleasure you are yearning for is part of the path toward a safe reputation, or conversely. So if reason directs desire, then it also sometimes thwarts desire.

61   MAYBE so, it will now be replied; maybe it is at reason's hands that the defeated desire suffers. Still, reason is then only acting at the behest of another desire, and so the conflict is really between the two desires, not between reason and desire. This, however, is to try to squeeze more out of the slavery image than it will warrant. Desire does not order reason to determine the path toward the thing desired (§ 42). Desire is for boys or reputation or whatever, and to say that it has in addition power of command over other faculties is to turn metaphor into mythology (§ 33). Desire and reason are just working side by side on their mental assembly

line, one producing impulse, the other giving it direction, but none of them commanding the other. So reason thwarts one desire in directing another one, but not at the behest of the latter; the thwarting is reason's own. Hence, if reason directs desire, as Hume claims it does, there will be cases of genuine conflict between reason and desire, his denial of such conflicts notwithstanding; and this alleged difference between Hume's and Plato's theories (§ 58) dissolves.[11]

ANOTHER difference remains. As suggested earlier (§ 59), Plato and Hume   62
do differ on what sort of thing it is the sight of which prompts reason to direct desire in a certain way. Reason being for both the discovery of truth or falsehood, they differ on what kind of truths are going to be practically important, and Plato is the more catholic in this respect. He envisages that even something like seeing beauty and moderation in their holy places will sometimes alter somebody's course of action, whereas Hume probably expects only the recognition of less elevated truths, like sexual intercourse jeopardizing a reputation, to influence people. However, that difference is irrelevant here. Whatever the truths in question be, important here is their role in determining action; and with regard to that role Plato and Hume agree.

THE ASSIMILATION of Plato's and Hume's theories of action will be attacked   63
from the opposite side as well, not only from Humeans pretending to despise Platonism (§§ 58–62) but also from Platonists hostile to Hume. According to an influential view in current Plato scholarship,[12] it is a mistake to assimilate Plato's and Hume's conceptions because it is a mistake to think that for Plato "reason simply reasons and desire desires," as Giovanni Ferrari puts it.[13] Rather, reason itself has desires, or even, with Charles Kahn, reason is a form of desire,[14] and desire in turn has a cognitive capacity.[15] By contrast, Hume and his followers' conception requires desires and beliefs to be disjoint classes of mental entities (§ 15). As such a distinction between desire and belief is precisely undermined in Plato, according to these scholars, Plato's and Hume's conceptions of action, for all their "misleading superficial similarity,"[16] differ fundamentally.

THERE is no doubt that, read literally, Plato's text says or implies that the   64
charioteer, or the calculating part, has desires (leaving aside Kahn's claim that he or it is desire), and that the horses, or the desiring and the spirited part, are engaged in reasoning, in the sense of discovering truth or falsehood. Thus the charioteer is said explicitly to be filled with desire on seeing the boy (253e5–254a1), and when later after the interrupted ap-

proach he is said to be begging the bad horse to defer another approach, he must be understood to wish for such a delay (254d2). The bad horse in turn is represented as a rather reasonable creature, entering an agreement with the other two (254b2), upbraiding them after they break it (254c7–d1), yielding to their request for deferring another approach (254d2);[17] and these things could hardly be ascribed to a creature incapable of discovering truth or falsehood.[18]

65 NONE of this settles the point at issue, however. Plato does say or imply that reason has desires and that desire reasons, but what needs to be determined is whether his saying or implying so is part of the image or part of the message. Somewhere this line must be drawn, and it takes further argument to show that reason's desires and desire's reasoning fall, together with reason's awareness of beauty as it truly is, on the side of the message or rather, together with desire's whinnying (254d4), on the side of the image. Nor does the *Republic*, dispensing with horses and charioteer, fail to be subject to that distinction. Presumably it is supposed to be literally true that action contrary to what we would like to do is sometimes due to reason (439c9–d1), but it is not supposed to be literally true that the spirited part takes up arms on reason's behalf (440e5–6). So here as well the question arises whether reason's desires and desire's reasoning are part of the architecture or only part of the decoration.

66 THE LATTER, it would seem. The trouble with desiring reason and reasoning desire is simply that we no longer know what we are talking about: applying the predicate denies the condition that served to identify the referent of the subject term. It must be conceded that what the term "reason" refers to, that of which the charioteer in *Phaedrus* is the image, is not the faculty, or power, of reasoning, as a traditional reading supposed.[19] A faculty is that property of a person that makes it true to say of her that she can do what the faculty is a faculty for. To such a property it makes no sense to ascribe the directing of desire. Yet Plato, through the image of the charioteer, does ascribe the directing of desire to reason. So a person's reason is not her faculty of reasoning. It is her reasoning. Of a person's reasoning it can indeed sensibly be said that it directs her desire. This phrase means that some piece of reasoning of hers determines to what action she is moved by some piece of her desiring. However, if reason is a person's reasoning, then to say that "reason has desires of its own"[20] is downright incomprehensible, for it is incomprehensible to say that a piece of somebody's reasoning desires something. A corresponding argument holds for desire. It is incomprehensible to say that a person's desiring something is engaged in some reasoning.

To AVOID this consequence people have tried two ways of reinterpreting 67
the phrases "desiring reason" and "reasoning desire." John Cooper favors
the rational nature approach:

> The desires of reason are thus implied to be strong impulses of some
> kind which we experience simply and directly because we possess the
> power of reason.[21]

So the alleged desires of reason are not, speaking strictly, desires that
reason has. We have them. What justifies the expression "desires of reason" is the fact that our having them is due to our rational nature alone:
any reasoner experiences these desires. This interpretation pursues an Aristotelian line. "Every human being by nature strives for knowledge,"[22]
the opening statement of Aristotle's *Metaphysics*, puts forward a claim of
this sort: the desire to gain knowledge is part of our nature, and in particular, it may be presumed, of our rational nature.

TALK of reason's desires certainly becomes intelligible in this way. Nev- 68
ertheless, this reading suffers from various difficulties. For one thing, it
saddles Plato with a claim that seems difficult to justify: what should lead
us to believe that indeed each and every reasoner on earth experiences
such a desire? For another, this interpretation, while explaining reason's
desires, leaves unclear what desire's reasonings are. After all, it could not
be held, analogously, that all desiring creatures engage in these reasonings,
since most desirers do not reason at all. Given that desire's reasonings
appear to be as much or as little part of Plato's account as reason's desires
are, it counts against the present interpretation that it works for the one
and not for the other. However, most important in the present context is
the fact that, third, the interpretation fails in its task of "de-Humeanizing"
Plato. The argument against assimilating Plato's and Hume's views on
action was: Plato undermines the very distinction between reason and
desire on which Hume's account is based (§ 63). On the present reading,
Plato does no such thing. He only maintains, on however good or bad
grounds, that all reasoning is accompanied by certain desires. Maintaining
that, he is not undermining the distinction, he is employing it. So while
Hume is likely to disagree with the view here ascribed to Plato, namely,
that reasoners as such are bound to experience certain desires, this disagreement does not affect the basic agreement in the conception of action,
epitomized in Hume's phrase that "reason directs desire."

THE SECOND way to deal with the problem (§ 67) is to go for a full ho- 69
munculus theory. This interpretation admits smaller creatures existing
within ourselves, little men or horses or whatever, not by way of a mere

manner of speaking, but literally, and their interplay is taken to produce action.[23] On this interpretation, "reason" does not, as just suggested, denote a person's reasonings. It denotes such an inhabitant of the soul. This again solves the problem: if there are such creatures in the soul, then there is no further problem about understanding how the one named "reason" should, in accordance with Plato's description, be capable both of reasoning and of desiring. As capable are we after all. Similarly for spirit and desire, other inhabitants of the soul: once admitted, they can also safely be claimed, in accordance with Plato's description, to be capable both of reasoning and of desiring.

70 THIS interpretation does succeed in de-Humeanizing Plato, but it suffers from other defects. First, a part of the soul that is capable both of reasoning and of desiring may be subject to the same sort of internal strife that such parts were just called on to explain in the full person. Second, to invoke homunculi deprives Plato's theory of explanatory power. Julia Annas defends the explanatory capacities of homunculi against this objection: "there is nothing wrong with talking of the explanatory parts of a whole person as though they were themselves people of a very simple kind."[24] She quotes Daniel Dennett: "if one can get a team or committee of *relatively* ignorant, narrow-minded, blind homunculi to produce the intelligent behavior of the whole, this is progress."[25] This much is true: there are no strictures in principle against explaining the doings of persons by appealing to the doings of smaller persons within them. However, there is something wrong with such an explanation as long as no better reason is given for assuming such smaller persons than the fact that, if true, the assumption would provide a satisfactory explanation. If no independent reason for assuming the homunculi is offered, if Dennett's committee remains just fantasy, albeit fantasy in terms of which action can be explained, then many of us will fail to see the progress in understanding that Dennett celebrates. Many of us will argue that the explanatory task is to say how we act, and not only to give some story on how action might be brought about by whatever fictional entities one cares to invent. Third, it is not even clear on this interpretation what a part of the soul is. Talk of parts normally can be explained by reference to spatial or temporal discriminations. Spatial ones presumably do not apply to the soul, and temporal ones are too weak, since the parts of the soul are supposed to coexist. Nor can the parts be distinguished by function, as they all execute more than one. Indeed they all execute more or less the same set of functions: they all reason and desire. Thus we do not have criteria for the expression "parts of the soul." We do not know, once again, what we

are talking about in speaking of reason that desires and desire that reasons.

To SUM up this part of the discussion, Plato evidently says or implies that reason desires and desire reasons (§ 64). This seems to refute the claim (§ 57) that "reason directs desire" is common doctrine between Plato and Hume, for it seems to show that Plato rejects the very distinction on which this doctrine rests (§ 63). In fact it does not show this. Plato's talk of reason's desiring and desire's reasoning is either part of the image (§ 65), and then it does not show this; or it is part of the message, but then it needs interpretation. There is only one interpretation, Cooper's rational nature approach, that succeeds in making acceptable sense of reason's desires, if not of desire's reasonings (§§ 67–68). On this interpretation, however, Plato's talk of reason's desires does not undermine, but presupposes, the distinction in question (§ 68). The fact, then, that Plato speaks of reason's desiring and of desire's reasoning does not cast doubt on the claim that he is defending a conception of action with which we are familiar through Hume. Nor is this claim, on the other hand, called into question by Hume's explicit denial of a conflict between reason and desire, since he cannot sustain this denial (§§ 58–62). So the interpretation proposed earlier (§ 57) stands. It is a Platonic tradition that lives on in what is currently called "the Humean theory of motivation," the conception of reasons for which people do things in terms of desires and beliefs of the agent.

THE DIFFICULTIES from which this conception suffers (§§ 31–39) can also be located in the original Platonic version. To recall, the difficulties consisted in both desire and belief being charged with incompatible roles, desire both setting a goal and moving the agent (§§ 31–33), belief both providing information and steering the agent to appropriate action (§§ 34–36). The same ambiguities mark the characters in Plato's story. The charioteer is supposed both to watch true being and to direct the chariot. The horses are supposed both to have aims, whether honour or boys, and to pull the chariot. To be sure, ordinary charioteers and ordinary horses can do both things, respectively. Charioteer and horses in the soul cannot. Of these we learnt only through their functions, and the functions, seeing the truth and directing action on the one hand, having an aim and initiating movement on the other, are different. In this simple sense we do not understand the account being given here. The identity claimed for the respective bearers of these functions is mythical. It owes its plausibility only to the terms of the story told here about the soul, not to its capturing the relevant experience. So it appears that this conception of reasons for action has ever been moving within the confines of Plato's myth.

73 To SHED the myth it would help to understand the need it was to satisfy. Here is a suggestion: the service of the myth was precisely to provide for that identity of what sees the truth and what guides, an identity not to be had other than by mythical means. That identity, after all, is the pivot of the story in the *Phaedrus*. Prompted by the sight of the boy's face, the charioteer remembers, that is, mentally sees, beauty as it is together with moderation on their holy ground, and that seeing is sufficient to make him pull back the bad horse. It is not that the charioteer in seeing beauty and moderation becomes cognizant of such information or such demands as to lead him to the conclusion that the boy had better not be approached, and therefore pulls back the horse. His pulling back the horses appears rather as an uncontrollable reaction, as something the charioteer cannot help doing—he is "forced" (254b8) to pull the bridles. In fact, as Ferrari has shown, the charioteer behaves just like a horse, "shying back from the starting line" (254e1–2). Ferrari takes this as evidence for the homunculus reading, just rejected (§ 70), of Plato's division of the soul. Better sense can be made of his observation if it is taken as indicating that there is to be no transition between the charioteer's perceiving beauty and moderation as they are and his determining appropriate action: it happens "at the same time," Plato says (254b8). In particular, there is to be no transition that consists of reasoning: this would not do justice to the supposedly overwhelming power of this sight, which just carries the seer. Awareness of beauty and moderation as they are is linked immediately in the charioteer to a restraint of desires from shameless behavior. In this way the person's actually refraining from shamelessness can count as action in accordance with what there is, as action appropriate to true being. The charioteer is what explains such action on the part of the subject, he is the conduit transmitting truth into the formation of action. Thus Plato's myth satisfies those demanding a concept of action that allows it to accord with what really is.

74 AND WHAT a strange need is that? Not all that strange, really. If you are convinced that the tradition of the community will no longer suffice to support the claims of morality against the challenge of rational arguments, and if on the other hand you are not prepared to give up the moral notions that are in the process of coming unstuck, you may try to give them a basis in what truly is. Not, to be sure, in the ordinary facts of life of which everybody is cognizant: what ought to be done, given these ordinary facts, is precisely what is at issue. Rather, you may try to found moral require-

ments in a realm of true being lying behind ordinary experience and accessible only to the educated. That would, first, give you a firm fundament, for what truly is would not seem to be liable to change. Second, you can beat the critics on their own field, in rational argument, by showing that rational investigation, continued methodically, will lead to the recognition of that order of things that, once seen or properly remembered, leaves you no choice but to behave. Now Plato was convinced that tradition would no longer do as a basis for morality. This is evident from the first book of the *Republic*, especially from the way the figure of Kephalus is treated there. On the other hand, Plato was not prepared to surrender morality to the sophistic challenge, as is evident from dialogues like *Gorgias* and again the first book of the *Republic*. So Plato chose the option indicated, founding moral notions on what truly there is. No doubt the difficulties on this path are considerable. It is not easy to see why what there truly is, beauty and moderation in themselves for example, should contain any requirement on people's actions. Suppose, though, that everything goes fine with showing that this is so: what is still needed is an account of agents sensitive to that sort of requirement; of agents, that is, who are capable of doing something because it is in accordance with what truly there is. This is the demand that Plato's myth is meant to satisfy. A charioteer is installed in our soul to allow for action that may be praised for being attuned to the truth; and we need to make room for such action so as to provide, in the face of the waning power of tradition, a basis for morality.[26]

IF THAT is indeed what recommended the myth, we may now leave it   75
behind. True, in our days as well many are worried that traditions are losing their power to keep people on track. However, practically everywhere the hope is lost to find a remedy in the idea of action in accordance with what there is. Metaphysical ethics is all but dead. Emotivists and utilitarians, moral constructivists and moral nihilists all agree that what there is is silent on what we should do. The moderns have buried this idea, and difficult though such a diagnosis be, there is at present no reason to think that it will come to life again. As little therefore do we need a charioteer in the soul, or any one of his successors. Their job is gone, that of turning insight into guidance; and we can dismiss these figures from our self-conception.

INDEED we should, for the myth brought additional costs. With the char-   76
ioteer comes domination within the soul. Horses good or bad are lowly creatures, being unable to see what is (§ 53), and so the charioteer, seeing what is and set to steer the chariot in accordance with what he sees, needs

to be master over them. He is a mild master as long as the horses comply anyway, but he exerts power to the point of violence against the recalcitrant (§ 51). Thus for the privilege of acting in the face of beauty and moderation as they really are, people pay the price of oppression within themselves. The idea of the philosophers, the ones who see what really is, becoming kings in the cities has been the butt of disbelief or ridicule from the moment it was conceived.[27] The corresponding idea of reason being master in our souls was widely accepted, by contrast, and has remained in force ever since. As noted, even Hume, his slavery rhetoric notwithstanding, speaks of reason's directing the impulse of desire (§ 41), and directing makes directors. Currently the word "control" is the more usual one,[28] but that makes little difference: we are still speaking of a relation of subordination and of power. Condorcet, in the closing chapter of the *Esquisse,*[29] looked forward to the time

> when the sun will shine only on free humans who know no other master than their reason.

It is paradoxical to call those free who consider themselves subordinated to a master within. Thus a better time is that when the sun will shine only on free humans who, understanding that reason has nothing to do with domination, know no master whatsoever. It is a better time, since we may be living then in peace with ourselves.

77   To SUM up. The doubts about the desire/belief thesis put forward in chapter 1 led to the question why that thesis is nevertheless so popular, and the suspicion was raised that it is popular in part because it is traditional (§ 40). It seemed appropriate, therefore, to consider that tradition in more detail. David Hume is its central representative in the modern age, but his argument for the thesis is again not convincing (§§ 41–47). Actually, however, the tradition comes down from ancient philosophy: Plato's division of the soul, presented in *Phaedrus* and in the *Republic*, is its origin (§§ 48–56). Assimilating Plato's and Hume's views on this matter can be defended against both Platonist and Humean objections (§§ 57–71). In Plato, in turn, the idea is founded on a myth, on a story that recommends itself not by capturing certain features of our experience, but by fulfilling a moral need (§§ 72–74); and a legacy of the myth is domination within the soul. Given that this is so, it seems recommendable and indeed possible now to give up the myth and whatever depends on it (§§ 75–76).

80 So TO understand this conception of doing something for a reason it is necessary to understand what a maxim is. Kant explains that a maxim is "the subjective principle of action."[6] So first, a maxim is a principle. This means that it is general. It specifies the *sort* of thing an agent is to do under some *sort* of circumstances. Kant mentions as an example somebody's maxim "to enrich myself by every safe means" (KpV 27): this agent, finding a fat wallet in the park at night or being given more than the right change at the post office counter or holding an unrecorded deposit the owner of which has died, and so on, is supposed to keep the wallet, pocket the money, embezzle the deposit, and so forth. Interestingly, even the man considering suicide is presented as holding the principle to shorten his life when continuing it promises more evil than pleasure (GMS 422), and that is a general principle, notwithstanding the fact that one cannot act on it more than once.

81 SECOND, a maxim is a *subjective* principle. This means more than one thing. It means in the first place that a maxim is somebody's, like a belief. True, different people may hold the same maxim just as they may share a belief, but that is only to say that the maxims they individually hold coincide, just the way their beliefs may. It means in the second place that, by contrast to the case of beliefs, people are master over what maxims they hold. You normally do not have the beliefs you do because you decided to have them; disregarding extraordinary cases like that of Pascal's infidel who acquires a belief in the Christian doctrine because he finds it prudent to have it.[7] You do have the maxims you do because you decided to have them. A maxim is yours because you made it yours; and it ceases to be yours as soon as you abandon it, which you are free to do at any time. Accordingly, that the maxim is a subjective principle means in the third place that the authority it holds over you is merely subjective. Nothing in the world committed you to enriching yourself by every safe means, if that should be your maxim. You alone did, and you can revoke your commitment at any time. You are subject to this rule, but it is your own. It is in this respect that Kant contrasts the subjectivity of maxims with the objectivity of practical laws. (GMS 420n.) If you also have a maxim of truthfulness, then you are subject to the rule not to lie, as before. However, in this case you are not only subject to your own rule, because there is a practical law prohibiting lies. Thus you are subject to a rule not to lie that holds independently of whether you yourself imposed it on you. So even if you revoke your commitment to truthfulness, as you well may, the requirement on you is not thereby lifted, as it is in the case of the maxim of greed. It stands regardless. That is to say, it stands objectively.

THIRD, a maxim is a subjective principle *of action*. However, it is a prin-   82
ciple of action not in the sense in which Newton's laws are principles of
motion; not in the sense, that is, of a statement that is fundamental for a
theoretical account of the phenomenon in question.[8] Kant's exact phrasing
here is all the more revealing as it is grammatically dubious: "Maxime ist
das subjektive Prinzip zu handeln" (GMS 420n.), which says: "a maxim
is the subjective principle to act." A "principle to act" is a principle from
which to act. It serves primarily to generate action, and only therefore
may it then also serve to explain it. A "principle to act" is a principle for
"acting on principle."[9] It is a principle in the sense in which one says
things like "I do not eat meat on principle."

IN SUM, then, a maxim is an individual's self-imposed principle, speci-   83
fying some sort of action to be taken under some sort of circumstances,
and generating action in accordance with it. Such a principle may
well be the reason for which one does something. I ask you why you
do not get yourself out of some difficult situation by a harmless lie, and
you tell me that it is your principle never to lie: in saying that, you
have indeed answered my question. I may then take issue with what
you said. For instance, I may call into question the wisdom of such a
policy. That does not alter the fact that what you said is an appropriate
answer to my request to see the reasons for which you did what you
did. Nor is it only conversationally proper to regard reference to a
maxim as an answer to the question for reasons. It makes sense to do
so. If a reason should be something that both is the origin and makes
transparent the action, then maxims seem to be excellent candidates for
being reasons.[10]

IT MAY be held against this suggestion that, first, as the maxim of greed   84
mentioned earlier (§ 80) shows, there are maxims which it is not reasonable to act upon. Thus, if maxims are reasons, we get unreasonable
acting on reasons, which sounds odd. It may be urged, in addition, that
maxims themselves are adopted for reasons, and these reasons, not the
maxims, should be taken as the reasons for which people do what they
do, if they act in accordance with maxims. It may be insisted, finally,
that the maxim account of action needs to be complemented by an account in terms of the agent's desires and beliefs. Why after all does an
agent act on some maxim he holds? Surely because he wants to comply
with the maxim, and thinks that the action in question would be a case
of complying with it. Thus the maxim conception appears not even to
be an independent competitor to the conception of reasons as pairs of
desires and beliefs.

85   To RESPOND to the first point, unreasonable acting on reasons will have to be admitted on any account of reasons. Some things people do are done for reasons, others are not, and perhaps we praise people sometimes for acting on a reason in some situation rather than "being carried away." However, we also draw a line among the things people do for reasons, and some of them we praise as generous, or courageous, or indeed reasonable, by contrast to others that we consider petty, cowardly, or foolish. The fact, then, that doing something for a reason does not guarantee the action to be reasonable cannot be held against the maxim account of reasons in particular. (This matter is taken up again in §§ 129 and 220.) With regard to the second point, it is not clear whether maxims are in turn adopted for reasons, for it is not clear what adopting a maxim really amounts to (of which more later in this chapter). However, even if maxims are adopted for reasons, there are no grounds for saying that it is these reasons, rather than the maxims themselves, that people act upon. The person referring to her principle never to lie does seem to have fully answered the question why she does not take that way out (§ 83). As for the third point, it is merely dogmatic to claim that the maxim account of agency needs to be complemented by some story about the agent's desires and beliefs. No reason is to be seen why things could not work just this way: the agent holds a maxim, recognizes a relevant situation, and, on account of his maxim, produces appropriate action. No reason is to be seen why in addition to the maxim a desire of the agent has to be brought in.

86   To THIS reply it may be objected in turn that for Kant himself it is necessary to complete the maxim account of agency by referring to the agent's desires, at least in cases of action on material practical principles, as he calls them (KpV 22). To be sure, these can become an agent's maxims, and so the relevant action is action on a maxim, in accordance with Kant's general view of agency. Yet the condition for their adoption as maxims, he maintains, is a prior desire (KpV 21). So the maxim in turn depends on a desire, in these cases at least, and that desire needs to be included in a full account of the reason for which one did something.

87   HOWEVER, the fact that Kant speaks of a prior desire being the condition for adopting some rule as one's maxim does not settle the issue about the role of desire in a Kantian conception of agency. We still need to understand, consistently with such a conception, in what sense the desire is supposed to be a condition of the maxim. Andrews Reath and Henry Allison have argued convincingly that taking desire to exert a force on the will is incompatible with practical freedom in Kant's sense; and Allison

in particular showed that this is so independently of whether desire's push is supposed to produce action immediately or to result in the adoption of a maxim on which the agent then acts.[11] It is less clear how to characterize in positive terms a Kantian agent following desire. Desire does not push agents either into action or into adoption of a maxim for action, granted. Yet what *does* it amount to that desire is the condition of an agent's adopting a maxim, as on Kant's view in human agents it often is? Reath and Allison answer that desire is such a condition just in case a maxim is adopted that "stipulates a policy of acting in such a way as to satisfy it";[12] the adoption of this maxim still being an act of spontaneity on the part of the agent. This answer is convincing as well: various passages in Kant support it, foremost among them the statement of 1792 that "an incentive cannot determine the will to an action unless the agent has taken it up into his maxim";[13] and it is very hard to see any other answer that would not violate the demands of practical freedom. Reath and Allison do not seem to recognize the costs of this answer, however:[14] it puts paid to all Kantian notions of a will that is sensuously affected, susceptible of pathological determination or subject to incentives, and thereby to the distinction between human and divine will. This is so because, according to this answer, the adoption of any maxim is spontaneous, hence undetermined and not subject to whatever affection. An incentive that cannot determine the will unless the agent has taken it up into his maxim is in fact an incentive that cannot determine the will, period. Desire's contribution comes to no more than this on the present picture: people often select maxims of which they expect that action in accordance with them will help satisfy their desires. So *what* people choose to do is actually correlated to some extent to what they desire, yet their choosing is in no way influenced by their desiring. Thus desire is not an additional factor to be included in a full account of the reason for which one did something. On a considered Kantian view it is never true that people do what they do for the reason that they desire this or that. It is true only that what they do sometimes agrees with what they desire.[15]

PUSHING the line of the last objection (§ 86) further, one may even deny   88
that the maxim account is in fact Kant's doctrine of agency, as claimed earlier (§ 78). Ralf Meerbote and Hud Hudson take Kant to hold an account of agency in terms of the agent's desires and beliefs, on the lines of Davidson's.[16] Meerbote bases his interpretation primarily on § 10 of the "Critique of Judgment," Kant's discussion of "purposiveness in general." According to Meerbote, this text says that humans act "from propositional representations of what they desire and from beliefs about means sufficient, or likely to be sufficient, in bringing about what is desired." Thus

an agent's reason for performing an action is constituted by a conjunction of desires and beliefs concerning means;[17] and, to follow Hudson now, the propositions expressing the means–end relations believed to obtain are Kant's maxims.[18]

89   THE ISSUE here is not only about how correctly to read Kant. If an interpretation on Meerbote's and Hudson's lines is right, the main representative of a maxim conception of reasons for action will be gone, and that will reinforce the suspicion (§ 84) that this conception is not even an independent competitor in the business of explaining what reasons are. There are grounds to believe, however, that the Meerbote-Hudson interpretation is not right. First, § 10 of the third *Critique* is not an impressive witness in matters of action.[19] Kant is delineating here purposiveness in general for the sake of his aesthetics, not in a practical context, and that is why he is merely repeating standard school formulae here.[20] Second, it is very hard actually to recognize the desire/belief account of reasons, which Meerbote and Hudson claim to find there, in the text of § 10 of the third *Critique*; a difficulty, however, that can only be mentioned, not elaborated here. Third, what Kant says about maxims cannot be accommodated on this interpretation. A maxim is, for Hudson, a proposition like: "One way to get this place warm is to make a fire." Yet this proposition can hardly be called a principle, which is precisely the term Kant consistently applies to maxims (§ 80).[21] Furthermore, maxims should be (according to KpV 19) *practical* principles, but there is nothing practical about that proposition. It is merely a statement about what the world is like. Agents may be well advised to take note of the fact expressed in it, but that does not suffice to make it practical. Otherwise every proposition will be practical, since for every proposition circumstances may arise in which agents are well advised to take note of it. Finally, Hudson's description of a maxim as a proposition expressing a means–end relation does not fit Kant's actual examples of maxims, like "never to leave an offence unavenged" (KpV 19) or again "to enrich oneself by every safe means" (KpV 27). It seems safe to conclude, then, that the considerations advanced by Meerbote and Hudson do not undermine the idea that Kant did propose an account of reasons for which people do things in terms of maxims.

90   THE QUESTION now is whether this account is viable. Two things are difficult to understand in it: first, what it is for an individual to have a maxim, and second, what it is to act on a maxim. First, then, having a maxim. An account of acting for reasons in terms of maxims needs this concept. On this account, agents act the way they do because they have

the maxims they do. If there is no such thing as having a maxim that is distinct from, and intelligible separately from, acting on it, this claim about agents becomes empty, and the maxim turns into a bare *virtus dormitiva*. Also, ordinary talk of maxims, and of rules and principles generally, relies on a notion of holding a maxim independent of any action ensuing. We speak of adopting, of being committed to, and of discarding a principle, and none of these expressions requires that any acting on the principle occurred. All this you can do in your heart. The proverbial hollowness of New Year's resolutions bears witness to this fact. If you resolve to clean your place every week, you have adopted a rule, you hold it, it is a rule you now have; and if the account of agency in terms of maxims has any chance of being true, something must now be different about you because you so resolved. Notoriously, however, this does not say anything about what actually you are going to do. After all, you may quietly discard the rule again when the time comes for completion. Also, you may just die on New Year's day. (Thus, Kant's claim [GMS 421n.] that a maxim is a principle "on which the subject *acts*" is too strong. Somebody may hold a maxim and still not act on it, because no occasion presents itself during her time.) So we both do distinguish between holding a maxim and actually following it and need to do so if talk of acting on maxims is to be informative. Thus it is appropriate to demand that the account of agency under discussion explain what it is to hold a maxim.

From the foregoing it is evident that for holding a maxim it is not nec- 91
essary to act on it. This is so even if sometimes failure to act in conformity with a maxim is rightly taken as a sign that the agent does not hold it. Nor is it sufficient for holding a maxim that one's actions exhibit the relevant regularity. The things we do, indeed the things we do intentionally, exhibit plenty of regularities that we have not dreamt of making it our rule to produce. Even known conformity is not enough. We sometimes watch ourselves getting into habits, for instance of reacting with petty censoriousness, while being far from having it as a maxim to exhibit these reactions. It does not help, either, to say that a person holds a maxim just in case she has expressly adopted it. If this means that the person has done whatever brings about her holding the maxim, then the explanation is going in a circle, for holding a maxim is just what needed to be understood. If on the other hand it means that the person has made an inner declaration, has "said in her heart,"[22] that such and such is henceforth to be a course of her action, or has in some other way promulgated within herself that law, then it is not clear why it should be true to say that a person holds a maxim just in case she has done one of these things. It is not clear why these inner dealings should bring it about that the person

now does hold the maxim in question. The dealings are not suspect because they are inner. Their effectiveness is what is in doubt. There is no connection to be seen between talking to yourself *ex cathedra* and the maxim in question being actually yours. To use a phrase of Wittgenstein, such gestures may be just a ceremony,[23] which is to say, something purported to be pregnant with meaning, but actually lacking a recognizable effect.

92 THE NATURAL proposal is: to hold a maxim is to want to act in accordance with it. However, this is ambiguous: acting in accordance with a maxim can be understood as compliance and as conformity. It can be understood, that is, as acting *on* the maxim and as acting that exhibits the regularity enjoined in the maxim. (You may have a principle of taking revenge whenever offended and act on it, which is compliance, and you may have no such principle, but still take revenge whenever offended, which is conformity.) Now to say that to hold a maxim is to want to comply with it is unsatisfactory, for, as indicated earlier (§ 90), we do not understand compliance, that is, acting on a maxim, without an idea of holding a maxim, and so to explain the latter by reference to the former is to go in a circle. Thus the answer under discussion should be understood, rather, in the sense of conformity: to hold a maxim is to want one's actions to exhibit the regularity specified in the maxim. However, this explanation appears to be incorrect. We recognize a distinction between wanting my behavior in the future to be of a certain kind and having it as my rule to act in that way. Somebody could say: "I do want to be a sensitive teacher, paying attention to the individual shape of my students' accomplishments, deficiencies, and promises. However, I know from experience that, at least under present conditions, I just cannot do it. A pile of only twenty papers invariably bores me stiff, so that all I produce are routine reactions to certain signals in the writing. And knowing that I cannot, I have stopped setting myself the rule to do it." This person wants to be an attentive teacher, but does not hold the maxim to be one. To be sure, he may be mistaken about the facts. Perhaps with a different approach he could after all do what he wants. Yet that is not the issue here. What he is saying, factually mistaken or not, does not seem to be incoherent, as it would be if holding a maxim were the same thing as wanting oneself to act in conformity with it.

93 IT MAY be insisted against this that strictly speaking the resigned teacher is indeed talking nonsense and confuses wishing and wanting: having given up trying, he can by right only say that he wishes to be a sensitive teacher. The trouble with this response is that the confusion, if it be one,

is ingrained in the ordinary concept of wanting. It is not bad English to use the verb "to want" the way the resigned teacher does. Thus the objector's notion of wanting as opposed to wishing, departing from ordinary usage, needs itself explaining, and that is as hard a task as the original one of explaining what it is to hold a maxim. In fact, under the maxim conception of agency it may well be the same task. That is to say, wanting in the sense in which, according to the present objector, the resigned teacher lacks the want to be a sensitive teacher, may indeed come to the same thing as holding the relevant maxim. If this is so, we have not made any progress: the former idea is as hard to understand as the latter.

ONE MIGHT try to improve the criterion by requiring of a maxim-holder, 94 in addition to wanting her actions to conform to the rule, the belief that this is possible for her. That takes care of the resigned teacher as described: he lacks the belief that he can be the attentive teacher he wants to be. It does not take care of another who wants to be an attentive teacher and knows that he can do it, but lacks the strength of will requisite for setting himself to do it. It is not that he backslides occasionally. In that case it may be argued that at the times in question he ceases to want to be an attentive teacher. It is rather that, although wanting it constantly, he fails to form the appropriate policy. Such a state of mind may not be common; it is certainly not unheard of. People suffer from depression, self-doubt, inner fatigue, or what the monks called *acedia* to the point of being unable to set themselves on a certain track, while no less wanting to be on that track in their actions. On the other hand, belief that she can do it may also be too stringent a requirement on a maxim-holder. As in the case of Davidson's typist who intends to make ten legible carbon copies, but does not believe with any confidence that she will,[24] it seems possible to adopt a maxim without positively believing that one will be able to stick to it. Perhaps one should not believe that one won't; but without a settled view either way a maxim certainly appears to be within reach. This might suggest the following condition for maxim-holding: wanting one's actions to conform to the rule and absence of a belief that one cannot do it. That, however, is clearly too weak as a sufficient condition. A resigned teacher may, unlike the one in the example earlier, have no views about what he can and cannot do and still be resigned, that is, fail to adopt the maxim of being an attentive teacher, while all the time wanting to be one.

So ONE might hope that intending rather than wanting (§ 92) provides the 95 key for an analysis of holding a maxim. One might suggest, that is, that to hold a maxim is to intend to act in conformity with it. There are two problems with this idea, however. First, we may not intend or have intended to do whatever we do intentionally,[25] and so to tie maxim-holding to intending may give us too narrow a conception of the former, one on which it is no longer true that for every action there is a maxim (§ 79). For example, you enter the room where you will be giving a talk, and there you see an old friend in the audience of whom you had long lost sight—you immediately greet her with joy. Was greeting her an intentional act? Certainly. You did not do it inadvertently, nor was it a mere reaction on your part. Did you intend to greet her? No. When you saw her, you greeted her right away, you did not go first through a phase of intending to do so; and before you saw her, you did not intend to greet her either, since you did not think of this possibility. Nor do you go to your talks intending to greet any old friend who might happen to show up, or with other general intentions of this sort.[26] Is your greeting her open to moral assessment? Yes, it should be, and so there should be a maxim you acted upon, even though it may be difficult to tell what it was. Thus you held a maxim, but there was no intending on your part to act in conformity with it. Hence, maxim-holding cannot be analyzed in terms of intending.

96   THE SECOND difficulty about this proposal lies in the fact that maxims are supposed to be binding for the agent who holds them, whereas intending to do something in the future is not. True, maxims are binding in a curious way, for the agent, master over his maxims (§ 81), can remove the bond at any time. Still, as long as he does not, he is held to its demand. Thus Kant consistently uses the vocabulary of obligation to describe maxim-holders. For instance, he explicates "maxim" by "self-imposed rule," (GMS 438) thus indicating that such a rule, while self-imposed, is therefore no less imposed, so that the agent on his part is subject to it.[27] Maxim-holders already are, to use Paul's phrase, "a law unto themselves."[28] By contrast, an agent is not bound by what previously he intended to do. Michael Bratman, it is true, suggests that there is "a characteristic kind of commitment" involved in intention. However, what he has in mind here is this: untoward circumstances apart, intention will determine and control action, and intention will guide reasoning toward forming suitable subintentions, toward forming only such other intentions as are consistent with the present one, and so on.[29] There is no idea here that an agent, by virtue of intending such and such, is under some kind of requirement to do such and such. The agent holding such and such a maxim, however, *is* under a corresponding requirement, even if it is only self-imposed. Therefore again, maxim-holding cannot be analyzed in terms of intending.

If correct, these considerations show that intending to act in conformity 97
with some rule is neither necessary nor sufficient for holding the appropriate maxim. Wanting to act in conformity, however, while not sufficient,
as the case of the resigned teacher shows, does seem to be necessary. Let
us say that the maxim you acted upon when you greeted your friend in
the audience was this: within the limits of custom always openly to express
your feelings. You may not have at any point intended to do so. Still, if
this is your maxim, it seems that so to act must be something you want.
So one wonders what needs to be added to wanting to act conformingly
to get full maxim-holding. In what does the resigned teacher differ from
an unresigned one who not only, like him, wants to be sensitive to his
students' individual achievements, but also, unlike him, holds this as his
principle? One might say that the latter is already engaged in the project
of attentive reading, while the former is not. It is true, the teacher who
makes attentive reading of his students' work his rule has not thereby
done any attentive reading (§ 90). What he has done so far is something
like enlisting himself for it. He is, in a stronger sense than Bratman's
(§ 96), committed to it. Kant at one point calls the acceptance of a maxim
"the formal ground" of action in accordance with it.[30] Thus it may be said
that the teacher who holds the maxim in question has given himself as
an agent the form of an attentive reader. If he does not change his rule,
as he is always free to do, then, once papers are coming in, his actually
reading them attentively will be a mere matter of carrying out what he
already set himself to do. It will be a mere matter of fulfilling his self-
given form.

This reading explains what may otherwise appear as a piece of strange 98
reasoning in Kant's thought on religion.[31] If an evil man, he says, turns
around the highest ground of his maxims through one immutable decision, he thereby is, as far as his principle and his attitude is concerned, a
subject receptive for the good, but a good person only in continuous working and becoming. For God, however, who sees the intelligible ground of
all maxims and in whose view, therefore, the infinity of progress is unity,
this counts as actually being good.[32] The present idea of holding a maxim
explains why God is not just mistaken on this score. The person who has
chosen a good maxim is, to that extent, already good in his form as an
agent. Not that he could save himself the trouble of actually doing good
things now. That would show that he did not after all take on the form
of the good, or has discarded it meanwhile. The point is that for God
that person's doing good things is no news. It was all formally there
already in his heart.

99   To PUT it in different terms again, the agent who holds a rule is embarked
on some course of action even before relevant occasions arise. One might
say, taking the phrase quite literally, that there is something that "he is to
do": in doing it when the time comes he will be fulfilling what he is.[33]
To exploit another phrase, sometimes it is said of a person that "she owes
it to herself" to do this or that. The person holding a maxim may indeed
be described as owing it to herself that she act in the way indicated by
the maxim, once the occasion arises. She only owes it to herself, that is,
she may actually not be going to do it. She owes it only to herself, that
is, she does not stand under others' requirements or expectations. Yet she
does owe it to herself, for she *is* under a requirement to do it (§ 96), and
did not just produce words or thoughts saying that she owes it, or saying
that she is going to do it. The maxim-holder differs from the person
ordinarily said to owe something to herself only in that the latter's "debt"
arises from some dignity or other quality the person just has, whereas the
maxim-holder freely imposed the "debt" on herself by adopting the
maxim.

100   THIS, it seems, is the best explanation that can be given of what holding
a maxim amounts to, but it is not good enough. We cannot substantiate
in our experience the distinctions and metaphors on which this explanation
relies. We do not know form, in this sense. We do not know what it is
to be an attentive reader in one's form as an agent and what it means to
say of some piece of attentive reading that it fulfills that form. We do not
know what it is that God is supposed to see in people's hearts, never mind
whether there is a God to do the seeing. And we do not know what the
bond could be to which a person by an internal fiat would make herself
subject. We do not know what it would be for a person in that sense to
be committed to some course of action; since that is a sense that goes
beyond Bratman's commitment involved in intention (§ 96), beyond Nancy
Schauber's "active commitment," one's assuming special obligations toward others,[34] and beyond one's caring about something or somebody, in
Harry Frankfurt's sense.[35] In the end, Romans 2:14 and the long time it
has been with us notwithstanding, we do not know what it is to be a law
unto oneself. So we do not know what is true of a person by virtue of
the fact that she has adopted a maxim. We are familiar with those things
from which maxim-holding needs to be distinguished. We are familiar
with people doing something, people saying or thinking that they are
going to do something, people being required or expected by others to do
something. We have no idea what it is that one is to do something, if it
is nothing of these. This is not an argument from queerness.[36] Arguments
from queerness suffer from assuming, first, that we know what kind of

entity is queer, and, second, that what is queer probably does not exist. The point of the present argument is more modest. It is not that maxim-holding would be a strange inhabitant of the universe. It is that on reflection we must say that we have not come across such a bird. In the end, the argument boils down to saying that the request for an explanation (§ 90) has not been met. "A person holds a maxim"—we still do not know what is meant by this phrase.

THE SECOND difficulty (§ 90) in the maxim account of reasons is to understand what it is to act on a maxim. Assuming, contrary to the argument so far, that we do know what it is to hold a maxim: the question now is what precisely the relation is between the maxim a person holds and an action on that maxim. The question is in fact what the word "on" means in phrases like "acting on principle." It is evident that the present account of reasons needs an answer to this question, too. Otherwise we will be barred from understanding its central doctrine that to act is to act on some maxim (§ 79). 101

KANT's writings contain the material for two different answers. One is given in "Foundations" (GMS 412), and considering the fact that this passage opens the main argument of Kant's principal text on moral philosophy, it may be called the official answer. 102

> Everything in nature works according to laws. Only a rational being has the capacity of acting *according to the idea* of the laws, i.e. according to principles; which capacity is a *will*. Since *reason* is required to derive actions from laws, will is nothing but practical reason.[37]

These sentences explain what action is by distinguishing it from mere working, that is producing effects, of which every natural object is capable. The difference lies in how action and mere working are related to laws. The mere working of natural objects only falls under laws, that is, can be correctly described by them. Agents by contrast may produce action so as to conform to a law. When they do, their action is not only correctly described by laws. Rather, there is a law such that the action is produced by the agent so as to instantiate it. Of this law the agent accordingly needs to have an idea, whereas mere natural objects do not have to be aware of the law they exhibit in what they do. To act so as to conform to a law, of which one therefore needs to have an idea, is to act according to principles, and these are the principles Kant calls maxims. Thus on this reading the passage is further evidence for the claim (§ 80) that for Kant to act is to act on some maxim.

103   THE ANSWER to the question what it is to act on a maxim is contained in the last sentence of the passage quoted. That it takes reason to derive actions from laws is an argument for identifying will and practical reason only on the understanding that to derive actions from laws is what will does. Will was introduced in the previous sentence as the capacity to produce action so as to conform to a law of which the agent has an idea; in short, as the capacity to act on maxims. So the implicit claim of the passage is that acting on maxims is a matter of deriving actions from laws. In standard philosophical terminology, to derive is to infer. To derive is to infer here in particular, because that explains Kant's saying that reason is required to derive actions from laws. On Kant's view, reason, "considered as the faculty of a certain logical form of cognition," *is* the faculty of inferring (KrV A330/B386). So this is what acting on a maxim amounts to: the action is inferred from the maxim. Kant's theory of acting on a maxim is the traditional doctrine of the practical syllogism.

104   ACTING on a maxim, then, works as follows. You have adopted some rule as your maxim. Now circumstances arise for which the maxim specifies a certain response on your part, and you notice that this is the case. So you draw a conclusion from the maxim together with a statement of the relevant facts; and your drawing the conclusion is your bringing about the action that instantiates the maxim. True, you can also bring about an effect instantiating some law in the way natural objects do. After all, you are a natural object, too, and your behavior could simply fall under the law. Yet when you bring about an effect the way only rational beings can do it, then your bringing it about *is* your drawing a conclusion from the maxim you hold. This is why only rational beings can do it this way: they alone can grasp universals and can infer from them. The syllogistic order is on display in Kant's example of the deposit:

> For example, I have made it my maxim to increase my wealth by every safe means. Now I have a deposit in my hands the owner of which died without leaving a record of it. (KpV 27)

Evidently the second sentence describes a circumstance belonging to those for which the first sentence specifies a kind of response to be taken (§ 80). If it were not for the moral reflection suggested by Kant that at least temporarily invalidates the agent's maxim, the agent would "straightaway," to use Aristotle's term,[38] embezzle the deposit. It would simply be a matter of putting two and two together; that is to say, of drawing the consequence from the principle together with the relevant circumstances. The very term "maxim" indicates this syllogistic function. "Maxima" is superlative of "major," which is the standard term for the first premise of a syllogism.

THIS account of acting on a maxim, it has to be admitted, is difficult to 105 reconcile with Kant's doctrine of the opacity of the human heart. This is so because acting on a maxim, so understood, requires agents to be aware of their maxims. It is not that agents have to go through an explicit reciting of the premises of their syllogism at the time of acting. Still, they need to have an idea of the sort of thing they are doing, or else it will not count as action. Indeed, Kant insists in the passage quoted earlier (§ 102) that action, unlike the mere working of natural objects, involves an agent's idea of the law that the action is to instantiate. Agents make things happen on the basis of an understanding of the laws exhibited in the things they make happen. However, Kant also rejects the requirement that agents be aware of their maxims when he maintains that

> the most painstaking examination can never lay open entirely the secret incentives, for, when moral worth is in question, it is not a matter of actions which one sees, but of those inner principles which one does not see. (GMS 407)

The context of the passage shows that these inner principles are to be understood as maxims. Thus Kant is saying here that we never know the maxim of an action, be it our own or somebody else's. We only know the action. Thus even the agents do not know what maxim they are acting upon.

THE CONFLICT between the present account of acting on a maxim and the 106 doctrine of opacity should be resolved in favor of the former, for there are independent reasons against the latter. If you can never find out what maxim you are acting upon, the task of acting only on a morally worthy one becomes as desperate as that of obeying a God who is radically inaccessible to human understanding; and Calvinism may indeed be the historical source of Kant's insistence on opacity. However, this is an element alien to the fundamentally rationalist outlook of Kant's enterprise. For him, it is not hidden to us what we ought to do. As the moral law is a demand of reason alone, we know it, all of us.[39] Yet he would be taking back with one hand what he gave with the other, if he were to claim that we can only know what we ought to do *in abstracto*; if he were to claim, that is, that we know a general criterion for identifying morally worthy maxims, but are unable ever to tell whether the maxim we hold is among these or not. "What man morally is or should become, that he must make or have made *himself*," Kant wrote.[40] Clearly this making is not meant to be a lucky or unlucky stab in the dark, as it would be if we could not check on how we are doing. Hitting or missing a target is not of our own making, in the sense relevant here, if, while having the target in full view, we never see what our shots are. No doubt we may be occasionally unclear about our maxims, but it would be devastating for a moral outlook if we could never be anything but unclear about them. Recently Onora O'Neill suggested that opacity of maxims, while diminishing our chances of explaining action, does not impair our striving to live up to morally worthy principles.[41] Yet again it is hard to see how it does not, for if you cannot tell, at least occasionally, where you are and what progress you are making, you can hardly be said to be striving somewhere. In fact, in unguarded moments Kant himself rejects opacity. In a late note he says that without a cheerful state of mind

> one can never be certain to have come to the point of *loving* the good,
> i.e. to have taken it up into one's maxim.[42]

So presumably *with* a cheerful state of mind one *can* be certain of having taken up the good into one's maxim. Indeed, if one could not, morality would be a matter of "fear and trembling," rather than of being cheerful.

107   THE PRESENT account of acting on a maxim (§ 104) does not suffer, then, from being in conflict with the doctrine of opacity, for that doctrine has to go anyway. It suffers from internal problems. There is no recognizable sense of "inferring" in which ordinary cases of following a maxim can be described as cases of inferring (except, say, that one is practicing logic). The person who has the principle to enrich himself by every safe means and recognizes that the deposit in his hands is a safe means is not, in an intelligible sense, inferring in embezzling it. Whether that person's maxim is formulated as an "ought"-statement: "I ought to do everything safe to enrich myself," as an imperative directed to himself: "Do whatever is safe to enrich yourself!" or perhaps in some other way, what can be inferred from one of these, given the safe means at hand, is at most something like "I ought to embezzle the deposit" or "Embezzle it!" So the agent muttering to himself: "Let me get it!" or whatever is colloquially equivalent, may indeed be drawing a conclusion. The agent embezzling the deposit is not. However, it is the agent who actually embezzles the deposit, not the agent who tells himself to do so, who is acting on the maxim to enrich himself by every safe means. Thus, there is no reason to think that to act on a maxim is to draw a conclusion from it. The difficulty is well known to students of Aristotle's theory of action. It is the difficulty of making sense of Aristotle's repeated assertion that the conclusion of a

practical syllogism is the action:[43] how could an action be inferred? The answer is that it cannot. The practical syllogism is not a viable account of acting on a maxim.

HERE, then, is the second (§ 102) account of acting on a maxim that can be construed from Kant's writings. He maintains that

> the universal of *our* (human) understanding does not determine the particular. (KdU 406)

108

Thus a maxim, contrary to what was stated in the first account, does not determine what particular thing to do in this or that situation. To determine what to do judgment is required. Judgment is different both from taking in the situation (what Aristotle calls "perception")[44] and from holding the rule (which Kant, at least in the context of the first *Critique*, ascribes to the understanding; A132/B171). Thus it is different both from the capacity to form the major premise (like "I should enrich myself by every safe means") and from the capacity to form the minor premise (like "Here is a deposit in my hands whose owner died without leaving a record") in a practical syllogism. Judgment is, rather, "the capacity to *subsume* under rules, i.e. to distinguish whether something is a case of some given rule (*casus datae legis*) or not" (KrV A132/B171). That is to say, judgment applies the rule to the situation. It is what draws the conclusion from the premises in a practical syllogism. In order to act on a maxim, then, a person needs, first, to hold the maxim, second, to take note of the situation, but third and independently, to select a particular action for the perceived situation by means of judgment. So once your maxim is in place, and you realize what the situation is, then it is judgment that accounts for your acting on the maxim. This is O'Neill's view: judgment, she writes, "is always needed when principles are applied to particular cases."[45]

THIS second answer to the question what it is to act on a maxim, by contrast to the first, does not take the transition from general rule to particular action as unproblematic. The plausibility of the first account depends precisely on there being no gap between a rule and its instantiation in action. This is the point of Aristotle's "straightaway he acts" (§ 104): to hold a rule and to see circumstances obtaining for which the rule specifies action is, on Aristotle's view, sufficient to go off and do it, no extra step required; just as, on his view, to think the premises of a theoretical syllogism is sufficient for thinking the conclusion.[46] By contrast, Kant, in the sentence from the "Critique of Judgment" just quoted, opens a gap between universal and particular. For him, therefore, deriving the

109

action from the law ceases to be (as GMS 412 had it) a matter of course. Going from law to action takes an extra step, and thus it takes an extra capacity. It takes judgment.

110 WHILE the notion that, for our understanding, the universal does not determine the particular is fundamental for the whole enterprise of a Critique of judgment, Kant himself does not actually show a great deal of enthusiasm for applying this idea to matters of action. He does embrace it in the opening paragraphs of the essay on theory and practice, but in the *Foundations* and also in the second *Critique* the practical syllogism dominates as an account of acting on a maxim.[47] The reason for Kant's reservations may be the following. Kant knows of two explanations for a person's outstanding judgment. The first is rich experience. The notion of a person's judgment being sharpened by experience is standard with him.[48] Thus, the judgment account of agency commits him to saying that some people are better than others in figuring out what to do, so in particular better in figuring out what to do on moral grounds, because they know more of the world. To many this may seem a very sensible thing to say, but for Kant it is an unwelcome consequence. It clashes with his conviction, gained no doubt in his encounter with Rousseau's Vicar from Savoy,[49] that "no knowledge and no philosophy is needed to know what one has to do in order to be honest and good and even wise and virtuous" (GMS 404). MacIntyre means to say something devastating when he concludes that "for Kant one can be both good and stupid,"[50] and O'Neill defends him against this charge.[51] Yet in one sense Kant is happy to accept it: Yes, I need not be clever—"inexperienced in the ways of the world, unable to prepare myself for every event that may come about, I just ask myself: Can you will your maxim to become universal law?" (GMS 403) However, once judgment is required even to reach action, as it is on the account under discussion, this attitude becomes untenable. Inexperience in the ways of the world will then be a drawback, and indeed a moral drawback. A second explanation of somebody's excellence in judgment is simply that it is a talent, a gift of nature (KrV A133/B172). On this line of reasoning the judgment account of agency leads to the consequence that some people are by nature better than others in finding out what to do, and in particular what to do on moral grounds. True, for Kant it does not completely depend on nature how good your judgment is, as O'Neill points out.[52] Judgment can be educated, for instance it can be sharpened by examples. On the other hand, if you simply lack this talent, practice will not help you: "there is no cure for this deficiency" (KrV A134/B173 and note). So the consequence is that some people are by nature better equipped than others to be morally good. This is unacceptable for Kant, and in this case

many will agree with him. Perhaps it was on account of these consequences that Kant did not wholeheartedly endorse a judgment conception
of acting on a maxim.

IT IS in fact not a satisfactory conception. In the first place, it is incomplete   111
the way the first account of acting on a maxim was. The objection there
was: the conclusion of a syllogism is a statement, or perhaps an imperative,
it is not an action; and so we do not know what "inferring an action from
a rule" should mean (§ 107). The objection is similar here: the faculty of
judgment presumably puts out judgments, and in the context of action it
should put out judgments to the effect that this or that ought to be done.
However, what a judgment to the effect that this or that ought to be done
has to do with doing this or that is precisely what needs to be explained
to answer the question what it is to act on a maxim. In the second place,
one would like to know more about how the faculty of judgment manages
to reach even the judgment to the effect that this or that should be done.
Absent some information on this point, judgment looks like a *virtus dormitiva*. It is not the fact that the same term, 'judgment', applies both to
the faculty and its output, it is the fact that we learn no more about the
faculty than that its employment has that output, which arouses suspicion.
Kant argues that you cannot teach judgment by offering rules for judging,
since rules are useless if the recipient does not have judgment already.[53]
Maybe so, but this does not show that it is unreasonable to ask for an
account of what a person is doing who exercises judgment. Without some
further explanation it will be merely a word, not a theory, that we have
been given.[54]

PERHAPS, however, no more is commonly said about the exercise of judg-   112
ment because the very idea of such a faculty is incoherent. Here is the
argument for this contention. Judgment is supposed to take us from a
rule together with a statement of relevant facts to the specification of an
action. Now if, in Kant's phrase, the universal of our human understanding does not determine the particular (§ 108); if the rule, with a suitable
minor premise in place, does not straightaway yield a particular statement
or imperative; if a particular statement or imperative can be reached only
by employing in addition an independent faculty of judgment, then it
becomes unclear what significance the rule still has in the process. It becomes unclear what it means to say that it is that rule that is being applied.
An independent faculty for applying rules is paradoxical. If that faculty,
being independent, all by itself determines what particular statement or
imperative is to be the result of the application process, then it is indeed
not applying the rule; and if it just enunciates what the rule is saying in

cases of this sort, then it is not an independent faculty, but superfluous. There is in fact no genuine problem of application. If the rule, fed with a suitable minor premise, tells us what to do, the purported problem of application is solved, and if it does not, then we may well have a practical problem, that is, we may not know what to do, but we do not have a problem of application, since the rule does not speak to the matter. Application is easy; if it is not, it isn't application. So to hold a maxim and to see that the relevant circumstances obtain must be sufficient to conclude that such and such action is to be done. There is, in this sense, no gap between the universal and the particular: to understand the universal includes the ability to make the transition to the particular. A universal that does not determine the particular is no use.

113   IT WILL be objected: "Sure, there is no problem of application once a suitable minor premise is in place. The problem of application is precisely how to get one. The problem is to recognize those features of the situation that make a principle relevant for it. And this is what it takes judgment to do." This much is true: the first and often the most difficult problem agents face is that of recognizing what kind of situation it is in which they find themselves. The maxim of greed mentioned earlier offers a trivial example of the difficulty: sometimes it is very hard to tell whether some means of enriching yourself is safe. Maxims of being helpful or loyal present deeper examples: often it is difficult to see what helping somebody, or being loyal to somebody, would consist in. O'Neill puts the point convincingly: "To suppose that they can instantly recognize their situation as having a certain specification simplifies, indeed falsifies, the predicament agents face."[55] This is why, incidentally, advice is sometimes helpful to a degree that surprises the adviser: to advise is not primarily to tell someone what to do, it is in the first place to help someone to understand his situation. However, the problem of understanding one's situation is not a problem of application. It is not a task that calls for a special faculty of judgment. It is a problem of cognition, of finding out how things stand. To be sure, to find out how things stand is not just a matter of opening one's eyes and looking. It takes practice, it takes education, to see what in some situation needs seeing. Yet it is an accomplishment separate from, and preliminary to, figuring out what according to one's maxim one should do in this situation. Hence it is irrelevant for the present task, which is to explain what it is to act on a maxim.

114   TRUE, we sometimes call, misleadingly, the difficulty of finding suitable minor premises a difficulty of application. For instance, if you tell some-

body that she should always do what in the end makes her happy, you may hear that unfortunately your rule is difficult to apply. Actually it is not, speaking strictly. The process of applying that rule is not liable to go wrong if you don't do it very carefully (the way it *is* difficult, say, to take a watch apart and put it together again). The process of applying that rule will not even get started, for lack of a trustworthy minor premise, and so it will not be a process that is difficult to run. In such a case it is a straightforward cognitive problem that you have, it is not a problem of application proper. The trouble is simply that it is hard to tell whether some course of action will make somebody happy in the end. To speak of a difficulty of application in these cases is misleading in the same way as it is, for example, to say that it is difficult to build a house these days, while meaning that building lots are hard to find: the fact that preconditions are not fulfilled is confused with a difficulty in the process itself. Because of this confusion it can appear as if it were the task of judgment, "a peculiar talent," as Kant puts it (KrV A133/B172), to supply an appraisal of the situation, while actually to have an appraisal of the situation in place is a precondition for applying a rule.

THE UPSHOT is, there is no faculty of judgment because there is no particular accomplishment that would call for such a faculty. Once a suitable appraisal of the situation is in place, to understand the rule *is* to be able to apply it, no additional step being necessary (§ 112); and if an appraisal is lacking, our ordinary capacity for finding out about things is called upon to supply one, judgment again dropping out of the picture (§ 113). As for the special condition of a lack of judgment in people to which Kant draws attention,[56] the learned stupidity of those who know a lot about medicine or law, say, but are poor doctors or judges nonetheless, this can be understood on similar lines. Such people need not be taken to be deficient in the alleged natural talent of judgment. While knowing a lot, they may be knowing the wrong lot; for instance highly specialized rules that do not help in dealing with the ordinary doctor's or judge's bread-and-butter cases. Or they may know a lot of rules while being blind to those features of situations that make them cases of these rules; which is to say, they may be no good at finding the relevant minor premises. So there certainly is a difference between people who are commonly said to have good judgment and others whose judgment is said to be poor. Yet contrary to what this common way of talking suggests, the difference should not be understood as a difference in people's supply of a particular faculty of judgment. It can be understood, more simply, as a difference in what rules they know and what things they see.

FOUR

Doing Things for Reasons— The Idea

ONCE more: what is a reason for which somebody does something, and how is the reason related to the action? Alternatively, given that sometimes actions are explained by means of the reasons for which they were done, by reference to what do such reason explanations of actions explain, and what is the relation between the thing explained here and the thing by means of which it is explained?

HERE is an example. We are playing chess. You move your bishop to b4. There it threatens my castle on f8. Then I move my pawn to d6. It blocks your bishop's road toward my castle. Under these circumstances it will sometimes be true to say: I moved my pawn to d6 because your bishop on b4 was threatening my castle. It will sometimes be true to say, equivalently, that your bishop's threatening my castle was a reason for which I moved the pawn. This does not exclude, to be sure, that I also moved my pawn to d6 for the reason that this would give my bishop on c8 greater mobility. There may have been a variety of reasons for which I did what I did. Still, to keep things simple, let us assume that the threat from your bishop was the only reason for which I moved my pawn. The question then is how these two, the reason and what was done for the reason, your bishop's threatening my castle and my moving the pawn to d6, are related. One answer is: my moving the pawn was a response to your bishop's threatening my castle. Indeed, this is not just one answer beside others. It is the answer that illuminates what reasons are for which people do things. The bishop's threat and the pawn move not only can be described both as the former being the reason for the latter and the latter being a response to the former. The two descriptions amount to the same thing: to say that the reason for which I move the pawn is your bishop's threat is to say that my moving the pawn is a response to it. And this is so, not because of a peculiarity of the example, but generally: to be a reason for which an action is done is to be something to which the action is a response. This, at any rate, is the idea to be developed here and to be defended against various objections. A number of problems will suggest themselves to readers right away, such as the question whether agents need not also be aware of what their action is a response to, and how to describe agents who are in error about the relevant features of their situation. These problems are taken up in the course of the argument that follows.

119   First of all, however, talk of one thing being a response to the other needs elucidating. Examples abound in games: to your sharp serve I respond with a long return, you draw spades and in response I trump with a jack, and when you leave me, in dominoes, with a three, my response is to get rid of my double three in turn. Examples occur outside games. You insult me, and I respond in kind, or else I respond by walking away silently. You sell me a lemon, and I cut up your tires. The lights turn red, and I step on the brakes. You do me a favor, and I do you a favor in turn. You publish a book in philosophy with big claims and little argument, and I write a scathing review. Simply, you ask me what time it is, and I tell you. Perhaps in each of these cases, except the last one, calling an action a response will be deemed metaphorical. It is hard to tell whether it is, literal and metaphorical usage often shading into each other. However, it does not matter as long as calling an action a response is appropriate in these cases, be it metaphorical or not. In many of these cases there will then be a characteristic history comprising both what you did, or more generally what happened, and what I did. There is your threat, and I turn it into a threat parried. There is your insult, and with what I do it becomes the initial part of a shouting match. There is your serve, and it becomes a service returned, and there is your question, and it becomes a question answered. "This statement must not go uncontradicted," we say: there are, as it were, two lives open for that statement, one with and one without being contradicted, and the speaker prefers the former to become real. The same way I could say to myself that this ace of spades must not go untrumped, and that your question must not go unanswered; and when I tell you the time, your question then does "go answered."

120   THIS will all seem trivial. Sure, I incorporated your bishop's threat into the history of a threat parried, but so did I incorporate your castle's sitting on a1 into the history of a castle sitting there followed by a pawn move to d6, and so indeed did I incorporate any state of affairs under the sun into a history of its being followed by my pawn move. Yet not to all those

things did I respond in moving the pawn. It is true, we do not have a handy expression, like "a threat parried," for all these courses of events, but that should not be relevant. The question, then, is how the relation between my pawn move and your bishop's threat, to which supposedly it is a response, differs from the relation between my pawn move and some other state of affairs, like your castle sitting on a1, to which it is not a response.

It is as historians of chess games that we can find the answer. After all, 121 we do not describe games of chess only by listing moves. We describe them also by marking out paths among states of affairs obtaining and moves made at various stages in a game. We describe them by showing histories in games. A history may comprise a large number of positions and moves: "The strong center established at the beginning gave Black the upper hand throughout"; or it may be a fairly detailed one: "White immediately attacked the gambit pawn." In particular, some histories link moves as being one the response to the other. Thus in our game my pawn move is linked as a response to your bishop's threatening my castle. My pawn move is not so linked to your castle's sitting on a1. There is nothing about my move or the castle's position that excludes their being linked in this way. They just are not, and with some experience in chess playing we know that they are not. This is all the difference between the two relations. Your castle's sitting on a1 and my pawn move merely occur in the same game and are otherwise unconnected, but your bishop's threat and my pawn move are linked as state of affairs and response.

It is as historians generally that we can find out which action is a response 122 to what. After all, we hardly ever describe what is going on by listing isolated events. We describe it by marking out paths among states and events, in particular actions. We describe what is going on by showing histories in it. That is, we describe it by telling stories. Some histories do not involve an action and a state or event to which the action is a response. For example, when you washed, dressed, went downstairs, and picked up the paper this morning, it was not in response to your having dressed that you picked up the paper. Other histories do involve an action and a state or event to which the action is a response. For example, it was in response to your insulting me that I shouted back. And we know the difference between the two kinds of history. We can tell a mere chronicle from an account of what happened. Sometimes we indicate the difference expressly. We are likely to say: ". . . and then I picked up the paper," but ". . . and so I shouted back." Thus the distinction between what an action is a response to and what is irrelevant for it is part of what we know of the histories making up the world. And we come to know it, certainly not by intuition, by merely looking at the events in question. We come to know it through our ordinary experience of how the world goes.

123   AND IT is only in our quality as historians that we can find out which action is a response to what. It is an empirical matter. We can only gather from cases which things make up a history, and in particular a history consisting of a state or event and an action that is a response to it. Admittedly, this is to shift the burden of explaining what a response is, hence what a reason is, to the relevant stories. We learn to play chess and to describe chess games in part by learning to respond, and to recognize responses, to states of the game. That is to say, we learn to understand games, our own and others', in terms of histories involving responses. Thus, if you really do not understand the difference between the two relations, that of my pawn move and your bishop's threat, and that of my pawn move and your castle's sitting on a1, then you need some more chess training. You need to become acquainted, or better acquainted, with histories in chess involving responses. Since I shall not run out of relevant stories that might help you to grasp the point, I need not ever be remiss in my explanatory duties, even though I shall not offer you a general criterion of what it is for an action to be a response to something. At some point, it can be expected, you will recognize, thanks to the stories I gave you, that in the original case the pawn move responds to the threat, and not to the castle's position on a1. True, that point may never come: there is no guarantee that eventually you will get the idea. But then there is no guarantee of success in explaining anything to anyone, by general criteria or otherwise.

124   WHAT holds for games, holds for life. We learn to do things and to describe what is being done in part by learning to respond, and to recognize responses, to what happened. Life is hardly ever lived or described one action at a time. We engage in whole courses of action, and understand ourselves to be so engaged; and some of these courses of action, like driving through town, leading a discussion, or indeed playing chess, characteristically involve doing things in response to something that happened. Thus again, if you really do not understand the difference between how my stepping on the brakes is related to the lights' turning red, and how it is related, on the other hand, to something irrelevant, like the sunset's being red, then you need some more experience of life, that is, of people's practices. You need to improve your historical understanding. You need to get a better grasp of what is done given what. And there is no dearth of stories that might help you to grasp that.

The term "historian" is understood here, evidently, in a broad sense. It 125
does not refer only to members of an academic discipline. It refers to
whoever gives a story of "what really happened,"[1] or tries to do so. So we
are all of us historians. The three-year-old is who tells what they did in
kindergarten this morning, the doctor is who tries to put together the
patient's anamnesis, the engineer is who explains the engine's breakdown.
In fact, we are all more or less specialized historians, on mornings in
kindergarten, on courses of diseases, on harmonic developments in music,
or on chess games. Thanks to such expertise, specialized or shared, we
know what belongs together in a history and what is irrelevant, and we
know what is a response to what. Which is to say, of course: sometimes
we know.

Are there limits to what sort of thing an action can be a response to? It 126
seems there are: only states and events qualify. Try objects, or in particular
persons: it is hard to make any sense of a statement that says that such
and such a thing was done in response to my car, say, or to the United
Nations or to Kate. Naturally one would suspect that what is meant in
these cases is rather, let us say, my car's being dirty, the United Nations
having imposed a restriction or Kate's asking me to help her with her
move, respectively, to which some action is a response; and with these we
are back with states and events. On the other hand, facts are candidates;
and we easily make sense of a statement that says, for example, that it
was in response to the fact that the lights turned red that I stopped the
car. This just means that it was in response to the lights' turning red that
I stopped the car; and with this again we are back with states or events,
facts dropping out of the picture. Strictly speaking, it would indeed appear
to be false to say that my action was a response to the fact that the lights
turned red. After all, I did what I did in response to what was happening
there in front of me at that time, but the fact that the lights turned red
is not something that happened anywhere or at any time.[2] Neither objects
nor facts being eligible, then, it seems safe to assume that it is only states
and events in response to which we do things. (Chapter 6 will investigate
whether there are further restrictions on the sort of thing in response to
which we may be doing something.)

This being settled, there is no need to observe scrupulously the appropriate 127
linguistic regime. It does not do any harm to say that I stopped in response
to the red lights, or to say that the reason for which I stopped was the
fact that the lights were red. After all, these are common ways of speaking.
It does not do any harm as long as it is understood that, strictly, the reason
for which I stopped was either the lights' being red, a state, or their

turning red, an event. Nor will it be necessary constantly to refer in this text both to states and events; often enough reference to one of the two will do. In fact, Jonathan Bennett argues persuasively that there is no interesting difference between states and events anyway,[3] but as this is a matter of some controversy,[4] and a controversy immaterial to present concerns, states and events will here officially be treated as different. It may also be worth noting at this point that the expression "state of affairs" is not used here in the technical sense it acquired in the tradition of Wittgenstein's *Tractatus*. There a state of affairs can only either obtain, in which case it is a fact, or not obtain, but it cannot have a beginning, duration, or end. By contrast, "state of affairs," as the expression is used here, simply refers to states, with the added convenience that it need not be specified whose states these are. To say that the lights are red is to report on the current state of the lights; to say that it is Wednesday is to report on the current state of affairs. And these states of affairs clearly last for a time and come to an end.

128   RETURNING to the task of elucidating the idea of a response (§ 119), it must be admitted that in one way it may mislead to call my pawn move a response to your bishop's threat. It may be thought, in the case, say, of your asking me what time it is and my telling you, that by responding I did not only make what you said part of a history of a question answered, but gave it its proper completion. A question, one may think, is something incomplete or, with the logicians' metaphor, something unsaturated, waiting for the appropriate answer. After all, we do speak of questions "calling for" or "requiring" answers. So the idea would be that a response basically is some kind of fulfillment of that to which it is a response. However, this is in itself already a dubious idea. It could well be argued, by contrast, that questions and answers are all, Humeanly speaking, distinct existences, none waiting or calling for fulfillment by the other, but just receiving different continuations in the course of events. It may be argued that figures of speech like "a question calling for an answer" are merely that, figures of speech, expressing the fact that *people*, under certain circumstances, expect or require other people to answer questions. However this may be, when it comes to moves in games or to things like shouting back to an insult, it is clear that these are not responses in the sense of giving the first thing any sort of fulfillment. It may be advisable for me to move my pawn to d6 under the circumstances, but if I don't, your bishop's threat will not stand unsaturated, waiting for completion. There is nothing defective about an unanswered question or about an unparried threat. My pawn move is a response to your bishop's threat only in the sense of turning it from a mere threat into a threat parried.

A RESPONSE need not be appropriate, it may well be foolish. For something   129
to be a way, and for something to be a good way, of responding to your
bishop's threat, are two things. Histories, in chess games and elsewhere,
are not sequences of things done well. They are sequences of things done.
To be sure, it may be difficult sometimes to decide whether something is
an utterly foolish response or no response at all, but this is no more than
an ordinary empirical difficulty of classification, like the difficulty of telling whether the color of a car is blue or violet. The fact that sometimes
there is this difficulty does not justify the assumption that foolishness
undercuts an action's response status. It does not show that a requirement
of appropriateness is built into the idea of one thing being a response to
another.

FOR SOMETHING I do to be a response to something that happened it is   130
not necessary that I think of it as a response. Seeing the threat I may just
move the pawn, without entertaining any thoughts as to what the relation
is between what I saw and what I do, yet even then not producing a mere
reflex movement. Neither is it sufficient for something I do to be a response to something that I think of it as such. I may be, like anybody
else, a poor historian of my deeds, connecting them with states or events
to which they bear no relation. Rationalizations, in the ordinary sense of
the term,[5] are a case in point. On the other hand, we do not consider an
action a response to something of which the agent is not in any way
cognizant. Thus if I fall into a trap you laid for me, my doing so is not
a response to the trap. It is if I see the trap and "fall" into it to please
you. Nor is it in response to the "splendid occasion" of the stove still being
hot that I burn my fingers on it, given that I had not noticed that it is
still hot. "Not in any way cognizant" is, admittedly, vague, but that is as
it should be, since it is a matter of dispute what kind and degree of
recognition to require here. Psychoanalysts, for example, are by and large
more generous in this respect than other people. On their view, it may be
in response to what his mother did to him that a man treats his wife
badly, though he is now not conscious of those things for which he is
taking revenge; whereas others may dispute that account precisely because
he is not conscious of them. How generous one needs to be here to do
justice to what people do and why they do it, and how generous one can
be here without effectively giving up the idea that people need to be
cognizant in some way of the reasons for which they do what they do,
should be determined by those actually working in the field of understanding people. Clearly, some things will be out, that is, will not be
acceptable as reasons for which one did something. After all, even psychoanalysts require that the subject be cognizant of the things for which

he is taking revenge in *some* way, namely, in the unconscious. So nobody will admit what is altogether beyond one's ken as something responded to in action, but what the limits of one's ken are is a matter of dispute.[6]

131   IT MAY seem that an agent's being cognizant of what the action is supposed to be a response to is really just the belief element in the standard desire/belief account of doing something for a reason, so that what is being proposed here amounts to no more than a change of terms. This is not so. First, for the standard doctrine a suitable belief is part of the reason for which one does something, whereas on the present account the agent's awareness of some state or event is merely necessary for that state or event to count as a reason for which that agent did something. That makes a difference. On the standard doctrine, when you have listed suitable beliefs of the agent, you are halfway through with the task of giving us the reasons for which that agent did something. On the present account, you have not even begun to do so when you have indicated what the agent was cognizant of at the relevant time. Second, on the desire/belief doctrine it takes a special sort of belief to form part of the reason for which somebody does something, namely, a belief to the effect that to do that thing is a suitable way to fulfill a desire of the agent (§ 2). On the present account, by contrast, the agent just needs to be cognizant of the state or event to which the action is supposed to be a response. This is certainly a less demanding requirement. The present agent only needs to register what, relevantly, is going on around her. The agent of the standard doctrine is presumably going to register that as well, but in addition that agent needs to entertain beliefs about the suitability of his actions for the fulfillment of his desires. Thus the beliefs of the desire/belief doctrine differ from the awareness required here both in their role in the theory and in what is being believed; and the latter difference makes the beliefs of the desire/belief doctrine rather more expensive, theoretically, to ascribe to agents than this awareness, which is quite cheap.

132   IN A more general vein, it may be objected that the notion of a history involving a response to a state or an event lacks the objectivity required for an account of reasons for which people do things. It may be argued that the chronicle of the game, that is, the list of moves, does record what actually happened, whereas stories in which an action is presented as a response to something are mere interpretations. So histories in which something is done in response to something else do not belong to the facts of the game, they are constructions imposed on the facts. In particular, then, it is only a construction, not a fact, that my pawn move is a response to your bishop's threat. Yet presumably it is not a mere construction that

the reason for which I moved the pawn was the bishop's threat. Hence, reasons for which people do things cannot be analyzed in terms of histories involving responses.

THIS reasoning is unconvincing. It rests on a distinction between stating facts and interpreting, which makes no sense. The point is not that, as some writers have held,[7] it is hard or impossible to sort out the statements that are interpretive from those that are not. Whether this is so in general or not, with regard to some descriptions of chess games it is not so. Here it is often easy to sort out the interpretive statements: any member of some such series as (1) e2–e4, e7–e5, (2) d2–d3, and so on, is not an interpretive statement, all the others are. Since many descriptions of chess games mark this distinction by printing the noninterpretive chronicle in bold and the interpretive text in regular type, sorting out the two kinds of statements cannot be frightfully difficult. The point is, rather, that it makes no sense to characterize the sets of statements so distinguished, the noninterpretive and the interpretive ones, as, respectively, stating facts and imposing constructions on the facts.[8] As for stating facts, any true statement, interpretive or not, says how things are and in that sense states a fact. If it is true to say that I moved my pawn to d6, and also true to say that the move was a response to your bishop's threat, then, trivially, it is a fact that I moved the pawn to d6, and it is also a fact that the move was a response to your bishop's threat.[9] As for imposing constructions on the facts, it is unintelligible what this could be. True, in saying that my pawn move was a response to the bishop's threat one claims that there is a certain relation between these two things, and the relation holds, if it does, in addition to, hence, if you like, on top of, the pawn move being a move to d6; which is all the sense that can be made of "imposing" in this context. Yet both these things are true, that the pawn move was a move to d6 and that it was a response to the bishop's threat; and what it means to say that the latter relation is a construction rather than a fact, is not clear.

133

IF THE distinction between stating facts and imposing constructions on the facts makes no sense, why is it so popular? Here is a guess. Things that are commonly put under the heading of facts and under the heading of constructions imposed on the facts are found out, in many cases, in different ways and with different degrees of difficulty. Typically, one quick glance at the board before and after the move will suffice to ascertain that I moved my pawn to d6, but many people will need to take a somewhat closer look and to consider possible further developments in order to find out that my move was a response to your bishop's threat. Hence judgments of the latter sort are more liable to error and so can become the subject

134

of a reasonable dispute, which the former often cannot. These and similar differences are then taken as grounds for concluding that only the first kind of inquiry, where basically you are supposed just to open your eyes and look, makes accessible the facts, and that the second kind, more dubious and debatable, only construes them one way or another. You become, finally, a radical constructivist, or perspectivist, on realizing that nothing meets the description "just to open one's eyes and look", that we always approach things informed by experience. Thus the first disjunct, stating facts, becomes empty for you, and you are left with the second exclusively, imposing constructions on the facts. However, the mistake in this reasoning comes one step earlier. Mistaken is the idea that what you can only find out with difficulty, by taking a second look or by going through some calculation, is therefore any less a fact. The underlying assumption seems to be that what really is a fact should be evident and so indisputable. Admittedly, that accords with the classical philosophical tradition that being is essentially knowable, but nothing else recommends this view. The truth is: how, and with what difficulty, we figure out the facts is our problem. It does not affect the fact status of what we figure out.

135   SUPPOSE now we understand what it is for something to be done in response to some state or event. You will then want to know why doing something in response to some state or event should be the same thing as doing it for a reason that is that state or event (§ 118). The answer is that this makes the best sense of how we ordinarily think and speak of reasons for which people do things. First of all, in explaining what people did by the reasons for which they did it, we do refer, in a vast number of cases, to the states or events in response to which they did it. Statements of the kind "I pulled over because the police ordered me to" (§ 5) appear to be the most common type of reason explanation. This claim, admittedly, is not based on counting cases. It is based on the experience that, with the motorist pulling over and with the chess player moving the pawn and in many similar cases, explanations referring to the police' order, to the bishop's threat, and so on, appear, again and again, to be the most natural ones to give, and explanations referring to the agent's desires or beliefs or to the agent's principles would, for the most part, appear stilted or far-fetched. We just do not say, normally, that I stopped the car because I thought the lights had turned red, or because I wanted to avoid driving into the intersection while the lights were red, or because it is my rule to drive safely. We normally say that I stopped the car because the lights were red, or had turned red.[10] To be sure, this alone does not decide the matter. Argument could be offered to the effect that appearances are deceptive here and that reason explanations really are explanations in terms

of the agent's desires and beliefs, or in terms of the agent's maxims. However, chapter 1 showed that the argument for the primacy of reason explanations by desires and beliefs fails, and chapter 3 showed that an understanding of reasons for which people do things in terms of the agent's maxims is not viable. Under these circumstances the fact carries some weight that in a vast number, and perhaps in the majority, of cases we take the reason for which somebody did something to be the state or event in response to which she did it. And the natural way to account for this fact is to say that something's being the reason for which somebody does something just *is* it's being the thing in response to which she did it.

IN THE second place, while admittedly we also refer frequently to agents' beliefs or wants in indicating the reason for which they do something, many of these cases, if not all, can readily be explained other than by supposing that speakers take beliefs and wants to be the reasons for which people do things. It is natural to say: "I am taking the oleander into the kitchen, I think there will be frost tonight," and it would take a rather self-confident (or forecast-confident) speaker to drop the "I think." Yet by inserting "I think" this speaker does not suggest that his belief is the reason, or part of the reason, for which he takes the oleander into the kitchen.[11] By inserting "I think" he recedes from saying "There will be frost tonight" to "There will probably be frost tonight"; and the probability of frost, which is a state of affairs, is the reason for which he takes in the oleander. (This is to assume objective probabilities, an assumption that will not be defended here.)   136

SIMILARLY for wants. Anscombe's farmer fully and perspicuously told us the reason for which he is going to Hereford, by saying: "There are good Jersey cows in the Hereford market,"[12] but it is true that he could have said instead: "I want to get a good Jersey cow." In saying that, however, he would not have suggested that his want is the reason, or part of the reason, for which he is going to Hereford. He would indeed have led us to understand the reason for which he is going, which is the availability of good Jerseys in Hereford, but he would have done so indirectly, by representing himself as someone sensitive to that state of affairs.   137

So TO construe things may appear dogmatic. If farmers sometimes say that there are good Jerseys in Hereford, and sometimes say that they want a good Jersey, why insist that the availability of good Jerseys is, and their wanting good Jerseys is not, the reason for which they set off for Hereford?[13] Because their using the phrase "I want to get a good Jersey" can be accounted for by a general tendency in how we speak, a retreat to   138 subjectivity, as it may be called. Phrases like the following, occurring in contexts unconnected to reason-giving, are very common:

- We regret to inform you that your application has not been accepted.
- He is not in, I am afraid.
- I understand that Mr. X is being considered for tenure by your department.
- I suppose I *am* saying that.
- I should like to have apple juice.

All these speakers literally report about their actual or potential states, but we are not taken in: by representing themselves as having some attitude or other to some state of affairs, they convey a different message, and that is not about them. It is as if the speakers showed us the imprint some state of affairs has or would have on them, and in this indirect way told us of that state, or, in the last example, asked the interlocutor, as indirectly, to bring that state about. Why we often speak in this roundabout way need not be considered here. Here it is only important that the farmer's saying "I want a good Jersey cow" can be understood on the same lines. In using this expression he is not, strictly, answering our question as to why he is going to Hereford, but by telling us how he feels about good Jerseys, that is to say by telling us of a subjective counterpart to the reason, he indicates, indirectly, what the reason is, namely, that there are good Jerseys available there. And if the farmer's saying "I want a good Jersey cow" can be understood as an instance of the retreat to subjectivity, a phenomenon that has nothing in particular to do with reason-giving, then it no longer bears witness to the assumption that we commonly consider wants to be reasons for which people do things. We do not: reference to the speaker's attitude is otiose in these cases.[14]

139 THESE considerations should throw into relief how strange an idea it really is to take the reasons for which people do things to be their wants and beliefs. After all, the reason for which one does something should be that on account of which one does it,[15] but one does not, in general, do things on account of one's beliefs or wants, one does them on account of what happened or what the current situation is. That is to say, even if, contrary to the argument just given, "I think there will be frost tonight" and "I want a good Jersey cow" were taken as stating the reason, or part of the reason, for which the respective agents do what they do, these would be odd reasons, given normal circumstances. One's belief that there will be frost tonight is not something on account of which one would, normally, take in the oleander. The frost is such a thing, or the probability of frost. So will the farmer go to Hereford for the sake of the good Jerseys available

there, not for the sake of his wanting one. And if wants and beliefs would regularly be odd reasons, it is rather more likely that they are not reasons for which people do things at all.

Using what is perhaps a mere pun, perhaps a piece of sound etymology, one might say that a reason should be something *for* which, and thus literally, before which, in front of which, facing which, one does something. ("Therefore" carries the same suggestion.) In what she does, the idea would be, an agent meets some state or event, which is the reason for which she does it. Yet under normal circumstances we do not, in this sense, meet our wants and beliefs. We are not facing them. They rather characterize us as we are facing the world.   140

The idea of a reason as that confronting which one does something comes out clearly in a passage in the King James Bible. Jesus tells Peter to do another round of fishing; Peter replies that they have been fishing all night, but he continues: "nevertheless at thy word I will let down the net" (Luke 5:5). Peter is saying here that, while there is a reason against another try, their fatigue, Jesus' speech is a reason for it; and that it is for this reason that he will do it. The reason is not the probability of a good catch at this time and in this place, for Peter does not infer such a probability from Jesus' word, nor would this inference be reasonable. The reason is just Jesus' saying what he did. And Jesus' word is that *at* which Peter will let down the net. That is to say, it is that facing which, or confronted with which, he will do it. So if what Peter says is true and he is going to let down the net for the reason of Jesus' saying what he did, then his letting down the net will be a response to Jesus' saying what he did.   141

That this is our ordinary notion of a reason has been obscured by a widespread confusion of reasons and causes. The confusion is fostered by the fact that some expressions, notably "why?" and "because," can be used both when reasons and when causes are meant. Indeed, "reason" itself is often used in the sense of "that which explains," no matter whether it explains as a reason in the narrow sense, as a cause, or in some other way. The confusion is also fostered by the fact that older language can use "cause" in the sense of "reason." Hobbes, for instance, recommends that people leave to the sovereign to uphold or forbid unauthorized prophets "as he should see cause":[16] modern language would use "reason" here. Wilson uses the example: "A man's desire to preserve his marriage may *give him cause* to stop his excessive drinking,"[17] but this locution seems archaic as well. A similar shift occurred in German. Kant claims that we must assume "daß jedermann die Glückseligkeit in demselben Maße zu   142 hoffen Ursache habe, als er sich derselben in seinem Verhalten würdig gemacht hat," that is, "that everyone has reason to hope for happiness just to the extent that he made himself worthy of it in his actions,"[18] and modern language would use "Grund," that is, "reason," here rather than "Ursache," that is, "cause." For all that, the demarcation of reasons and causes is clear enough in ordinary understanding to warrant the complaint about a common confusion between the two. One does not say: "I mention this matter for the following cause"; nowadays one uses "reason" in this context. Conversely, while not impossible, it is not quite correct to say: "The reason for which the car stalled was the humidity"; and it is impossible to say: "The car's reason for stalling was the humidity." That the humidity was the cause is what should be said here. It might be said as well that the humidity was the reason why the car stalled, but as the "why," pleonastic in any case after "reason," shows, "reason" is used here in the broad sense mentioned at the beginning of this paragraph, covering anything that helps to explain something. The distinction between reasons and causes evinced in these examples comes, roughly, to this: a reason for which somebody does something is that on account of which she does it; a cause of somebody's doing something is that which makes it happen that she does it. The confusion of the two does mischief by eliminating the former in favor of the latter; by suggesting, that is to say, that there is no reason relation specifically different from the cause relation. Once the reason relation is recognized as specific, however, it becomes much less plausible to identify reasons with wants and beliefs, and far more plausible to identify them with states and events encountered. Still, to warn against the confusion of reasons and causes is not to rule out beforehand that as a matter of fact reasons are causes. It may turn out that the things on account of which people do what they do are precisely the things that make it happen that they do what they do. Whether this is so or not takes further argument to decide.

143   So MUCH for an initial presentation of the basic idea proposed here. The chapters to follow will elaborate and defend the idea, by discussing a number of questions and objections that may be raised against it. The remainder of this chapter will give a brief review of passages in the literature where this idea has been touched upon. Thus Annette Baier, in a critique of Davidson's view of reasons for action, pointed out that in our normal understanding we take things like questions asked and orders given to be reasons for which people do things, not the agents' wants or beliefs.[19] Alasdair MacIntyre drew attention to sequences of actions in which one action is a response to a previous one, and claimed that at least in some cases the intelligibility of an action is due to its location in such

a sequence.[20] Apparently, he did not consider responses to things other than actions, which here are certainly included. Nor did he use this idea for elucidating reasons for action as on the present proposal. This is because for him "intelligible action" covers a far wider domain than "action done for a reason" does: doing what is routinely done at a certain time by members of one's social group is for MacIntyre an exemplary case of intelligible action, but not a case of an action done for a reason. For this view, however, it is difficult to find a justification. And Robert Audi at one point wrote that a person's action "is, in some way, a response to, and occurs because of, her reasons."[21] However, Audi's reasons then turn out to be states of affairs that the agent wants to become real,[22] and it is hard to see how the action could be a response to those: what something is a response to had better be around.

THE EARLIEST and most explicit hint in the direction taken here was given by Georg Henrik von Wright in his 1981 paper "Explanation and Understanding of Action." He distinguished internal reasons, construed on familiar lines of the desire/belief theory, from external reasons. External reasons are challenges, with things like orders, requests, and questions forming one type of challenge, and things like norms, customs, traditions forming another. Action for an external reason is action done in response to such a challenge.[23] One limitation of von Wright's treatment is the fact that his challenges are only one kind of reasons for which people do things. Admitting internal reasons alongside of external ones, however, leaves it obscure how to conceive of the relation between them. In many cases there will be both challenges and suitable wants and beliefs of the agent in place, but it seems implausible simply to add these and to say that such agents always do what they do for two reasons. Yet what else we should say is not clear. The present proposal takes the more radical line that reasons for which people do things are throughout external reasons in von Wright's sense. Second, and relatedly, von Wright only allows, apparently, challenges brought about by human action, and there seem to be no good grounds for this restriction. Finally, von Wright really deserts his own idea in the end. While at one point we are told that action may be taken on purely external grounds,[24] at another it appears that a challenge is a reason only if, thanks to the agent's acknowledging it as a reason, it has been made internal,[25] and with that the whole idea of an external reason has no longer any work to do. In fact it is worth staying true to von Wright's idea. Admittedly, agents need to be cognizant in some way of that which is the reason for which they do something (§ 130). They need not consider it a reason, though, and above all, whether they do so consider it or not, the reason does not thereby become an internal one. The reason

144

is not the acknowledgment, but the thing acknowledged, and that is the external challenge facing the agent.

145   THERE are, finally, three very recent studies of reasons for action, developing in different ways the same basic idea of reasons as advocated here. Frederick Stoutland, in his 1998 article "The Real Reasons," argues that external situations can be reasons for action. His approach differs from the present one mainly by his additional claim that external situations have content, and that it is because of their content that they can be reasons for action.[26] Marco Iorio's "Echte Gründe, echte Vernunft" of 1998 is focused on the problem of the explanatory force of reason explanations of actions as compared to explanations of natural phenomena in science. Arguing that reasons are states of things, and also using a far more liberal conception of causal explanation than is allowed here, Iorio unfolds a thoroughly naturalistic theory of action and of its explanation and justification. Jonathan Dancy's argument for the claim that reasons are not mental states, in his 2000 book *Practical Reality*, differs from the present one chiefly in his attempt to preserve a normative significance for reasons understood as states of things, his guiding idea being that courses of action are favored by the ways things are.

FIVE

The Explanatory Force of
Reason Explanations

THE PROPOSITION on the table is this: a reason for which an action is done 146 is something to which the action is a response (§ 118). The first question to ask here is how reference to a reason so understood can explain the action, since reference to a reason often does that. A rough answer will be evident from the foregoing (§ 124): explanations of actions by reference to reasons are historical explanations, for it is as parts of histories that reasons and actions are related. This is only a rough answer, because it is not clear what a historical explanation is and how it explains, a topic widely debated in the literature. From the following survey of this discussion it will emerge that it is also a preliminary answer only: there is no general pattern of historical explanations as such. Historical explanations do not owe the force they have to their being historical explanations, but to their following some more specific pattern (§ 159). And reason explanations, it will be argued, form precisely such a pattern of explanation: their force is not derived, but they hold it by virtue of being reason explanations.

IT WILL help to have an example of a historical explanation at hand. Here 147 is one:

> The custom of decorating evergreens at Christmastime has its origins in Alsatia. In the late Middle Ages, plays were presented there the day before Christmas (Adam and Eve's day) depicting the story of Paradise; and for scenic purposes apples were hung on trees, in this case evergreens, which would be the only trees bearing foliage at this season.

This is a neat explanation. Actually, professionals in cultural history may suspect it to be more neat than true. Arthur Danto, from whom it is taken,[1] does not indicate a source, and other evidence suggests rather that Christmas trees are originally winter Maypoles.[2] Never mind truth in this case, though. What is important is the fact that this text, if true, is splendidly successful. Christmas trees are an oddity in our world; people do not ordinarily put trees in their living rooms. Nor does one understand what Christmas trees have got to do with Christmas, the Christian holiday. So one asks what the origin of the custom is. The text quoted here gives an answer. It shows by what route people arrived at putting up Christmas trees. Thereby it sheds light on the present custom. It helps to understand it. It explains it.

148   IT IS a historical explanation because it explains the present custom by reference to an antecedent state of affairs or event. This is a generous way of counting explanations as historical. Explanations are not historical because of their subject matter, for instance because they explain things like wars or revolutions, which lie in the domain of the professional historian. Explanations are historical because they explain whatever it is they explain by reference to something happening or being the case before. Historical explanations in this broad sense do occur in history, the academic discipline, but they are not a special feat of historians. They grow in a variety of fields: linguistics, musicology, geology, medicine. They grow outside academia: a radiator cracks because the temperature dropped below zero,[3] a tablecloth is stained because a drop of red wine ran down the bottle, and so on. Taking "historical explanation" to cover so broad a range, rather than restricting the term, as the literature often does implicitly,[4] to, roughly, the sort of explanation professional historians employ, is justified by the fact that there is no sort of explanation specifically employed by professional historians. They do the same sort of explaining as everybody else.[5] They are just better at it, one imagines, and to be sure they explain events of greater consequence than a tablecloth having become stained. Historical explanation is not a thing like triple-tongue, the advanced flute player's special technique for fast *staccato*. Historical explanation is like flute playing: all sorts of people try their hands at it, and some are better than others.

149   MORTON White argued explicitly against such a broad understanding of "historical explanation." On that understanding, historical explanations "would turn up in all sciences," whereas White makes it a condition of a correct analysis of the expression "that we cannot say of an explanation, without impropriety, that it is both physical and historical."[6] It is not clear, though, why we should not be permitted to say that. True, in ordinary usage some explanations "are physical, others chemical, and still others

historical,"[7] but ordinary usage may be merely following here a traditional division of academic disciplines, and it is not clear whether there is good reason to draw the lines this way. There would be good reason to do so if historical explanation were a special technique of the guild of historians, but as just argued that is not so: the guild does not have special techniques in this sense. Alternatively, there would be good reason to do so if the term "historical explanation," as commonly used, were to single out a particular kind of explaining that, while not a speciality of historians, still forms a recognizable subclass of explanations by reference to things past, different for instance from physical explanations; but in that case it would first need to be shown what this particular kind is. Finally, it might be suspected that on the present broad understanding of "historical explanation" no explanation will be left that is not historical.[8] This is not so. To explain a proof, to explain the meaning of a word, to explain how a differential gear works, are all explanations, but not historical explanations, since they do not explain some state of affairs or event by reference to a prior one.[9] It is true, Hempel dismissed such explanations from the range of what he called scientific explanations, these forming the exclusive subject matter of his theory.[10] He never clarified, though, what distinguishes scientific explanations from explanations *tout court*, as it is certainly not its occurrence in scientists' speech or writing that makes an explanation scientific.[11] Thus, for all we know it might be true in the end that in Hempel's sense all scientific explanations, but not all explanations, must be counted historical, in the broad sense of "historical explanation" just proposed. If that were true, however, it would not be wildly implausible, the way it would indeed be wildly implausible to say that all explanations whatever are historical in character. It is not a common, but neither is it an absurd idea: that science should be, fundamentally, history. So this consequence, if it is one, does not threaten the proposed understanding with absurdity.

THAT there are historical explanations, in the broad sense of the expression, and that some of them succeed in explaining, there is no doubt, given examples like the one three paragraphs back. The controversial question is how they succeed. One would like to see their accomplishment explained in turn. A variety of such explanations has been proposed, but the following five represent the basic options on offer. For Hempel, the explanatory success of historical explanations is owed to a law, stated or assumed in the explanation, which, together with a statement specifying antecedent conditions, allows us to derive logically a statement that says that an event of the sort to be explained occurred.[12] David Lewis maintains that all explaining of particular events is causal explaining.[13] On Dray's

150

view, historical explanations succeed in the typical case because they exhibit the action to be explained as the action rationally to be done, given the agent's aims and the situation as the agent saw it.[14] Hayden White, while holding that historical explanations succeed in a variety of ways, highlights their "encoding a set of events in terms of culturally provided categories, such as metaphysical concepts, religious beliefs, or story forms," with story forms in particular being the focus of his interest.[15] According to Paul Roth, finally, explanatory success in a historical explanation is its acceptance by an audience as a paradigmatic solution to a current problem in the field.[16]

151   THESE accounts are unsatisfactory. As for the law conception, it is just not the case that an explanation like the one earlier (§ 147) involves a law. It does not state a law explicitly, but neither is a law "tacitly assumed" in it.[17] For a law to be tacitly assumed in the explanation, one of two things has to be the case. The first possibility is that people offering such an explanation generally have a suitable law in mind, but for whatever reason fail to make it explicit. This is not so in the present case. As Hempel points out, "it would often be very difficult to formulate the underlying assumptions explicitly with sufficient precision and at the same time in such a way that they are in agreement with all the relevant empirical evidence available."[18] So people by and large do not have a suitable law in mind. Alternatively, a law is tacitly assumed if what people offer as an explanation actually becomes an explanation only with the law added, whether they have it in mind or not. However, what was said earlier about Christmas trees effectively was an explanation already. To object here that, lacking a law, it could not really be an explanation is dogmatic. True, the dogma is common: Hempel notes that he shares the tenet in question, that "the explanation of a phenomenon . . . consists in its subsumption under laws or under a theory,"[19] with a broad tradition in the philosophy of science.[20] That does not make it any less a dogma, and one that does not stand the test of experience. Our experience is that a text like the story about Christmas trees earlier does explain, and does not need supplementing by a law to become an explanation. Historians in the professional sense at any rate have been quite vigorous in rejecting the idea that they need to rely, tacitly or not, on laws of history for properly doing their job of making us understand what happened. It may be worth noting here that Hempel's conviction that explanations need to be based on laws does not rest on a Humean theory of causality to the effect "that like objects, plac'd in like circumstances, will always produce like effects."[21] Even when in 1964 Hempel demotes causal explanations to being just a species of deductive-nomological explanations, he still "assigns to

laws or theoretical principles the role of indispensable premises in explanatory arguments,"[22] that is to say, in explanatory arguments of whatever kind. It is this assignment that is under dispute here.

DAVID Lewis's proposal, that to explain a particular event is to provide   152
information about its causal history, is attractively simple, but given our actual explanatory practice with regard to Christmas trees and the like, the simplicity appears Procrustean. Were the Alsatian paradise plays causes of people putting up Chistmas trees on December 24 ever after? Normally one would say that the paradise plays were the origin of that tradition. Is this a roundabout way of saying that they caused the tradition? It is difficult to see why this should be so. In our explanations of what people do we deal with traditions, imitations, resistances, and the like; and in some cases, as with the Christmas trees, we take ourselves to express in these terms a genuine understanding of what happened. To suppose that this understanding consists in our being informed of some feature of the causal ancestry of people's doing what they did seems contrived, especially since that causal ancestry is quite obscure otherwise. We actually know so little of the causal processes leading to the putting up of Christmas trees in the late Middle Ages that it is hardly natural to think that what we do understand is some character of these processes. Why should the explanatory value of our talk of people's practices, habits, traditions, and the like need to be expressible in causal currency, if we never come round to cash these checks? Initially one would think that causality is just one way to link items in historical explanation. It should take powerful argument to convince us that causal histories hold the privileged position Lewis ascribes to them, and Lewis at any rate does not offer positive argument for saying that they do.

DRAY's account is intended to cover only a subclass of what is here called   153
"historical explanations," namely, the explanations of actions and consequences of actions: only here is rational explanation appropriate. Thus with his account he singles out, in the way indicated earlier (§ 149), a particular kind within the larger group of past-referring explanations, a kind that, while not being the exclusive domain of historians, is yet specifically different from explanations in mechanics, say. However, it might be thought that the account is even narrower than that, and indeed intolerably narrow. The rise of the Christmas tree, it may be argued, is a consequence of actions, but it cannot be explained on the pattern of rational explanation, being an outcome that was never intended by any human agent. So in general what is called analytic history, structural history, or, modestly, fundamental history[23] may be claimed to fall outside

the range of Dray's account. Actually, this is not so. While indeed no agent planned for the Christmas tree to conquer the Western world, countless actions constituted its victory, and these might well be explained on the model of rational explanation.[24] The explanation given earlier (§ 147) would thus come out as a summary of many rational explanations for individual cases, the reference to the Alsatian paradise plays providing the vital piece of information about the situation of some of the earliest of these agents that makes their action rationally comprehensible.

154   THE REAL problem with Dray's account is different. In fact, there seem to be two. First, one wonders what justifies making rationality the standard by which all kinds of actions from all times and places can be measured. Why is it supposed to be an illuminating question to ask about anything people did anywhere whether it was the rational thing to do?[25] Dray must suppose that it is, or else the privileged position he gives rationality in historical explanation becomes arbitrary. What grounds he has for supposing it, however, is difficult to see. Perhaps the problem becomes clearer by reference to Max Weber's work (which surely influenced Dray). Weber taught that a basic historical tendency is the growing dominance of rationality, in particular means-ends rationality, in various spheres of human life, like economy, religion, and law; and that this historical process has its origin in Western civilizations.[26] Thus he considered the dominant role of rationality to be not a human constant but a historical achievement, and a local one at that. Weber taught on the other hand that to explain action we need to relate what actually was done to what would have been done by a fully rational and fully informed agent pursuing the same aims.[27] Evidently, however, there is a tension between these two doctrines. If the idea of rationality, for all its victory with people like us, is yet, by the first thesis, an idea of historically limited significance only, then it is unwarranted for an attempt to explain what people do and did to subject any action under the sun to that standard, as the second thesis requires. It is true, there is in our culture a whole tradition of thinking that human action as such aspires to fulfilling the demands of rationality, but this line of thought has become implausible precisely in the historical enlightenment of the nineteenth century, which has its chief representative in Nietzsche and is summarized in that first thesis of Weber. And if it has become implausible to think that rationality is something that human action essentially aspires to, then Dray's claim that historical explanation exhibits, as far as possible, the rationality of what people did, has become implausible as well. It is just not clear why putting, or trying to put, what they did into the mold of rationality should be the proper way to figure out why they did it.

THE SECOND problem concerns the explanatory power of judging an action   155
rational. Suppose it was rational for me to move my pawn to d6 in that
situation (§ 118), and I did so move it: it is hard to see how the first of
these should explain, or contribute to explaining, the second. In doing the
rational thing I was merely being "a good boy," taking what by my lights
would have appeared to be the best course; and that this is so is no
explanation whatever of my doing it. The point is not that sometimes I
do not do what is rational. This is so, but it does not suffice to undermine
the alleged explanatory power of my action's being rational in those cases
where it is. The point is that doing what is rational is just one type of
action, and to say of some given action that it is an instance of that type
is not in any way to illuminate us as to why it occurred, it is merely to
classify it. Things do not happen merely because they are rational. To be
sure, the classification as rational would hold explanatory power if we
knew already that this type of action predominates among whatever is
done in history, but we do not know that. At best we know, supposing
that Weber is right, that this type of action is becoming more and more
important in modern times, especially in Western countries. However, that
is too little to undergird Dray's proposal, which was intended to cover the
historical explanation of actions in general.

HAYDEN White's account of historical explanation is valid, at best, in a still   156
narrower domain than Dray's. It fails to cover even most of the explanations provided by historians. There is no reason to think that bread-
and-butter studies of historians like "Shifts in the Financial Situation of
Westphalian Monasteries in the Late Thirteenth Century," explanatory
though presumably they are, encode the events they report in terms of
some metaphysical category or literary story form, and neither is there a
"plot," one of White's favorite modes of encodement, underlying the history of the Christmas tree. White's idea is derived, apparently, from his
study of the great historians of the nineteenth century,[28] but its broader
application is dubious indeed. Given such doubts, however, it becomes
doubtful, too, whether "encoding" has any explanatory role even in these
cases. Some historians explain and encode. Other historians explain and
do not encode. So encoding may well be irrelevant for explanation. It may
be a device with only literary significance.

PAUL Roth explains "historical explanation" in terms of acceptance: "ac-   157
ceptance of a particular type of solution as paradigmatic is what it is to
have an explanation."[29] However, taking words in their ordinary meaning, this statement appears to be incorrect. For one thing, people sometimes have a historical explanation, but they do not accept it as paradig-

matic. One may think that the story of the Christmas tree is a good explanation, without being prepared to "conjugate" on this paradigm other cases that may come up. True, people by and large have the tendency to try a successful trick again. Thus they may be likely, as a matter of fact, to explain similar cases similarly. However, that they must sign a contract, as it were, to reapply the type of solution in order to be using it even once seems to be too demanding a condition. After all, in explaining some particular fact or event one need not even be aware of employing a type of solution that could be used again. Conversely, sometimes people accept an account as paradigmatic, but actually they do not have an explanation. An example are those who believe in the biblical account of the creation of the world. Many of them are happy to accept this "solution" as paradigmatic for other cases, but they do not have an explanation, the account being false. "But for them it is an explanation." Yes, but this means only that they think it is an explanation, and that is irrelevant for the point at hand, which is whether they actually have one, and they do not. Explanation and acceptance, then, are different things.

158   It does not follow from these objections, assuming them to be sound, that there could not be a general account of how historical explanations explain. It just seems wise to wait no longer and to settle for what we have got, which may well be all we are ever going to get. What we have got is a variety of types of historical explanation: explanation by laws, explanation providing causal information, perhaps explanation by encodement. Some historical explanations have force because they invoke a law connecting the antecedent conditions and the event to be explained. Some have force because they tell us about the causal history of an event. Perhaps some have force because they encode the event to be explained in some literary story form. None of these types, however, accounts for the entire field of successful historical explaining. That field is pluralist with respect to explanatory power. Historical explanations have force, if they do, not by virtue of being historical explanations, but by virtue of following some more specific pattern.

159   And one such pattern is the explanation of what people do by the reasons for which they do it. Reason explanations are historical explanations, in the broad sense of the expression given earlier (§ 148): they explain an action by reference to an earlier state or event, which is the reason (§ 126). They form a recognizable proper subclass of historical explanations: we are quite good at telling, borderline cases apart, whether some explanation is or is not an explanation by the reasons for which something was done;

that is, whether it is a rationalization in Davidson's somewhat misleading terminology.[30] Moreover, we take explanations of this type to hold the explanatory power they do precisely by virtue of being of this type. There surely are unsatisfactory reason explanations. They are not unsatisfactory, however, because they are reason explanations. They are unsatisfactory because, for example, they are only partial or superficial (§ 197). A reason explanation that does not suffer from this sort of contingent defects is as good and effective an explanation as any. Nor, finally, do reason explanations owe their force to some other type of explanation. A reason makes us understand something done for that reason not because there is a law to the effect that, given the state or event that is the reason, an agent produces action of this sort, for there may be no such law (§ 151). A reason makes us understand something done for that reason not because it informs us about the causal history of the action, since for all we know it may not do that (§ 152). A reason makes us understand something done for that reason not because reason and action can be encoded in some story form, for perhaps they cannot: people's doing things for reasons need not come in preformed plots. It seems, then, that the explanatory force of reason explanations cannot be reduced to that of some other type of historical explanation. It seems that the explanatory force of reason explanations is just their own.

MAINTAINING that reason explanations form one kind of historical explanation with independent explanatory force does not reduce one to saying merely that a reason is a reason. Reason explanations can, first, be identified and distinguished from others by the phrases characteristically used to express them, in English and in other languages. Such phrases are "for the reason that," "therefore," "on account of" in English, "deswegen" and "deshalb" in German, "propterea" in Latin, "heneka" in Greek. To be sure, languages being what they are, it cannot be expected that even one of these phrases is used exclusively for the reason relation. So it would take an extensive linguistic account to single out the contexts indicating the reason relation, and plenty of borderline cases may be left even on the best account. Still, no doubt need remain which relation we have in mind here. Second, reason explanations can be identified and distinguished from others by telling stories, true or invented, in which reason explanations do or do not apply, like the story of the bishop's threat in my chess game (§ 118) and the story of Peter's letting down the net at Jesus' word (§ 141). Reason explanations being historical explanations, we can appeal to our interlocutor's competence as a historian in leading him to see what a reason explanation is (§ 124). And we shall not run out of suitable stories to make our point.

160

161 REASON explanations are weaker than other kinds of historical explanation are often supposed to be, whether rightly or not. Reason explanations, in particular, do not show the actions so explained to be in any sense necessary. Seeing the reasons for which people did what they did we understand why they did it, but they did not therefore have to do it, given the reasons. It is true, some people think that nothing deserves to be called an explanation that does not show the thing to be explained as necessary.[31] However, David Lewis's reply is convincing here: a good explanation ought to show no such thing unless it is true.[32] Nor is it our ordinary understanding of an explanation that what is explained should thereby come to be seen as being necessary. Most of us are prepared to admit that historians, in the professional sense of the term, sometimes explain events, but few of us, and least of all the historians, take these explanations to show that things had to happen the way they did.

162 BY THE same token, explanations of actions by means of the reasons for which they were done are not strong enough to support the corresponding counterfactuals. If it is true that I moved my pawn because of your bishop's threat, we are not therefore in a position to say that I would not have moved that pawn had your bishop's threat not occurred. We do not know what would have happened in that case, and we do not need to know it to count as explaining what did happen. Nor are we in a position to say, with regard to a different game where in the same circumstances you do not threaten my castle with your bishop, but do something else instead, that I would have moved my pawn if your bishop had threatened my castle. We will just have to be silent about what I would and would not have done, if such and such an event would or would not have occurred. And those of us who are skeptical about the very sense of counterfactuals[33] will see little to regret here.

163 THE SAME goes for predictions. If my pawn move can be explained by reference to the reason for which I did what I did, namely by reference to your bishop's threat, that does not show that, once you had moved your bishop to its threatening position, it could be predicted that I would move my pawn the way I did. Perhaps it could. Perhaps such a threat of your bishop is a reason to which I respond unfailingly. Or perhaps people generally do so in such circumstances. But then perhaps it could not be predicted. Perhaps there is no relevant pattern in my or generally in people's reactions to this kind of situation, and yet it is for that reason that I did what I did. This is after all how we normally deal with explanations and predictions of actions by means of the reasons for which they are done. People kill themselves for reasons, and often enough we have af-

terward a fairly good idea of what the reason was, but in many of these cases we could not, given the reason, predict the event. Yet we do not therefore feel bound to withdraw the claim that what we figured out was indeed the reason. It is with actions and reasons as it is with people's faces. From the child's face you cannot tell what the grownup's will be, but in the grownup's you can recognize, sometimes, the child's.

ONE MIGHT say: if reason explanations do not show that the action in question had to occur, given the reason, if they do not support corresponding counterfactuals and do not guarantee appropriate predictions, what good are they anyway? Why would one want to have such an explanation? The answer is the usual one: one would want to have it to understand what is or was going on. To know the reason for which one did something is to know in one way why it happened, and so it is in one way to understand it. Necessity, counterfactuals, predictability may be nice things to get, but understanding does not depend on them. In understanding we see the way the world went. For that we do not need to know that it could not have gone differently under these conditions, that it would have gone differently under different conditions, or that its course could have been predicted. And to see the way the world went is a good thing. 164

IT MAY be thought that to take reason explanations of actions as a particular kind of historical explanation with independent explanatory force is to revive the redescription view of the explanation of action, as presented for example in A. I. Melden's book *Free Action*. On this view, there are two kinds of explanation, explanation by causes and explanation by reasons. Explanation by causes does not further characterize the event or state of affairs to be explained, it merely says how it came about. Explanation by reasons, conversely, further characterizes the action that is being explained, but it says nothing about how it came about.[34] It may be thought that on the present argument similarly reason explanations provide only a further characterization of the action, placing it in the context of a state of affairs or event to which it is a response, but do not say how it came about. Now there is indeed this parallel: both on the redescription view and according to the present argument, reason explanations are allowed that are not causal explanations. As for the positive claim of the redescription view, however, it has become clear in the ensuing discussion that the distinction between further characterizing an action and saying how it came about will not stand. Melden argued that reasons cannot be causes because, given that they do the former of these two, they cannot do the latter.[35] This argument fails, for you can further characterize something precisely by saying how it came about.[36] And that is what reason 165 explanations do. Indicating the reason for which something was done, they tell you how that doing came about, namely, owing to the reason; and at the same time they redescribe what was done, placing it in the context of the reason. So the redescription view is right in what it asserts: reason explanations redescribe actions. It is wrong in what it denies: reason explanations also tell how actions came about.

166   It is worth noting here that the argument on the opposite side, on the side of those who claimed to show that reason explanations really are causal explanations, suffered from a similarly hasty conclusion. They urged that merely to place an action in a setting that, while making the action understandable, does not include a cause of it is not to explain why the agent did what he did. Thus, the only way to understand the explanatory power that reason explanations after all do have is to take them to be causal explanations.[37] This argument simply assumes that descriptions other than in terms of causes do not explain, and that is the assumption Melden had precisely called into question. To be sure, Davidson is right to say:

> One way we can explain an event is by placing it in the context of its cause; cause and effect form the sort of pattern that explains the effect, in a sense of 'explain' that we understand as well as any. If reason and action illustrate a different pattern of explanation, that pattern must be identified.[38]

Quite so, and here it is: the pattern of explaining actions by reasons for which they were done.—And which pattern is that?—Well, I told you, by giving you stories exemplifying, and terms indicating, the relation in question (§ 160).—Could not this relation be reduced to others, to a causal relation for instance?—I know of no good argument to show that this could not be done. It just has not been done. So keep trying, if you like. I find it wiser to settle for accepting the ordinary distinction between reasons and causes (§ 142).—But the pattern of reason explanations is not as well understood as that of causal explanation.—First, that is disputable. In ordinary usage, reason explanations seem to work as smoothly as causal ones; and that the philosophical analysis of causation is in better shape than the philosophical analysis of reasons may well be doubted, given the state of the discussions: both areas are full of controversy. Second, even if true, the point is irrelevant. Suppose that we are further ahead in understanding causes than we are in understanding reasons: that is no support at all for thinking that reason explanations are really causal explanations. It is a pragmatic reason for trying especially hard to reduce the former to the latter. It is no sign that this attempt is going to succeed.

THERE may be some suspicion, on the other hand, that the present line of argument really returns to the old distinction between explanation and understanding; that it claims only that actions done for a reason need to be understood rather than explained, in the special sense these terms received in certain branches of the philosophy of the social sciences.[39] (It is a special sense as opposed to the ordinary one. In the ordinary sense, understanding is simply what is achieved by a good explanation. It is the ordinary sense that is employed for instance in § 147.) In one way, the suspicion is right. The contrast between explaining and understanding has been interpreted in various ways, but to follow Droysen, one of the authors originating the distinction, the basic idea is that explanation and understanding are different methods of inquiry leading to different ends. In understanding you come to see in some phenomenon an expression of humanity, in explaining you come to see in a phenomenon the instance of a general law.[40] Dilthey, another classical representative of the idea, sets up a similar contrast between uncovering the laws that govern the phenomena of the physical world and seeing the phenomena of the human world as expressions of human life.[41] What seems right here is the contention that subsuming phenomena under laws is not the only way of shedding light on them. Using words in what appears to be their ordinary sense, one might put the point by saying that there is explanation by indicating reasons no less than there is explanation by indicating causes and explanation by subsuming under laws. Using the established terminology of distinguishing explanation and understanding, one would have to say that explanation is not the only way to gain knowledge about phenomena. And mixing terminologies one might say, paradoxically, that explanation is not the only kind of explaining there is. Whatever the words, the important point is to recognize that indicating the reasons for which somebody did something has independent illuminating power. Recognizing that, however, does not entail acceptance of traditional doctrines of understanding as a special state of mind, giving access to something essentially inner, the individual mind or indeed human life or human spirit at large. There is nothing arcane about understanding what people do by means of the reasons for which they do it. It is just another way of making sense of what they do. The inner is really dispensable: in explaining what people do by the reasons for which they do it we understand them in terms of the histories of which these doings form a part. We can think of understanding by reasons as truly superficial.

To SUM up, the question of this chapter was how to account for the explanatory force of reasons, if reasons are understood on the lines indicated in the previous chapter (§ 146). The answer is that reason expla-

SIX

Any State or Event May Be a Reason for Which Somebody Does Something

THE PROPOSAL under discussion (§ 118) is this: a reason for which an action   169
is done is something to which the action is a response. The second (§ 146)
question to ask about this is whether a reason is a particular kind of
"something": to what sort of things is an action done for a reason supposed
to be a response? A first answer was given earlier: it is a response to some
state or event, not to a thing or a person or a fact, even though we
sometimes speak as if the latter could be reasons, too (§ 126). The further
question now is whether there are additional restrictions on what can be
a reason for what. Many writers have held that there are. Their idea was
that reasons and the actions done for these reasons need to be meaningfully
related; that not just anything can serve as a reason for which somebody
does something, but only things that the social setting of the action makes
eligible as reasons.

AN EXPLICIT argument for this idea is hard to find in the literature. Still,   170
a reasoning on the following rough lines seems to be what various authors
have in mind:[1]

1. Actions involve meaning.
2. In particular, actions done for a reason, and these reasons themselves,
   involve meaning.
3. Meaning comes in systems.
4. Systems of meaning are local.
5. Hence, given an action, only some states of affairs and events can be
   reasons for which it is done.

THE ARGUMENT needs elucidation. As for statement 1, "actions involve   171
meaning" means something like the following. After dinner in a restau-

95

rant you give the waiter a check. What you do can be described as handing over to him a piece of paper bearing various marks. This description, while correct, is inadequate. It does not capture what may naturally be called the meaning of what you do, which is that you are paying the restaurant a certain amount of money. So what you do *is* actually more than your handing over the paper, it also includes this element of meaning. "Actions involve meaning" says that this holds generally. Whatever can be called your action, includes some such meaning.[2]

172   REGARDING statement 2, let us say that the reason for which you pay the restaurant this amount is your owing them as much for your meal. The fact that you owe them this amount is again inadequately described by saying that you had a meal in a restaurant under ordinary circumstances without having so far paid for it. To say this is true, but it does not capture what again may appropriately be called the meaning of the situation, namely, your standing under a legal, perhaps also a moral, obligation to pay. Thus your reason like your action involves meaning; and not only in this particular case, it is claimed, but generally.

173   MEANING, according to statement 3, comes in some system. The idea here is this. Something is a payment only if there is a practice around of exchanging goods or services. You cannot pay in the middle of nowhere, socially speaking. A practice of exchange, consisting of actions, is again something that involves meaning. So here one thing involving meaning depends on another thing involving meaning. However, a practice of exchange in turn depends on other things involving meaning, on institutions and roles provided by them, on rules and sanctions imposed on violators, or on conceptions of oneself and of others; and while these again depend on other things involving meaning, still others in turn depend on them. So there is a system of such dependencies here, connecting meaningful items. This, it is claimed, holds generally: anything that involves meaning forms part of such a system. Authors differ about the basic elements in terms of which these meaning systems should be understood. Winch, a follower of Wittgenstein, favors social rules,[3] MacIntyre, with his Aristotelian outlook, opts for common practices,[4] and Taylor, continuing Hegel's project, stresses shared self-conceptions.[5] Yet these differences are secondary. The common idea is that something that involves meaning is possible only as part of a whole structure of things that involve meaning.

174   STATEMENT 4 says that there is not one comprehensive system of meaning for all mankind, there are several, and each is in force only in a particular time and place. As Hollis describes this view, "there is no single 'form of

life' in terms of which lesser forms make sense, not even one for each culture and still less one universal form of all cultures."[6] So while everything that involves meaning is related within some system to other things that involve meaning, it is not the case that there is one system in which everything is related to everything else. Pluralism is inescapable: the meaning involved in an action forms part of a particular system of meanings valid in that area only. How broadly or narrowly the area is to be construed, and whether the systems of meaning happen to be nested or to overlap, depends on the particular case.

STATEMENT 5 appears to follow from statements 2, 3, and 4. If (2) reasons involve meaning, (3) meaning grows only in systems, and (4) systems are local, then (5) the stock of meanings for reasons to draw on is limited for any given action, and so the range of what is eligible for being a reason for a given action is limited, too, limited by the system or systems of meaning valid in the area in question. Aristotle has the famous line: "The soul, in a way, is everything that is."[7] Never mind for now about the soul *being* everything. The important point in the present context is that Aristotle's dictum has humans stand amid whatever there is, capable of acceding, and accessible, to all things. The writers defending an argument like the one under discussion, however close to Aristotle their ideas otherwise are, depart from this Aristotelian vision. For them, our world is essentially a restricted one, a neighborhood. Heidegger has the similarly famous line: "Language is the house of being,"[8] and this house in which, presumably, we are living is a limited space, by contrast to Aristotle's totality. It is Heidegger's lead that the writers defending the present argument are following. The idea of the argument is: we are never acting, as it were, out of doors, in the open, but ever only in some house of being or other. Thus the reasons for which we do things are ineradicably local, tied to some particular system of meaning and intelligible only in such a context.

DOUBTS about the argument arise from the fact that it seems self-defeating. If giving reasons for something counts itself as an action, as some authors defending this argument insist,[9] one wonders how the general statements contained in the argument are even accessible. How, for example, can it be said from such a parochial viewpoint that no system of meaning is comprehensive? If, on the other hand, these general statements are taken as pronouncements with only local significance, then the force of the argument is blunted. It only shows, in that case, that people around here are apt to say that what they say has force only around here, which does not say anything about the force of what they say. Still, this sort of objection, which applies the conclusion of an argument to itself, is sometimes baffling, but hardly ever convincing. Something stronger is needed to give substance to those doubts.

177   LICHTENBERG wrote in his polemic against the physiognomists: "Suppose the physiognomist once captured man, it would just take a brave decision to render oneself incomprehensible again for centuries."[10] Physiognomy, Lichtenberg is saying, can at best point out such correlations between character traits and physiognomical features as have been found so far in human beings. It cannot determine which physiognomical features go, once and for all, with which character traits. A similar query may be raised with respect to the idea that a reason for which somebody does something is embedded in a local meaning system. Suppose it is all true: actions and the reasons for which they are done involve meaning, meaning comes only in local systems, so reasons form part of local systems of meaning. Why should this show that reasons are tied to such systems once and for all, to this or that system or indeed to any system? Why exclude Lichtenberg's brave decision to jump over the fence? If it is only our experience so far of what people do and why they do it that tells us that reasons are embedded in these local systems of meaning; we have no grounds for assuming that people are tied to this particular or to any such system in what they do and why they do it. We only have grounds for saying: that is an order that actions and reasons showed so far. We have no grounds for saying: that is an order beyond which they cannot go. Hence the argument under discussion does not show that, for a given action, only some states or events can be reasons.

178   DEFENDERS of the argument deny the crucial premise of the objection. They deny that it is only our experience so far of what people do and why they do it that tells us that reasons are embedded in local systems of meaning. They deny that this is something found out a posteriori. They claim that for reasons and actions to be so embedded is part of the a priori framework of doing something for a reason. Doing things for reasons does not just happen to involve meanings that form part of a local meaning system, it is of its essence to do so. In Wittgenstein's famous expression, "what has to be accepted, the given, is, one could say, *forms of life*."[11] That they have to be accepted means that there is no sense in the idea of stepping outside of them, whether in thought or in action. On this line of reasoning, Lichtenberg's brave decision is just not available. If this claim is true, then indeed not anything can be a reason for which a given action is done. Only that can be a reason that finds a place within some local system of meaning.

THE QUESTION, then, is what grounds there are for this claim. Why should   179
it be true to say that doing something for a reason cannot but involve a
meaning that draws on the resources of some local system of meaning?
An answer is provided by the doctrine of constitutive rules. This doctrine,
first advanced by John Rawls in 1955[12] and restated by many authors
since,[13] is now widely accepted. It says that there are rules that are constitutive of the actions instantiating them. That these rules are constitutive
means: without the rules, the actions instantiating them could not exist.
With a metaphor frequently used, constitutive rules "create" an activity.[14]
They are opposed to regulative rules, which specify actions that can exist
both with and without the rule. Standardly, the difference is explained by
reference to the rules of games. "Move the bishop diagonally only" is a
constitutive rule in chess, as without this rule there could not be such a
thing as chess playing, and neither, therefore, such a thing as moving a
bishop, in the sense relevant here. "Castle early" is a regulative rule in
chess,[15] for chess players can castle early whether or not there is this rule.

THE DOCTRINE of constitutive rules is brought to bear on the question   180
whether to be embedded in a local system of meaning is of the essence
of doing things for reasons (§ 178). Defenders of the argument under
discussion take this further step, which Taylor describes as follows:

> I am suggesting that this notion of the constitutive be extended beyond
> the domain of rule-governed behaviour. . . . Just as there are constitutive
> rules, that is rules such that the behaviour they govern could not exist
> without them, and which are in this sense inseparable from that behav-
> iour, so I am suggesting that there are constitutive distinctions, consti-
> tutive ranges of language which are similarly inseparable, in that certain
> practices are not without them.[16]

That is to say, there are meanings constitutive of action. Being constitutive,
they are indeed part of the a priori framework of action, and in particular
of action for reasons. Thus, given the local character of all systems of
meaning, the range of things that could be a reason for which somebody
does something is limited. So it is an argument by analogy that is supposed
to answer the question raised at the beginning of the last paragraph. Doing
things for reasons does not just happen to exhibit meanings, it cannot but
involve them, since doing things for reasons must be understood on the
analogy with action under constitutive rules.

ANALOGIES are more or less plausible, and certainly the present one is not   181
downright compelling. Taylor, moreover, fails to offer further reasons in
support of what he calls himself a suggestion only, and so leaves us with

as much conviction as the analogy by itself commands. Still, an analogy is better than no argument at all. The real problem lies, not in the argument's working by analogy, but in what the analogy is supposed to be an analogy with. The real trouble is that there are no constitutive rules. There are no rules such that the actions instantiating them could not exist without them. It is not true that without the rule about the bishop's moves there could not be chess playing and hence no moving of bishops. The actions instantiating the rules of chess, chess-playing in short, consist of moving pieces of wood on a board in certain regular ways, and certainly people could do that without there being rules of chess. No doubt people are not likely to move chess pieces around in these ways without there being rules to that effect, but this is irrelevant. If actually no chess-playing occurs without there being rules around, this does not suffice to make the rules constitutive: "not occurring without" and "being constituted by" are different relations.

182 To BE sure, everybody agrees that without the rules of chess in existence people could still move around pieces of wood on a board in those ways that are, as things stand, prescribed by the rules of chess.[17] For that reason the argument for the constitutivity of some rules was standardly shifted to the descriptions of the relevant actions. Rawls writes:

> Now what is meant by saying that the practice is logically prior to particular cases is this: given any rule which specifies a form of action (a move), a particular action which would be taken as falling under this rule given that there is the practice would not be *described as* that sort of action unless there was the practice.[18]

Perhaps it would not be so described. If so, this does not show that the rules in question are constitutive, but only that people who lacked for instance the chess rules would probably lack the chess vocabulary as well. That is to say, it is irrelevant for the question of constitutivity how any action is, or would be, described. It is irrelevant for the question of constitutivity whether people who lacked the rules, but moved the wooden pieces around in the right ways would call what they are doing chess-playing. It is irrelevant, because what descriptions people use is not a reliable indicator of what things there are or could be. What descriptions people use also depends on other factors, for instance on the vocabulary in which they have been trained. Constitutivity, by contrast, is about what things there could be. It is about whether actions that in fact are instances of some rule could occur even without the rule existing. So the fact, if it is a fact, that people lacking the rules would not describe the activities in terms with which we are acquainted through the rules does not show that these people could not carry out the activities themselves. That, however, is what would have to be shown to establish the constitutivity of some rule.

YOU WILL deny that the actions instantiating the rules of chess consist of moving pieces of wood on a board in those regular ways that we learned when we were taught the rules. You are right. For one thing, pieces need not be wooden, they may be of glass, too. That does not affect the point, though: people could without the rules move around glass pieces as well as wooden ones. Then there need not be a board, we may be playing correspondence chess, sending one another signals like "1. e2–e4" and imagining positions of pieces on a board, positions that are regularly connected with these signals. This again does not affect the point: people could without the rules send each other such signals and imagine positions of pieces on a board, positions that are regularly connected with the signals. (This assumes, it is true, that there may be regular connections where there are no rules, but you can hardly deny that: nature abounds with them.) In this way we can keep going. Take the preceding account of actions instantiating the rules of chess, the account according to which they consist of moving wooden pieces on a board in certain regular ways, and add or subtract conditions as you see fit. Throw in things like habits of the players, restrictions on the duration of a game, affective conditions like an eagerness to win. After each revision you introduce I shall be justified to reply that it does not affect the point: people could without the rules do what meets these conditions, that is, they could acquire these habits, keep within these time limits, be affected in these ways. Maybe the account of what instantiates the rules of chess will become unwieldy in the process, but this again does not affect the point. Our dispute is not about whether, without referring to the rules of chess, we can give a simple account of the actions instantiating them. We cannot. Our dispute is about whether there could be these actions without the rules of chess in existence. The game we have been playing in this paragraph shows that there could be such actions. Without the rules people could move around wooden pieces on a board in the regular ways that we are familiar with from having learnt the rules; and in whatever sensible way you refine this account of what instantiates the rules of chess, people could without the rules still do the things you specify.

IN THE course of our exchange you will be tempted to say that the actions in question are not mere movings of pieces of wood, or maybe glass, on a board, but, more specifically, an essentially rule-guided kind of moving these pieces. You will be tempted to say that, because it forecloses my standard reply to your proposals, namely, that they do not affect the point at issue. This one does. People could not without the rules do what is essentially a rule-guided kind of moving those pieces. Even so, resist that temptation. To say that the actions instantiating the rules of chess are essentially rule-guided actions not only affects the point at issue, it is the point at issue. Doubting your claim that the actions could not exist without the rules, I shall naturally doubt as well your claim that the actions are essentially rule-guided. So to say that they are does not advance our argument. Moreover, to speak of essentially rule-guided actions lands you in a Russian doll. Talk of rule-guidedness, essential or not, prompts the further question what it is that is being guided here. If you reply that what is guided are again essentially rule-guided actions, we are off on a regress in which you really never answer the question what the actions instantiating the rules of chess are. If on the other hand you specify the actions that are guided by the rules without again invoking rule-guidedness, you could as well have done so right away in answer to the question what the actions instantiating the rules of chess are, and the previous argument comes into force again: actions that you specify without invoking essential rule-guidedness could well occur where the rules do not exist.

185 In addition, you can save your point from doubts by making it a matter of definition. You can declare that you are not prepared to call "chess-playing" any activity that occurs without certain rules in existence, like that about the movements of bishops; and then you can safely claim that these rules are constitutive, since the activity in question, chess-playing, could not exist without the rules. That is an empty victory, though. We wanted to know whether it is true of chess-playing, in the ordinary sense of this expression, that it could not exist without the rules, and that question is not answered by your decision to use "chess-playing" only in such a way that it *is* true.

186 Given how influential the doctrine of constitutive rules has become, the critical point bears repeating. Searle writes:

> A marriage ceremony, a baseball game, a trial, and a legislative action involve a variety of physical movements, states, and raw feels, but a specification of one of these events only in such terms is not so far a specification of it as a marriage ceremony, baseball game, a trial, or a legislative action. The physical events and raw feels only count as parts of such events given certain other conditions and against a background of certain kinds of institutions.[19]

The first sentence is trivial: yes, to describe something as a physical movement is not to describe it as a ceremony. The second sentence, however, does not follow. What is described, and correctly described, as a movement may still be a ceremony, and not only count as part of one given certain conditions and against a background of institutions. Searle's idea seems to be that, under the right conditions and with the right background in place, to the mere physical thing, the movement, another part is added that is social; or even that there is some sort of transsubstantiation:

> It is only given the institution of money that I now have a five dollar bill in my hand. Take away the institution and all I have is a piece of paper with various gray and green markings.[20]

The truth is that Searle has something in his hand that is both a five-dollar bill and a paper with various markings both if the institution of money exists and if it does not. If it does not exist, we shall perhaps not call this thing a five-dollar bill, but that, as argued earlier (§ 182), is immaterial to the point at issue. To be sure, Stone Age Searle cannot do a great deal with the five-dollar bill in his hand, but that concerns the likely effects of this paper, not what it is. A hair-dryer lying on the bottom of the sea is therefore no less a hair-dryer. The idea that with the institution of money gone the bill withers into a mere physical thing is superstition. It is to mistake function for substance.

To SUM up. There are no constitutive rules, for there is no rule such that   187
without it the actions instantiating it could not exist (§ 181). Constitutive rules were called upon to support, by analogy, the a priori status of local meaning systems with regard to actions (§ 180). The a priori status of local meaning systems needed to be secured in order to defend (§ 178) the original argument (§ 170). This argument was intended to show, by appealing to the indispensability of local meaning systems, that there is a limited range of things eligible for being a reason for which some action is done. The argument needed defending against the Lichtenberg objection that, even if the actions we know do draw on local stocks of meaning, it is not indispensable for an action either to draw on these particular ones or indeed to draw on any (§ 177). With constitutive rules gone, the defense against this objection collapses, and so does the original argument. Thus no reason has been given for denying that, for any action, any state or event whatever might be a reason for which it was done. Anything might be a reason, for all we know: it is a matter of experience to figure out what, in a particular case, *is* a reason.

188   To DENY that there are constitutive rules, meaning systems with a priori status, and forms of life that just have to be accepted, is not to bar from reason status rules, customs, obligations, and other things deemed to involve meaning. You do something because you promised to; this statement may be taken precisely at face value. You promised, and this event, your promising, is just what your performing now is a response to. So it is the reason for which you now perform. To allow your promise to count as a reason does not require, contrary to what many writers suggested, an additional layer of "institutional facts,"[21] rules,[22] constitutive self-understandings,[23] or the like. Your promising is an event like any other, and therefore eligible like any other for being the reason for which you do what you do. It is true, you probably would not have promised if the practice of promising had been unknown in your area; and given that you did, we would have had a hard time figuring out that you did without some familiarity with the practice. However, these things are true only because people have the ways they do, both in recognizing and in doing things, in the sense in which geese and elephants, too, have the ways they do. Their truth does not need undergirding by meaning structures with a priori status. The same holds for the fact that things like your promise stand a much better chance of actually being a reason for which you do what you do than things like the extinction of a distant star. It is just our way, or that of most of us, that we often take account of promises and not of stars in what we do, but it is not therefore how we are bound to go.

189   NOR ARE there other reasons apparent for being illiberal about the range of eligible reason candidates. It might be complained, for instance, that a dubious state of affairs is used already in the initial example, when your bishop's threat is considered a reason for my pawn move. A genuine state of affairs, it might be argued, is in this case only the position of the pieces, not such a thing as a threat, and only a genuine state of affairs is eligible for being a reason for which somebody does something. However, it is hard to see what disqualifies threats as compared to positions. There is the argument that positions are facts, but threats are only interpretations of facts. This argument has been shown to be powerless: what is asserted in a correct interpretation is not therefore any less a fact (§ 133). Alternatively, it might be claimed that, if your bishop is threatening my king, nothing has happened so far, only something will happen, unless prevented; whereas the position is something that is the case now. This reasoning is circular. If your bishop is threatening my king, something actually has happened, namely, that threat arose; and why the presence of the threat should not be as good a state of affairs as the position of the

pieces was just the question. Again, it might be urged that threats are threats because they give rise to certain affects, like fear or disquiet, whereas positions obtain regardless of such reactions. Yet it is not true that I am threatened only if I am worried in some way. With your bishop on b5, my king actually is threatened, and so I as a chess-player am threatened, however coolly I take it. What is true is only that a threat *may* regularly give rise to certain affects, but that is true of positions as well. Arguments to the contrary failing, then, threats are welcome as reasons for which people do things, and so are, by parity of reasoning, promises, in the literal as well as in the metaphorical sense in which a high position on the barometer promises a beautiful day. We prepare ourselves to start very early for the peak tomorrow, because the barometer promises a fine day: that promise is the reason for which we prepare ourselves. Like Peter (§ 141) we could say to the barometer: at thy word we will get our boots ready.

SEVEN

Reasons for Which People Do Things Are Normally Not Qualities of the Agent

190   THE PROPOSAL as developed so far says: a reason for which something is done is a state or event to which the action is a response (§ 118), the explanatory force of reason explanations is specific to them (§ 159), and there are no a priori limits on what could be a reason for which something was done (§ 187). Now this is all very generous: there are all the states and events in the world any of which might become the reason for which something is done, and to be the reason they do not need to bear a special relation, of causality or of meaning, to the action in question. The natural question to ask at this point is: what makes it the case that an agent, facing this vast array of what might be reasons, is doing something for this or that reason in particular? The range of reasons for which agents do things is actually quite limited, whereas the range of reason candidates is broad indeed, on the present proposal: what is the source of that limitation?

191   THE AGENT is. Due to particular traits of the agent the range of things eligible to be reasons is narrowed down to the reasons for which that agent actually does something. One such trait was mentioned earlier (§ 130): a reason for which an agent does something cannot be something of which the agent is not in any way cognizant. And there are others. In the last example, the barometer's promising a fine day tomorrow is only a reason for which we get our boots ready if we are eager to reach the peak tomorrow, or feel it would be a shame not to go, or some other condition of the kind holds of us. It is not a reason for which you prepare your boots, since you want to spend a lazy day in the valley anyway. Thus, a state or event owes its position as a reason for which somebody does something to features of the particular agent; that this agent wants this

or knows that, for instance. Agents put out actions on being supplied with reasons, but which state or event it takes to have some agent do something that is a response to it, which diet of reasons an agent feeds upon, that depends on the particular agent, on her knowledge, eagerness, expectations, and so on. Agents are differentially sensitive action-producers, and the profile of the reasons to which someone is sensitive marks at the same time that person's practical blindness. In this sense, then, agent souls are not after all "in a way everything that is" (§ 175). The agent is a reason-selector, one could say, though this would be liable to misunderstanding. Selecting reasons for which one does something is not an extra activity over and above the ordinary ones. Selecting reasons is an activity like casting a shadow. There is selection in the sense that, due to some of your qualities, one thing is a reason for which you do something and another thing is not, just as due to other of your qualities your shadow is long or short.

IN THIS sense, then, reasons for which one does something are agent-dependent: something may be a reason for which I do something and not a reason for which you do that thing, or indeed anything; and this difference may be due to our knowing, believing, expecting, desiring, or being eager to do, different things. The agent-dependence of reasons does not mean that reasons are merely subjective, in the sense that it is not a fact, but only thought to be a fact by either the agent or an observer, that something is a reason for which that agent does something. Reasons for which somebody does something are agent-dependent the way neighbors are. Anybody might be someone's neighbor, but only some people actually are somebody's neighbor at a certain time, and which are may depend on the person's position. Thus anything might be a reason for which someone does something, but only some things actually are such reasons at a certain time, and which are depends on the person's particular practical stance. It depends on the person's particular disposition, in the old sense of the term that does not refer to a tendency, but to the way a person thinks and feels about what happened and might happen. None of this entails that either neighborhood or reasons are only in the eye of the beholder. (Not that it is easy to see what it should mean to say that beauty is in the eye of the beholder—unless it were to mean that beholders have beautiful eyes, which apparently it is not supposed to mean.)

FROM the fact that it depends on qualities of the agent what is and what is not a reason for which that agent does something, it does not follow, either, that these qualities themselves are the reasons for which that agent does something. We need to be eager to reach the peak tomorrow, or

192

193

something similar, in order to get our boots ready today for the reason that the barometer promises good weather, but that does not show that we really get our boots ready for the reason that we are eager to reach the peak tomorrow. And ordinarily at least it is not true that we get our boots ready for the reason that we are eager to reach the peak tomorrow. Ordinarily things like our eagerness do not come into account. Ordinarily agents doing things for reasons are turned toward the world. They get their boots ready on account of the barometer's promise, not on account of their eagerness to reach the peak. Often they do not care, sometimes they do not even know, about their eagerness. Their eagerness is merely that feature of them to which it is owed, in this case, that the barometer's promise becomes a reason for which they prepare their boots. Their eagerness is, as it were, transparent, like a telescope: through it some things are singled out as reasons for which one does something, but it, the eagerness or the telescope, is not itself among the things so singled out.

194   IT SHOULD be easy to distinguish these two things: a reason for which we do something, and that about us due to which such and such a state of affairs is a reason for which we do something. Yet confusion of the two is common. It arises, presumably, from the similarly common confusion of reasons and causes (§ 142). Our eagerness to reach the peak tomorrow, supposedly an inner state and thus capable of setting our outer machinery moving, therefore seems to be a cause of our getting the boots ready, and it seems to be its real cause, since the barometer's promise, even if it also is admitted as a cause, moves us only via our eagerness. The eagerness thus being considered a cause, it is inferred, by the confusion of reasons and causes, that it is a reason, too, and indeed the real reason.

195   STEPHEN Darwall argued for a third position on the question what sort of thing a reason is for which we do something.[1] From the fact that reasons are "what people are to take account of in evaluating choiceworthy alternatives," he concluded that "they must be the sort of thing that can be thought or said on behalf of an act," "*dicta*" or "considerations," as he calls them.[2] On this ground he rules out a priori the notion that a reason for which somebody does something is a desire, since a desire is not a consideration. The premise of this argument, slightly weakened, seems to be correct: a reason for which one does something is the sort of thing that typically comes into account if, prior to doing it, one considers whether to do it. One may not consider, perhaps because there is no time, and still do it for a reason. Indeed, sometimes we consider whether to do something, and then do it for a reason that never figured in our consideration, perhaps because we are ashamed of the reason (of which we are never-

theless cognizant). Even so, one would think that typically reasons for which we do things do come up in considerations beforehand, if such consideration occurs at all. Darwall's negative conclusion seems right, too: desires of the agent are not, normally, things that count in a consideration of what to do. Should we consider whether to get our boots ready, it is not our eagerness to reach the peak tomorrow that counts, but the promise of fine weather. Doubtful is Darwall's positive conclusion that, since reasons are the sort of thing that comes into account in considering what to do, they are considerations, things said or thought. That is an oddly Berkeleian argument. The idea seems to be that people can only consider considerations when evaluating practical alternatives. It would seem more natural to think that what people consider are, rather, actual states of affairs, the dangerous situations or promising opportunities existing. If Darwall insists that what people consider should be described with a 'that' clause, that is no problem: we will be considering, then, that the barometer promises a fine day tomorrow. Even so we will not be considering a consideration. We will be considering how things are.

THERE *are* cases in which one's desiring something is a reason for which   196 one acts, but their special character rather confirms the point that in general desires are not fit for the reason job. A friend of mine used to put the fresh pack of cigarettes he had just bought into the mailbox downstairs in his apartment building, so as to make it more difficult for him to get hold of them when he wanted one.[3] Here a reason for the action was indeed his desire. He took the desire into account and responded to it, just as I take into account and respond to your bishop's threatening my castle. Similarly, there are cases in which one's believing something is the reason for which one acts. If you find yourself believing that you are so worthless as to deserve being killed, this may be a reason for which you go to see a doctor. However, these are clearly special cases.[4] I do not in this way take my desire into account and respond to it when, craving a beer on a hot summer's day, I finally get myself one from the refrigerator. Nor do I treat myself for bishop-related anxiety when I move my pawn to c6. At least it would take pretty weird clinical circumstances for that statement to be true. In the normal case such states as desire, belief, intention may be present, but they are not that on account of which I do what I do. Thus they are not the reason for which I do what I do.[5] To suppose that they are is to picture an agent who is the practical counterpart of a Cartesian consciousness, dealing primarily with his or her own states of mind and additionally only, by happy coincidences, with things like what the weather is going to be or threatening bishops. In fact we are agents right in the middle of things. To put a grand phrase to a proper and modest use, we are world-historical agents. Accordingly, we understand our actions primarily in terms of their place among things happening, not in terms of our attitudes with regard to things happening.

197   A FURTHER argument for thinking of reasons as states of things rather than states of mind is given by the fact that such a conception readily makes sense of the idea of a deeper reason for which somebody did something. For instance, trying to understand why a man injured his wife we may not be satisfied to be told that he did it because she had asked him how much the car repairs had cost. There may be good evidence that this actually was a reason, and indeed not just one reason among various parallel ones. Even so we are likely to ask what the deeper reason was. An answer will call to our attention such things as the injuries to his vanities or the professional insecurity he suffered. Such an answer need not falsify the initial claim that it was his wife's question that was a reason for his outburst. Both answers may be true, yet one of them more revealing than the other and discoverable only by digging back further into the circumstances that prompted the man's response. Actually, the metaphor of depth comes in handy here, as the upper parts of a fundament are no less supporting for being in turn supported, together with what they support, by the lower parts. So a deeper reason is, roughly, a bigger chunk of world being responded to in the action. An account of reasons in terms of desires and beliefs, by contrast, does not open a dimension of depth. The man's desire to silence his wife's question and his desire to prove himself against many defeats suffered are just two desires standing beside each other. To be sure, the content of the second desire comprises that of the first in this case, but this does not help as long as we think of the desires as being the reasons, or part of the reasons, for which people do things; for the desires are not related as one underlying the other. The dimension of depth, then, being available on the one account and not on the other, the case is strengthened for saying that in general a reason is some state or event in the world, and not a state of the agent's mind.

198   THIS view is further supported by the fact that in this way several agents can act for the same reason, whereas if reasons are states of the respective agent, we never do things strictly for the same reason, only for similar ones. Ordinarily, however, we do say that you and I act for the very same reason, as when we both get our boots ready because of the barometer's promise of fine weather tomorrow. We do say that there can be such a thing as a common cause. Admittedly, this is not a very strong point, given how unreliable ordinary speech is in matters of identity and similarity. Still, it is an advantage of the present view of reasons that it allows

reason-sharing. It may be replied to this that we also speak of shared beliefs and common wishes, and if such locutions are available, so should be, explained in terms of these locutions, talk of shared reasons. However, the usual reconstruction of these locutions, by identical content, does not help those who take reasons to be states of mind in overcoming the present difficulty. Contents after all, whatever they are, are not states of mind of agents. The believings, desirings, and so on are supposed to be states of mind, and if states of mind are what reasons are, then reasons remain different between different agents, the identity of their contents notwith-standing.

HOWEVER, there is one serious argument for saying that, for example, the   199
bishop's threat cannot be the reason for which I move the pawn, that the reason must be, rather, some state of mind like a desire to counter the threat. It is the argument from the case of error. Henry thinks that a thunderstorm is approaching and asks for shelter in the house on the hill. As it turns out, no thunderstorm comes, he only thought there would be one. To indicate the reason for which Henry went up to the house on the hill we cannot refer to a thunderstorm coming that night, there being no such thing. We can only refer, it seems, to his belief at the time that a thunderstorm was coming. This is how indeed he may describe the matter once he has recognized his error. He may say: "I asked for shelter because I thought a thunderstorm was coming." However, if his belief, not the approaching thunderstorm, is the reason for which he went up to the house in this case, then also his belief, and not the approaching thunder-storm, is the reason for which he goes up to the house in case a thun-derstorm does come. After all, he is in the same state, whether a thun-derstorm is actually coming or not. It seems then that with and without a thunderstorm we need to refer to Henry's belief in giving the reason for which he went up to the house on the hill.

ONE MAY dispute the argument on the grounds that, even if Henry is in   200
the same state whether or not a thunderstorm is actually coming, it does not follow that the reason for which he goes up to the house on the hill is the same in both cases. This follows only under the assumption that a reason for which one does something is a matter of the state one is in, and the truth of this assumption is just what is at issue. Yet even if his reasons are allowed to be different in the two cases, there is still the challenge: what is the reason for which he goes up to the house, if he is wrong about the thunderstorm approaching? If he is right, then this is his reason, that a thunderstorm is coming, but if he is wrong, that cannot be, as none is coming. On the other hand, it is uncomfortable to follow

the argument just given and take Henry's belief as the reason, for the objections to that idea (§ 196) have not been invalidated. After all, that "at" which he asks for shelter in the house on the hill is not his belief that a thunderstorm is coming. Henry does not come across this belief in his mind and find he had better do something about it, the way the potential psychiatric patient does come across a belief in his mind and decides he had better do something about that. What he comes across, or actually, what he takes himself to come across is an approaching thunderstorm, and it is at that that he should ask for shelter. Yet that cannot be, with no thunderstorm coming.[6]

201   IF THERE is no thunderstorm coming that could be a reason for which he goes up to the house, and if a belief that a thunderstorm is coming is not such a reason, either, it seems inevitable to conclude that there is no reason for which Henry goes up to the house on the hill. He thought that a thunderstorm was coming, and at the time he might have taken himself, and might have been taken by others, to be going up to the house for that reason, namely, that a thunderstorm was coming. Now that his thought about the thunderstorm turns out to be mistaken, so does that understanding of his action. If the cow is lost, so is the calf: reason-ascriptions collapse as well, once the purported bearer of the reason-predicate fails to materialize.

202   REJECTING precisely such a view as this, Bernard Williams writes:

> The difference between false and true beliefs on the agent's part cannot alter the *form* of the explanation which will be appropriate to his action.[7]

It *is* to alter the form of the appropriate explanation to say that the reason for which Henry asked for shelter was the thunderstorm approaching, in the case of his belief being true, but that there was no reason for which he asked, in the case of his belief being false. It is not clear, though, why Williams's statement should be accepted. He does not defend it explicitly, and the only argument that comes to mind is the one touched upon earlier (§ 199): what the reason is, and indeed whether there is any reason, for which somebody does something should depend on the state of the agent, not on the state of the world; and since the truth or falsity of the agent's beliefs depends, ordinarily, on the state of the world, the form of the appropriate reason explanation should not be affected by switching the truth values of some of his beliefs. However, this argument merely assumes that reasons for which somebody does something must be located within the agent, and that is just what is being disputed. Taking reasons rather to be something encountered in the world, as proposed here, makes it quite natural to think that appropriate explanations of an action will have different forms, depending on whether the agent's relevant beliefs are true or false.

THE PARALLEL with the theoretical case is again (§ 196) illuminating here.   203
The Cartesian tradition saved the natural light of reason from skeptical attack by setting up the inner theater of ideas, or impressions: your judgments about these, unlike your judgments about things in the world, are supposed to be error-proof. Similarly, the dominant view of action saved practical reason by having inner states like belief function as reasons: even if, given how things go, your action turns out to be foolish or superfluous, it was still done for a reason. Yet the device provides false comfort in both cases: it is an uninteresting achievement for inquirers merely to be right about their ideas, unless that happens to be the object of inquiry, and it is an uninteresting achievement for agents to act reasonably with respect to their inner states. What is of interest is to be right about things and to act reasonably with respect to how they are. Instead of setting up the specious safe haven of ideas and inner states, it would have been wiser simply to admit that both kinds of getting it right are not so frequent achievements.

THERE is Davidson's and others' argument to the effect that both kinds   204
of getting it right must be frequent achievements; that most of what we believe must be true and most of what we do must be done for a reason.[8] It is a transcendental argument, in the sense that it ascribes this perfection to people as a necessary condition of their being even understood. However, as I have argued in more detail elsewhere,[9] the argument, like the more traditional transcendental arguments offered for instance by Strawson in "Individuals" and "The Bounds of Sense," suffers, in the first place, from assuming a dubious verificationism.[10] The argument shows, at best, that we have no way to ascribe beliefs and attitudes to people one by one, but that we need to ascribe them in clusters. The argument does not show thereby that beliefs and attitudes grow only, or predominantly, in clusters: necessary conditions of finding out about something are not necessary conditions of its being what it is. The argument is defective, second, because it fails to show that such clusters, assuming that they need to be formed, must be formed in accordance with standards of rationality. There is no justification for giving rationality such a privileged status in the descriptions of people (§ 154).[11] The argument failing, then, we have to live with the possibility of being massively wrong, both in what we think and in what we do.

205   SAYING that it was not for a reason that Henry asked for shelter is also supported by some ways in which we normally describe such a situation. True, Henry may well say afterward that the reason for which he went up to the house on the hill was his belief that a thunderstorm was coming (§ 199), but he may also say that it only seemed to him there was a reason for doing so, or that he only thought he had one. These are locutions in terms of having reasons and there being reasons, hence not directly relevant to the present topic, doing something for a reason. However, it will be argued later (§ 220) that in order to do something for a reason it is necessary that one have a reason, and that there be a reason, for doing it. If that is so, the phrases just mentioned indicate implicitly that what Henry did was not done for a reason. Thus ordinary usage does support, if only ambiguously, the account proposed here.

206   HENRY did not do for a reason what he did, because there was no thunderstorm. So you can do something for a reason and on a different occasion do the same thing not for a reason, with only the circumstances and nothing about you being changed, except of course that some of your beliefs switched from truth to falsity. Doing something for a reason is like playing a piano concerto. Playing exactly the same, you may contribute to the performance of a piano concerto on one occasion and not contribute to such a performance on another: it depends on whether an orchestra joins you. So Henry, one could say, played his part of a concerto for hiker and thunderstorm, but as the thunderstorm missed its cue, what he did turned out not to be a contribution to a full performance of the score.

207   ONE MAY wonder, though, whether there is not an easier way to describe Henry's situation. True, his going up to the house was not a reponse to the approaching thunderstorm, since no thunderstorm actually was approaching. Still, there were signs of an approaching thunderstorm, dark clouds gathering, let us say. Why not have him go up to the house in response to them? Three cases need to be distinguished here. First, the suggestion may be that Henry went up to the house for the reason that dark clouds were gathering, no thunderstorm entering the picture. In this case no problem arises: dark clouds do gather, so Henry asks for shelter. However, the problem is avoided here, not solved: this is no longer the case of an erring agent, as it was supposed to be (§ 199). After all, Henry is responding here to what is actually the case, that is, the clouds gathering. Moreover, this story is fairly unrealistic. Henry is here suffering from cloudophobia, rather than seeking protection against a thunderstorm. Second, the suggestion may be that Henry went up to the house for the reason that, as indicated by the dark clouds gathering, there was a prob-

ability of a thunderstorm coming. This is a case similar to the one where we get our boots ready because the barometer promises a fine day, and again it raises no problem. If it was indeed probable to some extent that a thunderstorm would come, then Henry did not err when asking for shelter, even if the thunderstorm in the end did not come. He was just cautious, responding not to a thunderstorm, but to the likelihood of one, and likely the thunderstorm was after all. Third, the suggestion may be that, dark clouds notwithstanding, a thunderstorm was in fact never probable, or at any rate never probable enough to be a reason for which Henry would seek shelter. In going up to the house he was just mistaken about what was likely to happen. This is indeed the case of an erring agent, but here the original problem returns, and the clouds do not help. It is immaterial what misled him, whether he suffers from the mistaken idea that, in the original case, a thunderstorm is approaching or that, in the present case, a thunderstorm is likely. In either case the problem is whether anything, thunderstorm or likelihood of one or whatever, can, in spite of nonexistence, be a reason for which he goes up to the house. Indeed it cannot.

TRUE, to say that Henry did not do for a reason what he did may mislead. 208 It may suggest that his asking for shelter should be considered just a random movement of his, similar, say, to his eyes' blinking, which of course it is not. Still, that is not in fact what is being said; and there is no basis for thinking that what is not done for a reason therefore must be a random movement. Henry's asking for shelter does resemble a random movement in that it lacks a reason for which it was done, but otherwise it rather resembles people's asking for shelter when it is for a reason that they ask, for the reason, namely, that a thunderstorm is approaching; and it will ordinarily be more illuminating to classify it with these actions. Merely playing the piano part of the first Beethoven concerto resembles merely playing the piano part of the first Brahms concerto in that on neither occasion a full piano concerto gets performed. Even so it will ordinarily be more helpful to classify playing only the piano part of the first Beethoven concerto together with a full performance of this piece, taking it as an exercise for, or a truncated version of, the latter, rather than to join it, under the heading "Incompletes," to the defective Brahms performance. In this way, asking for shelter in the house on the hill without a thunderstorm coming is best understood as a truncated version of asking for shelter with a thunderstorm coming.

THIS is why saying that Henry thought a thunderstorm was coming helps 209 to explain his going up to the house. After all, to say what the agent took to be the case very often does help in explaining what the person did (§ 199). Saying that Henry thought a thunderstorm was coming is not to state the reason for which he went up to the house: his belief is not such a reason (§ 200). Saying that Henry thought a thunderstorm was coming does not single out a cause of his going: as long as physiologists do not establish causal connections between believings and doings, there are no grounds for assuming that Henry's belief causes him to go. Saying that Henry thought a thunderstorm was coming indicates that his going up to the house should be ranged with the goings up to the house done for the reason that a thunderstorm is coming, as a defective version of these. It indicates the concerto of which his performance was a supplementing or solitary part. To indicate that does help to explain his going up to the house. We may be baffled by his suddenly turning off the road, but now being told that it was a version, either straight or defective depending on what the weather will be, of an asking for shelter on account of an imminent thunderstorm, we may understand his doing so. We may understand it, for we are familiar both with such histories as somebody asking for shelter in response to an imminent thunderstorm and with people getting things wrong and preparing for events that do not come after all. So it is an explanation to say that Henry asked for shelter because he thought a thunderstorm was coming, but it is not an explanation indicating either the reason or the cause of his doing so. It is not a historical explanation (§ 148). It is an explanation indicating what sort of thing it was that he was doing. We are familiar with such explanations. "That's an eclipse," (§ 149), "They are already performing," "She is in her phase of defiance," uttered under suitable circumstances, are other examples.

210   THIS in turn may help to explain why we are so strongly inclined to say that a reason for which agents, and especially agents in error, do what they do is, or includes, their belief, a statement that on the present account is false in most cases. (See § 196 for special cases in which it is true.) We classify Henry's asking for shelter, as a defective version, together with people's asking for shelter when a thunderstorm does come, and we assume further that, similarly as well, there is a reason for which Henry asks as there is in their case. Now, since the reason for which the others act, the approaching thunderstorm, is not available for Henry to act upon, nothing seems to be left but to take his belief as a reason. Then, however, with the erring agent's belief being considered a reason, prudence seems to suggest applying the same pattern in turn to the veridical case. It becomes the cautious, the self-critical thing to say that reasons for which people act are always their beliefs; much in the way of the swift argument that led people from the experience of illusions to the conclusion that

sense-data are all we ever perceive.[12] In this way we end up with what is nearly the opposite of the truth. The basic mistake of this reasoning does not lie in ranging Henry's asking for shelter together with that of people who are right about the thunderstorm coming. After all, that assimilation is what gives us an understanding of what Henry did. He asked for shelter as those do who do it for a reason. The basic mistake lies in extending the assimilation to the point of assuming that, like those people, Henry did for a reason what he did. This assumption is unwarranted.

IF THIS accounts for Henry, what about Lucky Jim, who somehow gets it into his head that there is a dangerous bear round the corner of the path in front of him and, like Henry, asks for shelter in the house on the hill? As it happens, there is no bear there, but a heavy thunderstorm is actually coming that he failed to notice, and due to his asking for shelter he avoids it. Normally, we shall explain his asking for shelter by saying that he did it because he thought there was a bear round the corner, and perhaps our saying this, and the explanatory force of saying this, can be understood on the lines indicated two paragraphs back. Still, it may seem that on the present account we are bound to say, falsely, that he asked for shelter because of the approaching thunderstorm. After all, his asking seems to be as a matter of fact a response to the approaching thunderstorm, whether he thinks of it this way or not, and so it should count as done for that reason. Here there seems to be a case, then, which reduces the present account, if not to absurdity, at least to plain falsity.   211

THE ALLEGED consequence does not follow, however. As suggested earlier, agents are reason-selectors (§ 191), and for Lucky Jim the approaching thunderstorm is not one of the events to which his doing something could be a response, since he fails to notice it. It does not change matters that he actually does what would have been an appropriate response had it been done by somebody who did notice the thunderstorm approaching. His position is really the same as Henry's: there is no reason for which he asks for shelter, there being no bear round the corner and the thunderstorm falling outside his repertoire of reasons for which he might be doing something. With respect to the thunderstorm, Lucky Jim is just that, lucky. He does the right thing, though not for a reason. And that there are cases of this kind, cases where we do the right thing, but not for the reason that it is the right thing, can hardly be disputed.   212

TO SUM up. The question was what selects the reasons for which one actually does something from the broad range of what could be such a reason (§ 190), and the answer is that it depends on features of the agent,   213 in particular on such things as an agent's eagerness, belief, and expectation, whether something is or is not a reason for which that agent does something (§ 191). Thus, what is a reason for which I do something may not be a reason for which you do that thing, or anything (§ 192). However, features of the agent like eagerness, belief, and expectation are typically not themselves reasons for which that agent does something (§ 193), though sometimes they are (§ 196). Nor does the case of the agent in error show that reasons for which somebody does something are states of the agent. Rather, agents in error may not be doing what they are doing for any reason at all (§ 201).

EIGHT

Reasons One Has for Doing Something

THERE is a set of further questions about the proposal under discussion (§ 118). The proposal states what a reason is for which somebody does something and how such a reason is related to the action. However, we speak of reasons with regard to action in a variety of other ways, too, and an account of reasons for which somebody does something will not appear convincing as long as it does not also help to make sense of these locutions. Here is a survey of some of them. Not only do people do things for reasons, the case treated so far. It may also be that somebody has a reason, or reasons, or simply reason, to do something, or for doing something. Similarly, there may be a reason, or reasons, or simply reason, to do something, or for doing something; and there may be such reason, or reasons, for somebody in particular or not for somebody in particular. In addition, there are various qualities being ascribed to reasons, either by comparison or absolutely. Somebody has good, strong, sufficient, excellent, overwhelming reason to do something. Something is a bad, weak, poor, insufficient reason to do something. One reason is better, stronger, more powerful than another. Somebody has more reason to do one thing than to do another. And these various ways of speaking of reasons can be combined in a variety of ways.

THE DIFFERENCES are often only stylistic. Thus, there being reasons for somebody to do something and that person's having reasons to do that thing may be taken to amount to the same.[1] Nor is there any interesting difference between reasons to do something and reasons for doing something. Furthermore, that there is reason to do something can be understood as saying that there is at least one reason, possibly many reasons to do it. And where reasons to do something are said to exist, but not for anybody in particular, these reasons may be taken as reasons "for whom it may concern." Thus to say that there is reason to turn off the mains before changing a fuse is to say that anyone who is about to change a fuse has reason to turn off the mains. So the variety of phrases boils down to just two sets of important differences. There is, first, the difference between there being a reason for somebody, or alternatively, somebody's having a reason, to do something on the one hand and somebody's doing something for a reason on the other. There are, second, the qualitative differences mentioned at the end of the last paragraph. This chapter takes up the first of these differences and offers an account of reasons we have for doing something. Two far-reaching objections to this account, one raised by internalists, the other by defenders of the normativity of reasons, will be the topic of chapter 9; chapter 10 will suggest a way to understand the different qualities commonly ascribed to reasons.

216   A REASON for which one does something differs from a reason one has for doing something in that one may not do what one has reason to do. One may have reason to follow the doctor's advice, and still not follow it. It differs also in that one needs to be cognizant in some way of a reason for which one does something (§ 130), but not of a reason one has for doing something. There being poison in your glass is a reason for you not to drink it, even if you do not have any idea of that stuff being poison. A popular terminology calls a reason for which somebody does something motivating,[2] a reason somebody has for doing something justifying,[3] but both terms are unfortunate. As for the former, to motivate is to set moving, and so to call a reason for which somebody does something a motivating reason is to suggest that a reason is a thing that makes agents move. That is to say, it is to assume that a reason is a cause of an action done for that reason. This is a substantive claim (§ 142), and so it should be argued, not prejudged by the terminology. On the other hand, to call reasons one has for doing something justifying reasons is misleading because it suggests that these reasons always succeed in justifying the action concerned. They may not. For instance, they may be outweighed by reasons one has against that action. Yet reasons outweighed are no less reasons one has. Staying, then, with the terminology of reasons one has for doing something and reasons for which one does something, the problem at hand is to understand what it is merely to have a reason, by contrast to doing something for a reason. In particular, the problem is to find out whether reasons one merely has can be understood in a way similar to that which seemed to account for reasons for which one does something.

HERE is a case of having a reason. At another point in our chess game   217
(§ 118) you threaten me with a knight fork, a position in which the knight
attacks, for example, king and castle at the same time, thus forcing the
opponent to save the former and surrender the latter. Inexperienced chess-
player that I am, I fail to see the danger. Nor is there in this case any
further advantage to be gained from disregarding it. It will be just plain
stupid of me not to prevent your knight from forking my king and castle,
and I can prevent your knight from doing this by covering the square in
question. In this case it is true to say that I have reason to cover that
square. The question is what it is about the situation that makes it true
to say that. An answer corresponding to the previous account of doing
something for a reason (§ 118) appears natural. To do something for a
reason was to do something that is a response to the state of affairs that
is the reason. There merely being a reason for doing something, then,
would be for a state of affairs to hold in response to which one could be
doing something. It takes two things for something to be done for a
reason, the reason and the action that is a response. If there is only the
former of the two in place, then this is the situation of there merely being
a reason for doing something. The world has done its part for there to
be a history involving a state of affairs and a response on your part, but
as long as you have not done yours, there merely is, or you merely have,
a reason for doing something. The ball is in your court.

To USE some of the other examples mentioned earlier (§ 119): when in   218
playing dominoes you put down a three, that is a reason for me to put
down my double three in turn, even if I do not do it, and hence do not
do it for that reason, because we are interrupted, say. When you ask me
the time, that is a reason I have for telling you, even if it is not a reason
for which I do, since there is a stronger reason for me not to, my mouth
being stuffed at the moment. The initial part of a history that can be
completed with a response of mine is on the table: that is what it is to
have a reason for doing something. Thus the case of an agent having a
reason, but not acting for that reason, turns out to be the converse of the
agent in error. Henry produced action where there was no reason (§ 201).
Such an agent does not produce action where there is reason.

IN THIS way a reason I have for doing something can be the same thing   219
as a reason for which I do that thing, if I do.[4] This is as it should be. It
should be possible that I cover that square precisely for the reason that
earlier I only had, but failed to see. Therefore again, to speak of motivating by contrast to justifying, or normative,[5] reasons may mislead (§ 216),

since it may suggest that these are disjoint classes of reasons.[6] They are not: a reason I act upon is always a reason I have, though not conversely.

220 IT MAY be doubted that whoever does something for a reason also has a reason for doing it: what about somebody whose response to some state of affairs is crazy? On the account proposed, we would have to say that what the agent did was done for a reason, but in fact we may be unwilling to concede that there really was a reason for doing such a mad thing.[7] However, if we are unwilling to concede this, that is probably due only to a verbal disagreement: sometimes the phrase "having a reason" is used in the sense of "having a good reason"[8] and clearly in that sense it is false that whoever does something for a reason has a reason for doing it. Sometimes, though, "having a reason" does not imply that the reason in question is a good one, and that is how the expression is used here. On this understanding, however, the consequence holds: once it is clear, say, that the reason for which some people are doing a rain-dance is the current drought, it is, by the same token, also clear that there is a reason for them to dance, that is, the drought.

221 IT TURNS out, then, that "somebody has a reason" and "there is a reason for somebody" mean precisely what other phrases of this form mean. Having a reason is like having an opportunity, or having difficulties, and there being reasons is like there being opportunities and difficulties. Just as, in the case of an opportunity, something happened that by suitable action you can turn into the initial part of some kind of success story for you, or in the case of a difficulty, something happened by which you will be stymied in your course unless special effort is taken, so in the case of a reason you have, something happened that by suitable action you can turn into the initial part of a history of something done for a reason. This is not to say that reasons are a kind of opportunity or difficulty. It is to say that one has reasons, and there are reasons, the same way one has, and there are, opportunities and difficulties.

222 OBJECTION: why not say of anything that you are physically capable of that you could do it in response to anything whatever happening? Why not say that in response to yesterday's bad weather you could count the trees in Thetford Forest? And so we would have to say, on the present account, that you have reason to count the trees in Thetford Forest, but in fact you have no such reason.—No, I do not have such a reason, for it is not the case that in response to yesterday's bad weather I could count the trees in Thetford Forest. I could count the trees all right. I could not count them in response to yesterday's bad weather. As things stand, these

two do not connect in the way of event and response. It might have been the case that they do: anything might be a reason for doing anything (§ 187). There is no reason a priori against linking them in this way. It is merely a matter of what the world, including me, is like that it would be an error to do so. And we can tell that it would be an error by virtue of our knowledge of what the world is like. The objection here repeats, with respect to reasons one has, the objection raised earlier with respect to reasons for which one does something (§ 120): that anything can count as the thing in response to which something was done, so that, on the account proposed, anything can count as the reason for which something was done. And the reply is the same, too (§ 121): it is not true that anything may be the thing in response to which something is done by somebody. Not anything may figure in the reason position of an agent's history, be that the position of a reason merely had or the position of a reason acted upon. What may and what may not, however, is merely a historical matter.

IT IS easy to understand on this account how people may at the same time have a reason for doing and a reason for not doing something. There may be, indeed there constantly are, various initial pieces of histories opening the way for incompatible responses from the same agent. Reasons abound, reasons one has, that is: there are lots of threads at any point for agents to keep knitting on, and to go on with one may exclude going on with others. With a standard metaphor, reasons one has compete sometimes for getting acted upon, since not all can. On the other hand, there may be several reasons for which one does one thing (§ 118), hence several reasons one has for doing something that do not compete. One thing done can be a response to a variety of states of affairs. 223

IN ADDITION, there may be several reasons for doing one thing, and the person does it for one reason and not for the other. Davidson drew attention to this sort of case:[9] since you have an appointment already, you have a reason to decline that invitation, but as a matter of fact you do not decline it for that reason, but because of the unpleasant company you expect. Davidson suggests that the difference between the cases of having a reason to do something and doing it, but not for that reason, and having a reason to do something and doing it for that reason needs to be accounted for by saying that the reason one has is also a cause of one's doing it in the second, but not in the first case.[10] That argument, however, does not appear compelling. An agent who has a variety of reasons for doing the same thing is offered, on the present account, a variety of things to which his action could be a response. What he does then may in fact be a response to none of them, or to all, or to some and not to others.—And 224 how do we tell whether what he does is or is not a response to some reason he has for doing it?—The way anybody would: by asking him, watching him in similar situations, and so on. Nor would Davidson suggest otherwise. The dispute is not about how we figure out which of the agent's reasons becomes a reason for which he does the thing in question. The dispute is about what it is we thus figure out. And it seems sufficient to say that we figure out whether what the person did and the reason obtaining are indeed related as one being a response to the other, the way we figure out many other relations between things done and states or events, relations like simultaneity, similarity, repetition, superior significance, oddity, what have you. There does not seem to be a need for a causal substructure for things to be linked as a reason and what is done for that reason. Think of what professional historians are doing: among the things that happened they draw lines, one could say, lines of what was important for what, what developed into what, what prepared the ground for what. Just such a line we are drawing as well, only with an object of smaller scale, when we are saying that you declined that invitation, not because of the other appointment you had, but because of the unpleasant company you expected.

225 FURTHERMORE, what is a reason for one agent to do something need not be a reason to do that thing for another. This again is the same point as with respect to reasons for which people do things (§ 191). The barometer's promise of a fine day tomorrow may be a reason for you to get your boots ready, whether or not you actually do it, but it is not a reason for me to prepare mine if a lazy day is all I want for tomorrow. That is to say, people are as much selectors of reasons they have as they are selectors of reasons for which they do things: one subset of the facts there are is the set of reasons one agent has for doing something, another subset is the set of reasons another agent has for doing something. To repeat (§ 193), this does not mean that the qualities to which it is due that people have the reasons they do themselves are their reasons. It just means that, in accordance with their particular dispositions, they come with particular ranges of things that are reasons for them to do things. This also leaves open the possibility, though no more than the possibility, that some reasons are widely, or indeed universally, shared among creatures acting for reasons. Rationalist conceptions of morals, for instance, are not ruled out a priori.

226 MORE elaborately, one may distinguish between three levels of reason selection. First, among all the states of affairs obtaining, the set of reasons I have for doing something and the set of reasons somebody else has for

doing something will be different. The threat of the knight fork, for instance, is a reason I have for covering the crucial square, but it is not such a reason for somebody else who tries to please her opponent by losing, even when neither of us knows of the threat. Second, among the reasons we both have for doing something I am aware of some and somebody else is aware of others. Thus, assuming that we both have reason to protect that square, one of us may see that this is so and the other one may not. Third, among the reasons for doing something that we both have and both know, the set of reasons for which I actually do something and the set of reasons for which somebody else does something will be different. With both of us knowing that the threat of the knight fork gives us reason to protect the square in question, one of us may still not do it, whereas the other one may.

AT ANY time we have reasons for doing things, but the set of reasons we   227
have changes. In part it changes due to our own doings. For example, a task carried out now will not be awaiting completion in an hour. However, the set of reasons we now have for doing things is not up for grabs now. Think of it this way. If you are like me, at any point in your life since you were grown up there were letters left to respond to. The set of these letters changed: some dropped out because you finally did respond, others dropped out precisely because you never did, and time and again new ones were added. So to some extent it depends on you what the set of letters to respond to will be tomorrow: today that set is given. In this sense you already have a correspondence, you do not start it from scratch. To be sure, some people wipe the slate clean and do start their corre-spondence from scratch. Most do not, and their case provides the image: reasons you have are like letters the world has written to you. (The agent in error is, with this image, responding to a letter from Santa Claus: in fact no such message arrived.) True, there is this difference: unlike most of your correspondents, the world often addresses its letters to many of us at the same time.

A PROMINENT feature of reasons for which people do things was the fact   228
that by reference to them the action can be explained (§ 146). So in the case of reasons people just have but do not act upon, one may well wonder why they do not: why don't they do the thing that they have reason to do? After all, since sometimes we understand what they do by means of the reason for which they do it, we shall ask for an explanation if, with the reason for doing something in place, they still do not do it. Actually, nothing beyond ordinary ignorance prevents answering this question in any particular case. Agents are selectors of reasons for which they do

things (§ 191), and one may be able to explain in each case why some reason the agent had did not come out as a reason for which that agent acted. One will explain it in many cases by indicating relevant states of the agent. Thus unless I am given a hint, I fail to do something about the knight fork threatening me: that is because I do not see it. The state of my teeth is a reason for me to see a dentist, but I don't: that is because I fear the pain. I have reason for getting some exercise and still do not do a thing: that is because I have more important things to do. As before, though (§ 193): that a failure to act on a reason can be explained by reference to the fact that agents recognize, fear, care about, and so on, such and such things, does not show that what they actually do is done for the reason that they recognize, fear, care about, and so on, these things. It is done, rather, for whatever the material reason of the action in question is, if indeed it is done for any reason. My failure to protect that square against your knight is explained by my overlooking the threat of the fork, and that in turn is explained by my lack of experience in chess, but if I attack one of your pawns instead, a reason for which I do that is not my overlooking the threat of the fork, but for example the vulnerability of your center.

229   WE REFER to the reasons people have not only in explaining what they did, but also in advising them what to do, and it is worth showing how this practice can be understood in terms of the present account of reasons we have (§ 217). You tell me that there is reason for me to protect the square c7, and, let us say, you even tell me what that reason is, namely, the threat of the knight fork. The point of your telling me is to help me in finding the best way to deal with the situation. So one wonders how, on the present account of reasons one has, your telling me about that reason *can* help me. On the present account, my having a reason to protect c7 amounts to my being in such a position as, by protecting c7, to produce a response to the threat of the fork: why should your telling me about that be capable of helping me in finding the best way to deal with the situation? Because it may alter the range of what I am practically sensitive to. If people are reason-selectors, then your telling me may change my selection of reasons for which I do things. On all three levels just distinguished (§ 226) our selection of reasons can be changed by others. First, something may become a reason I have for doing something thanks to somebody's teaching me. Thus the offer of a cheap comprehensive railway schedule was no reason for me to buy one, but through that friend of mine I got to be a big railway fan and thus what had not been a reason became one. Second, somebody can make me aware of a reason I have for doing something, as you did in telling me about the knight fork.

Third, somebody can turn the reason I both have and know into a reason I act upon by making me attend to it vividly. In these ways the set of reasons for doing something that I have, or know, or act upon, may change. Thus I change, in my intake of reasons and in the shape of my practical blindness (§ 191). So changed I may be better able to deal with the situation.

There is nothing problematic about the general assumption at work here that through our words we should change one another. We do it all the time: we redirect another's attention, revive memories, allay fears. Given how pervasive these changes are, not only in extreme circumstances, but in the ordinary course of things, there is no reason to doubt that we change one another's reason-selection as well: through what we say, reasons one has become reasons one acts upon. It makes good sense as well to suppose that such change should be capable of helping someone to deal with a situation, which is a condition of its being advice. Again, we do it all the time. For instance, when you are flying, they tell you that, if there is need, you should fix the oxygen mask first to yourself, then to your child. Presumably the first time you heard this you came with reasons for doing things in reverse order, and presumably your coping with an emergency situation is improved by the change in your reason profile that the announcement effected. To be sure, your way to cope with an emergency may well not be improved by the announcement. For one thing, the words may not reach you, in one way or another, and your reason-selection may remain unaffected. For another, if your reason-selection changes, it may in fact not be for the better. You may be misled. Still, none of this shows that people do not sometimes succeed in changing you for the better.   230

It may be complained that a strange notion of advising is being employed here. On the account given, to tell me about reasons I have may be to advise me because it may change me for the better by changing my intake of reasons for which I do things. This, it may be said, is a strange notion of advising, as one would have thought that to advise is not straightaway to change people, but merely to present considerations to them on the basis of which they may then decide to change themselves, that is, change the selection of reasons for which they do things. After all, it is taken as the distinctive mark of advising as opposed, say, to indoctrinating that the considerations put forward are merely offered to the person addressed, the decision being left to her. In fact, however, it is doubtful whether an extra decision to accept it is necessary for taking advice, and so it is doubtful, too, whether a distinction on these lines between advice and indoctrination can be maintained. I may just come away from listening   231 to what you say with a different selection of reasons for which I act, without having expressly ratified the change, and still qualify as having taken your advice. Once you suggest to me, for example, that I should cover the square c7, I may immediately see the danger and move to protect the square: there may not be an extra act of deciding that this is a reason to act upon, but even so I shall be following your advice. Just as new beliefs need not be explicitly accepted, but may merely grow on a person in the course of her experience, so reasons one acts upon need not be endorsed as such, but may just come to acquire this status in the course of what happens to the person, and in particular through what she is told by others. To be sure, what people say may do its work slowly and indirectly. One may have to reconsider the matter, or again one may have to lay it aside for a time. Still, the range of reasons for which one does things will eventually have shifted, and that will be due to people having said what they did. Thus the present conception of advice is indeed not compatible with the widely held one according to which the person receiving advice is always master over what she accepts of it and what she rejects, but so much the worse for this widely held conception.

232   ONE MAY also be dissatisfied with this account of advising because it says nothing about what changes are for the better. Actually, that is a question that even to begin to try to answer here makes no sense. I do have views both about what in general is good in life and more in particular about how best to prepare broccoli. Thus I do have views, in these and in other matters, about which changes in people's reason selection are changes for the better. Still, your views are likely to be different, and we will have to argue it out, on the basis of material considerations about broccoli, life, and the rest. That will take time, and more than we have in the present setting. However, nothing other than the fact that it will take too long speaks against pursuing the question. The topic does not, by itself, resist argument, nor would it be unnatural to take it up in the present context. It is only too big. To be sure, things would be different if that old hope of philosophers from Plato on were true that there is a form of the good. Then one round of argument would suffice to decide which changes are for the better. Judging by what we have got so far under this heading, however, that hope seems to be forlorn. It seems that we will indeed have to argue it out case by case, for broccoli, for life, and for every other item on the agenda, what is good and what is better.

233   WE ADVISE others on what to do, but more important, we deliberate ourselves—more important, because advice will hardly be fruitful if the per-

son receiving advice is not at the same time a deliberator. So again it is worth showing how deliberation can be understood on the present account of reasons we have (§ 217). Let us say then that you have been offered a job at the University of Bielefeld. The Bielefeld department is higher than your present one in the informal ranking of your discipline, and as you are quite keen on being professionally recognized, that is a reason for you to accept the offer. It is a reason in the sense indicated: there is the enhanced reputation the Bielefeld job is going to give you, and you are in the position to respond to that by accepting. Then one afternoon you take the time expressly to consider what accepting would involve. You realize that it would probably mean that you will be living in a fairly uninteresting city. As you are a "cityzen" with all your heart, that is a reason you have for rejecting the offer. Again, it is a reason in the sense described: there is the lack of a city life that the Bielefeld job will inflict on you, and you are in the position to respond to that by rejecting the offer. It *is* such a reason and you *are* in that position independently of whether you notice it or not. That is to say, somebody else could have been quicker than you in detecting that there is this reason. It could have been news for you to be told about it. On that afternoon, though, you discover this reason yourself. You paint yourself a full picture of a grey life in Bielefeld. You imagine what it would be like to lack the choice between a variety of interesting things to do on any given evening and to run the risk of bumping into your students wherever you go. You contemplate that, and contemplating it changes you. The fact that accepting the offer would improve your professional standing becomes less important, and the fact that you will probably have to live in Bielefeld if you accept it looms larger and larger, eventually becoming, let us say, the reason for which indeed you reject the offer.

THIS is a case of deliberation. It is a simplified case, true, but it differs   234
from real cases only in reducing the number of reasons considered to two. One feature of the offer, overlooked so far or not taken seriously, becomes prominent to the point of overshadowing the other and determining the decision. Thus your reasons profile has changed. What you did to bring that about was to give these things some time and attention. That was important. Reasons we have do not exert their force behind our backs. It takes our open eyes, attention, and time, sometimes more, sometimes less, for them to become effective. Thus we may even know of a reason we have, but for lack of attention remain unimpressed by it. To deliberate is to consider things that you can do something with in response, and sometimes, thanks to such considering, one of these things becomes something

NINE

Are Reasons Internal?
And Are They Normative?

Two IMPORTANT objections will be raised against the account of reasons one has, as presented in the last chapter, one by internalists, the other by normativists. To start with the former, internalism is the view, advocated by Bernard Williams[1] and others, that one has a reason for doing something only if one is also motivated to do it or at least could acquire such motivation by sound deliberation on the basis of the motivation one has.[2] There has been some controversy about what this thesis entails, in particular about whether it rules out a Kantian conception to the effect that rational principles suffice to establish reasons for people to do and not do certain things, with Williams suggesting that it does rule it out,[3] and critics like Christine Korsgaard[4] and especially Jay Wallace[5] arguing that it does not. However, the thesis itself has been widely accepted. By contrast, the present account of reasons people have for doing things is externalist. No motivation on their part, actual or rationally accessible, is required for people to have a reason to do something. It suffices that something happened to which their action could be a response. True, somebody's desiring something, caring about something, or the like may figure, on the present account as well, in an explanation of why something is a reason for somebody, but whether such explanations of why something is a reason need to be motivational is left open (§ 191). Thus there is no conceptual link here, as there is on internalism, between having a reason and being motivated accordingly. So the question will be raised whether the present account of reasons can answer the internalist challenge: what could a reason to do something be that is not supported by appropriate motivation of the agent?

237   CHALLENGE against challenge: why should one's having reason to do something require one's having a motive, actual or rationally accessible, for doing it? To enter the discussion, not by way of Williams's official thesis, but by way of what he actually offers as an argument, the basic line of reasoning seems straightforward, even if commentators have offered a variety of reconstructions.[6] The basic line is this:

> 1. A reason one has for doing something could be a reason for which one does it, and in that case it would explain the action.[7]
> 2. "Nothing can explain an agent's (intentional) actions except something that motivates him so to act."[8]
> 3. Hence, there is no reason for somebody to do something without some sort of motivation to do it.

238   THE CRUCIAL question is what sort of motivation exactly the conclusion requires for there to be a reason for an agent to do something. In fact, a series of conclusions of increasing strength may be construed that might all be supposed to be established by the argument. On the weakest version, the motivation allegedly needed for a reason amounts to no more than the reason's being such that the agent could do the thing in question *for* that reason. Admittedly, the argument so construed would be gaining little ground. The conclusion would merely restate the first premise, just introducing the term "motivation" in addition. Nor would the argument so construed be in conflict with the account of reasons proposed here. That a reason one has for doing something might also become the reason for which one does it can be agreed on all sides. Stronger versions construe the motivation allegedly needed for one's having a reason as consisting in one's having a desire for doing the thing in question (or a personal loyalty, a project, an emotional reaction, or something of the sort). On the strongest version, such a desire, and so on, has to be actually present in the agent having a reason, whereas the weaker of the two stronger versions only requires the desire, and so on, to be either present in, or rationally accessible to, the agent. On both these stronger readings the argument would have major import. It would show the reasons an agent has to be contingent upon her current psychological state; for it depends on that state both what desires, and so on, she actually has, for the strongest version, and what desires, and so on, she could rationally acquire on the basis of those she actually has, for the weaker version.

239   IN THE strongest version the conclusion is clearly too strong to be true. We do not want to say that reasons exist only to the extent that the agent actually has a desire, or something like it, to do the thing in question. We do not want to say that unwillingness to go to the dentist makes void any

purported reason to do so. We do not want to say this because it would make nonsense of much of our practice of advising and deliberating. We consider whether there are reasons to do something especially when we, or the agents concerned, do not feel like doing it; and it would be foolish to consider that if in any case there were no such thing as a reason that one does not feel at all like acting upon.

WILLIAMS, as mentioned earlier (§ 236), does not defend the strongest version of the argument, but the weaker version of the two strong ones, the one that requires a desire or something like it either to be actually present or at least rationally accessible for there to be a reason. It is difficult to see, however, how to support this weaker claim without appealing to the argument in its strongest, and implausible, version. As Williams indicates, it is the explanatory role of reasons that the argument turns on,[9] but with regard to explanatory function it seems there should be no difference between the case of a desire or the like being not actual, but rationally accessible, and the case of it being not actual and not rationally accessible either. Rational accessibility is neither here nor there, one would think, when the question is about what explains action: if a desire or something like it must figure in such an explanation, then it must be an actual, not merely a rationally accessible desire. It may be replied that the agent having a reason is not after all required to be already moved to do the thing in question. What is required is only that it be true of her that, were she to act on the reason she has, there would be something to move her to do so. Yet this truth is not worth requiring; sure enough, something or other sets the person going who does something for a reason. This reply, then, takes us back to the weakest version of the argument, which says only that reasons need motivation in the sense that the agent might act on that reason. That is true, but nothing of interest follows from it. Leaving aside, then, this weak interpretation, Williams's argument seems to commit him to a conclusion much stronger than intended, and indeed unacceptably strong. 240

THE CULPRIT is premise 2. If only what motivates agents can explain their actions, then the motivation they do not have right now, but would acquire if they thought a bit more about the matter, is irrelevant. The agent's doing what, as of now, he is not motivated to do could not be explained, says premise 2; and so the offending conclusion follows, by premise 1, that this agent does not, now, have a reason for doing it, either, since any purported reason lacks, as of now, explanatory potential. It is difficult to see, however, why one should grant premise 2. We often explain people's actions by referring to their reasons rather than to their desires (or projects, 241 loyalties, etc.) We do say that I moved my pawn because of the bishop's threat, and so one wonders on what grounds Williams is ruling against this practice. Especially the defender of external reasons wonders. Since reasons in her view do not depend on the desires, and so on, of the agent, she can also be expected to maintain that one's reasons by themselves may suffice to explain one's action. That she is mistaken in maintaining that is something that Williams needs to show, not just to assume by way of a premise. Such an argument, though, is not apparent in Williams's text. He only reiterated his statement more recently, saying that what an agent "actually does has to be explained by his S," that is, by his actual motivational set consisting of his desires, and so on, and he added that "nobody denies this."[10] There certainly is wide agreement on this point, but even so the question remains what the reasoning may be that supports it.

242   THE ONLY one that comes to mind is this: explanation is by causes, and the causes of action are desires or something of the kind. The second of these appears false as stated, since there are, after all, physiological causes of action that are not desires or anything of the kind, but that may be irrelevant in the present context, given that not the explanation of action in general, but the explanation of action by reasons is at issue here. Precisely in the present context, however, the first statement, that explanation is by causes, may be contested. Precisely where the explanation of action by reasons is at issue, this statement begs the central question. We wanted to know by reference to what reason explanations explain, and simply to assume that explanation is by causes is to close that investigation before it started. True, there may be a general theory of explanation telling us that this is so, but in that case we should still want to ask whether that theory fits reason explanations of action in particular, or is rather refuted by them. Perhaps reason explanation of action is not by causes, but rather by aims.[11] Perhaps reason explanation is not by causes, but really only by reasons.[12] Given these possibilities, it is merely dogmatic to say that explanation must be by causes.

243   So WILLIAMS's claim is unjustified that only desires or the like, only members of one's motivational set, explain actions, and thus the internalist challenge (§ 236) has no force. Why that claim is nonetheless so widely accepted is easy to understand. Thanks to one dominant strand in the modern tradition, we have been brought up to believe that real, respectable explanation is by causes. Our intellectual conscience is worried as long as we cannot show, or rely on somebody to show, the mechanism that produces an effect. This belief makes suspect our practice of explaining what people do by the reasons for which they do it, since on the face of it

reasons are not causes (§ 142). That there was a reason for somebody to do something, says Williams,[13] that fact by itself would never explain anything that she did, not even her doing what there was reason for her to do. Why? Because it does not seem to be a cause of anything she did. So desires and the like are called in to take over the explanatory job commonly ascribed to reasons. That calms our conscience, since desires, and so on, are supposed to give us a psychological mechanism producing action, and it also very nearly vindicates our practice of explaining people's actions by their reasons, with the reservation only that the real explanatory work is done, not by the reasons, but by the appropriate members of one's motivational set. Thus it comes to seem natural to hold that only a desire or some other member of one's motivational set can explain action. Yet what we have been brought up to believe is not true. At least it is not justified. There are no grounds for suspecting that ordinary explanation of action by reasons, by reasons unreduced to motives, is less real and respectable, less good an explanation than any other.

So MUCH for the internalist challenge to the present account of reasons one has (§ 217). Another line of attack, perhaps an even more natural one, is the objection that this account of reasons one has fails to do justice to the normativity of reasons. If reasons one has are just initial parts of histories that one may complete with a response, then such reasons do not put any requirement on the person's doings. In fact, however, to have a reason for doing something is to be subject to some kind of requirement to do it, or so at least is the view of the majority of writers in the field.[14] Thus the present account of reasons, unable to accommodate this feature of reasons people have, is unsatisfactory.   244

THERE is no denying that on the present account there is nothing normative about reasons one has. Threads of histories begun may be completed, but it is not the case that they ought to be. So if reasons are normative, the present account of reasons is sunk. Still, it is not clear, the majority opinion notwithstanding, that reasons are normative, or so at least the following will argue. Two representative and influential conceptions of the alleged normativity of reasons will be discussed, those put forward by Christine Korsgaard and by John Broome; and the result will be that neither succeeds in substantiating the idea of reasons being normative. It will then be argued that, contrary to initial appearances, our ordinary ways of speaking and thinking of reasons to do something do not support that idea, either. Pending further argument on the question, then, the present account of reasons people have for doing things cannot be thrown out for its failure to cater for the alleged normativity of reasons.   245

246 AUTHORS often do not take the time to spell out what exactly they mean by saying that reasons are normative. Clearly, a rough idea is this: people ought to do what they have reason to do. This is rough, first, because the language of 'ought' is not the only contender, if a leading one, for capturing normativity. Jonathan Dancy, for instance, prefers to speak of states of affairs 'favoring' courses of action,[15] and it is not evident that such language can be reduced to the language of 'ought'. This complication, though, will be disregarded here, and the argument is going to be conducted only in terms of 'ought'. The formula just given is rough, second, because quite often people ought not to do what they have reason to do. Robbing a bank, for example, is certainly something I have reason to do, provided that I am likely to succeed, but it is not something I ought to do, as there are stronger reasons against doing it.[16] The natural way to avoid this problem is to say that people ought to do what, on balance, they have reason to do. Unfortunately, talk of a balance of reasons rests on an understanding of the idea of weighing reasons, thus on understanding what it is for one reason to be stronger, or weightier, than another; and that is going to be discussed only in the next chapter. The best course for the moment may be to ignore this complication and to pretend, contrary to fact to be sure, that in any situation people face just one relevant reason for action. And the question about the normativity of reasons is why it should be true that then they ought to do what they have a reason for doing.

247 IT CERTAINLY looks like being true. For one thing, somebody who is asking for advice in a difficult situation may very well express himself by saying: "What shall I do?" and in response to this question it would be perfectly appropriate to go through the reasons for and against the various courses of action offering themselves. Similarly, if the other person does not have a clear view of these reasons and their relative strength, it would be perfectly appropriate for her to say: "I have no idea what you should do." These locutions do suggest that what one should do depends on the reasons one has. For another thing, we sometimes blame people for failing to do what they know they have reason to do. For instance, we sometimes blame people pursuing an end for failing to take the suitable means. Thus we take such people not to have done what they ought to have done. We suppose, then, that by virtue of having a reason for doing something, they were under a requirement to do it.[17] However, these considerations do not decide the matter. We may be misguided in speaking the way we do and misguided in blaming people for failing to act on reasons they have, since actually they are subject to no such requirement. That certainly would be news for our ordinary ways of thinking about reasons, but news or not,

it may still be true. Argument is needed, then, to back the assumption that one ought to do what one has reason to do and no reason not to do.

THE MOST ambitious argument here is Christine Korsgaard's. Her view is   248
an extension of Kant's theory of autonomy. Kant held that we are subject to moral requirements because, as rational creatures, we impose the moral law on ourselves.[18] Korsgaard holds that we are subject to rational requirements of whatever kind, not only to moral ones, thanks to our imposing laws on ourselves.[19] Thus for her, reasons do not "exist independently of the rational will."[20] Rather, willing an end makes it the case both that the agent has reasons to take suitable means toward that end and that he is subject to a rational requirement to do so; always supposing contrary reasons to be absent. Thus one ought to do what one has reason to do and no reason not to do: one's having a reason and one's being required to act accordingly both result from one's own legislative act. Reason and requirement are twins: born at the same time from a rational agent's setting herself an end.

APPARENTLY Korsgaard takes herself to be expounding Kant's doctrine   249
here, and that claim would certainly be open to doubt. Reason and requirement are not twins for Kant: God has reasons for what he does, but he is not required to do it.[21] Korsgaard's suggestion that this notion is only a transient element of Kant's thought at the time of *Foundations*," superseded by his mature theory of autonomy, would seem to be historically untenable.[22]

NEVER mind historical accuracy, though: the question here is whether   250
Korsgaard's position is persuasive in its own right. That depends on whether we have grounds to believe that creatures who have reasons for doing things are also creatures who, by imposing laws on themselves, endow these reasons with normative status. Korsgaard calls the latter capacity a will, thus introducing a distinction between willing on the one hand and wanting or desiring on the other. In this terminology the question may also be put as follows: do we have grounds to believe that creatures having reasons are also creatures having a will? Korsgaard insists that having a will "is constitutive of being a person."[23] However, it is difficult to see the grounds for this statement. Persons, as one would ordinarily understand the word, are most, or indeed all, of one's fellow human beings, and to say that all these are self-legislators, and constitutively so, that therefore they all give the reasons they have for doing things normative import, does not, on the face of it, appear plausible at all.[24] Autonomy in this strong sense is just not visible or evident in the people

around us, and no further reasons are given that would make the idea any more credible. At times Korsgaard goes so far as to claim that, if you lack a will or abjure having one, there is really no you around,[25] but this appears merely dogmatic: that is actually not the way we think of people. To be sure, if it were established already that reasons are normative, self-legislation might turn out to be the best explanation for this fact; and Korsgaard sometimes speaks as if she were arguing for this more modest thesis.[26] Whatever her own aim, though, the present task is to find a justification for holding reasons to be normative in the first place. Such a justification she does not offer.

251 A MORE cautious and also a more promising theory has been advanced by John Broome in a recent pair of articles.[27] He distinguishes three types of normative relation:[28]

- the reason relation: something is a reason for a person to do something;
- the ought relation: something makes it the case that a person ought to do something;
- the relation of normative requirement: something normatively requires a person to do something.

And he argues for the following three theses:[29]

1. Practical reasoning must be understood in terms of normative requirement.
2. If one is subject to a normative requirement, then one ought to make true the following implication: if the condition normatively requiring one holds, then one does do what one is normatively required to do.
3. If one is subject to a normative requirement, then it need not be the case that one ought to do what one is normatively required to do, and it need not be the case, either, that one has reason to do so.

252 To ILLUSTRATE the import of these claims, suppose you have the aim to buy a boat, and the only way to do it is, as you know, to borrow money.[30] Then what is true of you, on Broome's view, is only this: under these circumstances your having the aim of buying a boat normatively requires you to borrow money. Practical reasoning does take you from willing the end to willing the means: you cannot rationally stay with the former and fail to proceed to the latter. You ought to make sure that, if you have the aim of buying a boat, you do borrow money. However, this is not to say that, simply, you ought to borrow money. Incumbent on you is only to make the conditional true, not its consequent.

253 IT MAY not be evident what bearing these ideas have on the question at hand, namely, whether reasons are normative. Indeed, this may become

quite obscure on reading Broome's statement: "By 'a reason' I mean a *pro tanto* ought."[31] So the question pursued here does not even arise for Broome, it is settled in the affirmative by definition! In fact, though, definitions do not settle questions; and while Broome is free to stipulate that the word "reason" in his writing is to stand for "*pro tanto* ought," this does nothing to show that what ordinarily is called a reason carries normative force. The question still stands whether it does, and to avoid confusion it may actually be better to translate Broome's talk of reasons back into talk of *pro tanto* oughts. So the first of the relations just mentioned becomes

- the *pro tanto* ought relation: something makes it the case that a person ought to do something, provided that she ought not to do something else.

To mark the contrast, the second relation could then be called the "all-out ought relation." And thesis 3, revised accordingly, says:

(3.) If one is subject to a normative requirement, it need not be the case that one ought, and it need not even be the case that *pro tanto* one ought, to do what is normatively required.

THE RELEVANCE of Broome's argument for the question whether reasons are normative lies, rather, in his conception of practical reasoning. This is so because ordinarily one would take a reason to be something expressed or indicated in the major premise of a piece of practical reasoning, and not, as on Broome's usage, something making it the case that somebody is subject to a *pro tanto* ought. Disregarding for the moment earlier quarrels about where precisely to locate reasons, in desires, in end states, or rather in states that the action is meant to remedy, ordinarily one would take the statement that you have the aim of buying a boat to indicate a reason you have for borrowing money. Reasons, on this understanding, would be something that figures in reasoning; and the very words suggest that this is a more natural construal than Broome's separation of reasons and reasoning.[32] Given this understanding, however, the relevance of Broome's theory for the present question becomes clear. The theory says that it is not the case that one ought, either all-out or *pro tanto*, to do what one has reason to do. The theory is saying that because reasons, on the present understanding, are what reasoning starts out from, and reasoning, as Broome insists,[33] yields no ought, not even a *pro tanto* ought. In that sense reasons are not normative. However, the theory also says that one ought, all-out, to make true the conditional: if one has a reason to do something, then one does it. The theory is saying that because again reasons are, on the present understanding, what reasoning starts out from,

254

and reasoning, as Broome insists,[34] is to be construed in terms of normative requirements. In this sense, then, reasons are normative.

255 THIS is the claim; what is the argument? It is fairly clear that practical reasoning, once construed in terms of a normative requirement, does not yield the conclusion that you ought, either all-out or *pro tanto*, to borrow money, to stay with that example. Under a normative requirement you only ought to make sure that it is not true both that you have the aim of buying a boat and that you do not borrow money, and from that you cannot infer that you ought to borrow money. You cannot even infer it if it *is* true that you have the aim of buying a boat, for then it may still be the case, not that you ought to borrow money, but that, while having the aim of buying a boat, you ought not to have it. So the first of the theory's two claims, namely, that reasons are *not* normative in the sense of yielding such an ought, plainly follows from statement 1 earlier; and the second of its claims, namely, that reasons *are* normative in the sense of a normative requirement holding, *is* statement 1, given the revised understanding of reasons suggested in the last paragraph. The crucial question, then, is why statement 1 should be true; why practical reasoning needs to be understood in terms of normative requirement.

256 BROOME may be read to be arguing as follows. The relation between your having the aim of buying a boat and your borrowing money is not the all-out ought relation. This is so because it may be that in fact you ought not to borrow money, perhaps because you ought not to have the aim of buying a boat in the first place. If that is the situation, then your having that aim does not, as on the all-out ought relation it must, make it the case that, simply, you ought to borrow money. Neither is the relation between your having the aim of buying a boat and your borrowing money the *pro tanto* ought relation. This is so because if you have that aim and do not borrow money, with circumstances as before, then "you are definitely not entirely as you ought to be,"[35] whereas with a *pro tanto* ought relation you may or may not be as you ought to be, depending on whether or not there is something else you ought to do. Assuming that the two ought relations and the relation of normative requirement are the only candidates for giving an account of practical reasoning, it follows that practical reasoning needs to be understood in terms of normative requirement.

257 AND PRECISELY this assumption may be doubted. The point is not that practical reasoning should be understood in terms of yet another norma-

tive relation. The point is that it should perhaps be understood in terms of no normative relation at all. Broome's argument is convincing as far as it goes: among the three normative relations considered, normative requirement wins the contest because of the defects of the other two. However, this is not an argument for the normativity of reasons. It is only an argument for understanding the normativity of reasons, if indeed normative they are, in terms of normative requirement. And for all Broome says, they may not be normative. If under circumstances as before you have the aim of buying a boat and do not borrow money, perhaps there is nothing at all wrong with you. Perhaps you are neither definitely failing in what you ought to do, nor failing provided that there is not something else you ought to do. Perhaps you are just fine. Sure, compared to people around you, you may be behaving strangely, but that is a different thing. Also, people may call you irrational. Yet if this only says that you are one of those who do not do what they have reason to do, this is true and admitted, but harmless, whereas if it implies that you are not as you ought to be, the comment is, for all we have heard so far, unwarranted.[36] Broome's argument, then, presupposes, but it does not show, that reasons are normative.

IN DISMANTLING the confusing accoutrements of the idea, Broome's argument rather makes evident how odd it really is to think of you as bound to make true the conditional: if you have the aim of buying a boat, you borrow money. Why should it be the case that in some way you are not as you ought to be if such a conditional does not hold of you? Who or what imposed that task on you? It seems easier and more natural to describe your situation in these terms (using again "reason" in what seems to be its ordinary sense, not in Broome's sense of a "*pro tanto* ought"): the advantages of having a boat give you reason to buy one and, your finances being what they are, they also give you reason to borrow money. Yet there is nothing that hereby you are called upon to do, neither to borrow money nor to see to it that it be true that if you have the aim of buying a boat, then you borrow money. Borrowing money is just something you can do in view of the attractions of having a boat: if you keep having that aim and still do not borrow money, you will not have failed to deliver something that is due. Sure, probably you will not have a boat then, and probably you will feel frustration, especially on considering that it is by your own hands that you suffer. Still, this does not show that you went amiss in what you did. And if I advise you to borrow money, as I well may if I care about you, I shall not be speaking in the name of a normative requirement to which you are subject whether I speak or not. I shall try,

258

by pointing out the reasons you have, to influence you so as to take the course where you probably will be better off. Normativity, that is, can be dropped from the picture.

259   To RECAPITULATE. Two theories about the normativity of reasons were discussed, Korsgaard's ambitious and Broome's more modest one. Neither supplied an argument showing that reasons are indeed normative, they only gave different accounts of a normativity of reasons they actually just assume, in terms of the agent's rational self-legislation the one, in terms of a normative requirement the other. Positive argument lacking, as far as one can see, it would seem that the idea of reasons being normative may be given up. It would seem that reasons can indeed be regarded, in accordance with the suggestion earlier, as mere proposals, offers, or invitations the world extends to you. The case of invitations marks the point. In the German system, members of universities are generally required to contribute to academic self-administration, so in this system the invitation to a committee meeting does have normative force, derived from that general obligation. Suppose now that obligation gone, and no "social" obligation or moral pressure taking its place, suppose a truly free invitation, merely announcing that here there is an interesting or important or tedious committee meeting for you, an invitation that you may take or leave without in either case failing in what you ought to be: then you have what a reason is like that is not normative. And given the lack of persuasive arguments for a more demanding conception of reasons as normative, that understanding of reasons would seem to hold the better position, were it not for the two phenomena mentioned at the beginning of this discussion (§ 247). First, if reasons are not normative, why do we think of pointing out the reasons one has as a proper answer to the question what one should do? Second, why do we blame people for failing to do what they have reason to do? The case against the normativity of reasons will only be complete with a satisfying answer to these questions.

260   To START with the first question, once we observe actual usage more closely, the problem may vanish. Unexpectedly you find yourself, together with a close friend, with a free evening before you. It will be natural to ask her in such a situation: "What shall we do now?" It will not occur to you to ask: "What ought we to do now?" Not even "what should we do now?" sounds right. It is not that this "shall" serves to form a future tense in this context. If your companion replies: "We will end up working anyway," this is not an answer to your original question, but the suggestion that the question is not worth considering, since you are both so unimaginative. A proper answer to your question will be one that states or

indicates a reason for doing this or that, for instance: "The film in the Moviemento is supposed to be outstanding." Alternatively, a proper answer to your question will be simply: "Let's go to the movies." The same holds for more serious cases. One who has suffered a great loss could ask: "What shall I do now?" and this would not be to ask "What is it that I ought to do now?" nor to ask "What is it in fact that I am going to do now?" Such a person simply wants to be told a course of action for her to follow, and as in the previous example, a bare imperative or the indication of a reason for doing this or that would be a proper answer. This suggests that in such contexts "I shall" does not have normative force; that it does not mean anything like "I am required by the norms applying to this case to do such and such." So even though we do properly refer to reasons somebody has for doing something in response to a question like "What shall I do?" this does not show that we think of reasons as normative.

THE SECOND question was why we blame people for failing to do what they have reason to do, if reasons do not have normative force. The answer is that, strictly, it is false or misleading to say that we blame people for failing to do what they have reason to do. First of all it should be noted that some of us, those of a strongly Stoic or Buddhist bent of mind, do not blame at all, or at least try to do without it. They have not surrendered the idea of there being reasons for doing things. What they seem to have in mind is rather that one's failure to do what one has reason to do belongs to the great whole of the world, by blaming which one only shows one's lack of wisdom. Second, in a large number of cases it may be suspected that people who are blamed for failing to do something that they have reason to do are not blamed *because* they failed to do something that they have reason to do, but rather because they failed to do what they ought to have done. After all, even if reasons are not as such normative, it is still true that many things that people have reason to do are things they ought to do, and conversely. Thus one may be blamed for what actually is a failure to do what one has reason to do, but not blamed on this ground. Therefore it is misleading to say that we blame people for failing to do what they have reason to do, since it suggests that normally we blame people, not only when, but also because they failed to do what they had reason to do, and that may well not be so. Finally, with regard to blaming people on the grounds that they failed to do what they had reason to do, consider Korsgaard's case of the ride on the roller coaster:[37] you have made up your mind to do it, and all you have to do is buy a ticket and get on, but you are prevented by terror. We may safely assume that there does not exist a general norm against riding on the roller coaster,

261

and we may also assume, less safely, that there is no other reason for you to shy back. Are we going to blame you for failing to do what, as far as we can tell, you have reason to do? The truth seems to be that some of us will blame you and some of us will not. Some of us will be tolerant toward those who do not follow reason. They will say that if you are not otherwise failing in what you ought to do, then the fact that you have, and know that you have, a reason for doing something and still do not do it, is nothing for which to blame you. Others will be exasperated by your unreasonableness. They will say that doing what one has reason to do is itself a character trait one ought to have, so you do deserve blame. Who is right need not be decided here. The point is that people will just react differently. Hence it is false to say that we blame people on the ground that they failed to do what they had reason to do. We do not, some of us do.

262 THUS the two phenomena mentioned earlier (§ 259) no longer protect from doubt the thesis that reasons are normative. It is not generally true that we blame people on the grounds that they failed to do what they had reason to do; and while it is proper to point out reasons somebody has in response to a question like "What shall I do?" these locutions lack normative import in many cases (§ 260). As on the other hand no persuasive argument in favor of the normativity of reasons could be found either in Korsgaard (§ 250) or in Broome (§ 257), it would seem sensible to conclude, as long as no better argument appears in the field at any rate, that reasons are not normative. And that removes the second important objection (§ 244) to the proposed understanding of reasons people have for doing something.

TEN

Stronger Reasons

THE REMAINING task distinguished two chapters back (§ 215) was an explication of the qualities commonly ascribed to reasons, as when reasons are called strong, good, overwhelming, and the like. There is certainly a wide stylistic variety of expressions available here, but it seems that substantially these characterizations all locate the reasons to which they apply on one dimension, that of strength. A good reason is a comparatively strong reason, a poor reason a comparatively weak one, an overwhelming reason is as strong as to be irresistible, and so on. True, some of these phrases are used in other ways, too. What is called a good reason is often simply a reason, by contrast to a merely apparent one. "Poor reason" and "bad reason" are often diplomatic expressions for what is not considered a reason at all. Still, these uses seem to be derivative; and the concept in terms of which the basic use of these phrases needs to be explained would be that of a reason's being strong. Or rather, that of a reason's being stronger than another: "strength," at least "strength of reasons," seems to be one of those cases where the comparative is conceptually prior to the positive.[1] At any rate, an understanding of one reason being stronger than another, an understanding compatible with the overall conception of reasons proposed here, is the aim of the following discussion.

To DISCARD first of all some unsatisfactory suggestions, a stronger reason need not be a reason looming larger in the agent's consciousness. People can deeply worry about trifling things, and treat casually what is all-important. Second, a stronger reason cannot be explained as a reason more likely to be acted upon. Maybe people quite often do things that they have stronger reason not to do. So strength of reasons cannot be effectivity, as one might call it. Nor, finally, should a stronger reason be explained as one accompanied by a more pressing normative claim for compliance. Not only the earlier doubts with regard to the normativity of reasons tell against taking this line. More important, it would be an explanation by the equally obscure. The question is what it is about a reason that makes it stronger than another, and to be told that this is due to a more pressing normative claim connected with the reason is disappointing: one would like to know then what it is about one reason that makes its associated normative claim more pressing than that of another.

265   An interesting proposal is offered by Joseph Raz. On his view, a reason is stronger than another by virtue of overriding it in cases of conflict. Reasons are in conflict if the one is a reason for doing, and the other is a reason for not doing, the same thing. And one conflicting reason overrides the other if the conjunct of the two is a reason to do what the overriding one by itself is a reason to do, whereas the conjunct is not a reason to do what the overridden one by itself is a reason to do.[2] Think of it as a seesaw for reasons: either reason makes the plank go down its way when sitting on it alone, but only the stronger one pushes the plank down its way when both are sitting on it at opposite ends. As Raz points out,[3] this account allows for ties and for incommensurable reasons: reasons may conflict, in the sense explained, and yet their conjunct may not be a reason for either course of action—again, as with people on a seesaw.

266   The problem with this criterion is that it may produce too many ties, or indeed only ties. Here is one of Raz's examples of one reason overriding another:

> The fact that my son has been injured is a reason for me to drive him to the hospital at 45 mph. . . . It overrides the only conflicting reason present: the legally imposed 30 mph speed limit.

On Raz's proposal, the former reason is overriding, the latter overridden thanks to this: the joint fact of his son's having been injured and of there being a legal speed limit of thirty miles per hour is a reason for him to drive to the hospital at forty-five miles per hour, but this joint fact is not a reason for him to drive to the hospital at thirty miles per hour at most. However, it is hard to see the joint fact of his son's injury and the legal speed limit of thirty miles per hour as indeed providing a reason for driving to the hospital at forty-five miles per hour. On being told that the legal speed limit of thirty miles per hour is part of a reason he has for driving his son at forty-five miles per hour to the hospital, an ordinary speaker will be baffled, or else will suspect him of an unusually rebellious temperament. In addition, consider the situation where he drives his son to the hospital, not because of an injury, but for a routine checkup: we do not want to say that some of the reason persists that he had in the previous case for driving at forty-five miles per hour. We rather want to say that the injury alone gave him reason to drive faster than permitted. Thus we want to say that it is false that the joint fact of injury and speed limit is a reason for him to drive fast. Nor, to be sure, is the joint fact a reason for him to drive more slowly. The joint fact, it would seem, is not a reason for anything. Hence on Raz's criterion the two reasons, injury and speed limit, come out tied, which they should not.

In defense of Raz's proposal it might be suggested that the situation should rather be described as follows. While it is both true that he has reason to drive his son to the hospital at forty-five miles per hour and to do so in violation of the legal speed limit, it is only true that he has reason to stick to the speed limit, but not true that he has reason to endanger the life of his son by doing so; and this difference accounts for the former reason's overriding the latter. This may not in fact be a friendly amendment, since Raz's proposal was about a conjunction of reasons, and here we are talking about a conjunction of action descriptions. Anyway, the main problem with the suggestion is that this account of the situation is not even correct. Only the first half is: he has reason to drive his son to the hospital at forty-five miles per hour, and he has reason to do so in violation of the speed limit. The second half is not correct. It is not only true that he has reason to observe the speed limit, it is also true that he has reason to endanger his son's life by doing so. The existence of the speed limit counts against violating it, however narrowly or broadly the violation may be described. Thus no difference emerges here that could be used for an account of reasons overriding and overridden.   267

Taking reasons as initial parts of histories to which agents may respond in action, as suggested here (§ 217), opens a more promising line of thought. The world normally offers you numerous threads to keep knitting on (§ 223), but the point is, some are more important to you than others. The practical field in which you move is not flat. Some of the states of affairs and events to which you may respond stand out, others recede into the background, and that is what makes them stronger or weaker reasons. In Raz's example, his son's injury is more prominent among the things inviting him (§ 259) to respond than the legal speed limit. No doubt the speed limit continues to matter, it just comes up against something counting for more. To rush to the hospital is a matter of "first things first." Assuming that a person does first what he has strongest reason to do, the proverbial formula expresses the point nicely: that a   268 thing is first, namely, in importance, that makes it first to be dealt with, namely, giving strongest reason for action. So here is the proposal: stronger reasons are states of affairs or events more important to the agent.

269　Thıs is not to explain the relative strength of reasons in terms of the relative strength of the agents' desires. That a reason matters to you is one thing; that you are eager to act on this reason, or eager to reap the benefits of doing so, is another. Sometimes we find ourselves wanting to do something very much, but we may admit, perhaps later, perhaps even at the time, that the reason for doing it is not especially weighty. And conversely: a reason for action can be significant without inspiring a particularly heated desire.

270　Indeed, this is not even to explain the relative strength of reasons in terms of what the person considers important. To be important and to be deemed important are two things. People can worry themselves out of their wits over insignificant things while neglecting what is really important, and that is no less true for having been used, often deceptively, as a topos in Christian homily. That in this way the relative strength of reasons does not depend on how the person judges the situation fits our normal understanding of reasons. We think that people may not only fail to notice the reasons they have (§ 226), but also may not be the best judges about which of the reasons they do notice are stronger and which weaker. That is why sometimes we offer advice, perhaps unbidden advice: we want our interlocutor to appreciate what really counts. ("You can go out with him, fine, but dropping out of college to live with him is crazy.")

271　Who, it will be protested, can overrule me on what is more and what is less important to me? The answer is that your biographer can. What is more and what is less important to you is a matter of what your life is like, yours in particular and human life in general; and so somebody knowing something about your life and about human life, your biographer, to use the term broadly again (§ 125), may know better than you do about the relative importance of things to you. No doubt for some matters you are going to be your best biographer yourself, but for other matters you may not be. It may just be the case, to take up the example of the last paragraph, that given what you did so far in your life, what you got involved with, what you became sensitive to, a completed education is in fact more important to you than living with James, and thus the reason for the former *is* stronger than the reason for the latter, even if you disagree with this judgment. You may be pursuing your plan merely in order to be the romantic, adventurous lover; a guise, however, that just will not fit you, given what you have become in your life so far. This is not to say, to be sure, that to keep going as one did has always the strongest reason for it. Sometimes it is more important to take off in a new direction, and again the agent may not see it. (Different case: "It is about time she moved out of her parents'.") Even less is it to say that education generally beats love in importance. Only, for some people sometimes it may, their own judgment to the contrary. Least of all is it to say that any of this is easy to tell. The point is merely that at times we may be right and you may be wrong about what is more and what is less important to you. We may *be* right; which is not just to say that events may prove us right, or that you will come round to share our view. Whether these things happen or not, it may be true that now you have a stronger reason for continuing college than for moving in with James, even though you think otherwise.

THIS explanation of "stronger reasons" as "reasons more important to the   272
person in question" is following to some extent Harry Frankfurt's ideas about caring and about things being important to us.[4] It is true, intent on bringing out "the importance of what we care about" (the title of the first of his papers on the topic), Frankfurt drew attention chiefly to cases of caring deeply about persons or causes, cases of love, for example, or cases of devoting oneself to the pursuit of an ideal. That restriction does not seem to be essential, though. In fact, Frankfurt's remark that there are "wide variations in how strongly and how persistently people care about things"[5] can be read as allowing one person to care about a large number of things with different degrees of intensity; so that for each person we get a landscape of things cared about, with a few peaks perhaps, a range of middling hills, and a large area of very low elevation. This is the idea that can be used to account for "stronger reasons": given such a landscape, now more broadly of things more or less important to somebody, a reason is stronger than another depending on whether it is located at a higher elevation in this landscape. Sure, some things will be important to you and yet not count as reasons, since there is nothing you can do about them. Still, if something is a reason for you to do something, you can locate it on your map of importance; and the elevation of that location determines the reason's relative strength. Thus in that example of Raz, you do care about the legal speed limit, and so the reason you have for observing it has some strength. Still, you care a great deal more about your son's health or perhaps life, and this is what makes the reason stronger for driving him to the hospital faster than permitted.

ON FRANKFURT's view, we must be prepared to overrule people on   273
whether they do or do not care about a certain thing,[6] and as argued two

paragraphs earlier, so we do with respect to what is important to them. Furthermore, for Frankfurt the order of what is important to us does not reduce to a moral ordering.[7] Something may be important to one without morality's telling her so; and conversely, something may still not be important to a person, even though morality claims that it is. To explain "stronger reasons" in terms of what is more important to people thus entails taking the relative strength of reasons they have to be determined not by moral considerations, or at least not by moral considerations alone. This is a welcome consequence. It allows us to ask what the relative weight of moral and of other reasons is, in a particular case or even in general, and that certainly appears to be a sensible question. Morality is not the arbiter over the relative weight of the various reasons one has. It is just one party to the dispute. Thus no doubt some of the reasons people have for doing things are moral reasons, and no doubt for such reasons they sometimes do what they do. Yet how important, and thus how strong, moral reasons are depends on the agent.

274   IT DEPENDS on the agent, but not, to be sure, in the sense that agents can set at their discretion how important some reason, moral or not, is to be. The relative weight of reasons is, as Frankfurt puts it in a different connection, "irredeemably a matter of personal circumstance."[8] What one is and has become—a music-lover, a miser, a truly political animal,[9] or an adventurer of whatever kind—determines which reason one has counts for more than another. That obviously is not to say that there is no fact of the matter here. Mahler's Ninth being broadcast tonight is for the music-lover a stronger reason to stay at home than the famous logician's lecture is a reason to go to the university. This is something that is the case, and anyone knowing enough about the music-lover's life can tell that it is. To make the relative strength of reasons agent-dependent in this way evidently accords well with the general line about reasons taken here. If reasons are pieces of histories to which one may respond in action, then it should certainly depend on the particular character of the one possibly responding which of these pieces predominates in the entire setting and which stands back.

275   ADMITTEDLY, Frankfurt himself insisted on separating our caring about things and their being important to us on the one hand from our having reasons for certain courses of action on the other. Thus he distinguishes acting under "volitional necessity," that is to say, doing something because one cares about something in such a way and to such a degree that one cannot forbear doing it, from acting for insuperable reasons, where one

"must reject the possibility of forbearing because he has such a good reason for rejecting it."[10] It may well be doubted, however, whether this difference is borne out by our experience. People who do what they do because they care so much and in such a way about something will often explain themselves by means of the reason vocabulary, saying for instance that they find the reasons for it incontrovertible. Similarly the other way round: those with overwhelming reason for some course of action may well express themselves by saying that someone or something is all-important to them. The same is true in cases falling short of any kind of necessity. The music-lover for instance, talking about why he intends to stay home to-night, may say equally well that he loves Mahler's Ninth Symphony, which is going to be broadcast then, and that he has excellent reason for listening to that recording. There is a difference of style between these two ways of putting things, the first sounding emphatic, the latter a bit frosty, but apparently no more than a difference of style. True, sometimes people will resist explaining themselves in the vocabulary of reasons. One may say for example: "I will stay with him because I love him, even though all the reasons tell against doing it." However, to speak this way is to betray too narrow an understanding of reasons: as if only the selfish sort counted. No doubt this person does have reasons for staying with her companion, her own words notwithstanding. Thus it can be suspected that those who insist on explaining themselves in terms of caring about things *rather than* in terms of reasons they have are only mistaken, one way or another, about what it takes for something to be a reason.

SPEAKING from a broader perspective, it may indeed be an advantage of the present line of thought that it does away with the difference between the order of reasons and the order of caring. Frankfurt, broaching the philosophical inquiry into what we care about and what is important to us, contrasted that inquiry with ethics, which deals with right and wrong and with moral obligation.[11] To leave it at this contrast, however, is hardly satisfying. Both the important and the obligatory are practical, they are concerned with what to do; and so some account of the relation between them would have to be given, which seems difficult to provide. On the present proposal things fall into place quite easily. There is, like a relief map, the range of things important to us in varying degrees. All the reasons for action we have are located somewhere in this domain, and their relative strength is determined by how important to us the thing in question is. Moral reasons are a subclass of the reasons we have. And as for the relative strength of moral and other reasons for doing things, that depends, on the person and on the case.

ELEVEN

Doing Things for a Purpose,
Doing Things for Fun

277   IT REMAINS to examine how much sense the proposed account of reasons
for which we do things (§ 118) makes of the various cases in which we
actually ascribe such reasons to people. Clearly it makes good sense of
quite a number. As indicated before (§ 119), it works particularly well for
moves in games. Thus if there is an ace on the table and for that reason
I play trump, it makes good sense to say that my playing trump is a
response to the ace lying there, and that this is precisely what my playing
trump for this reason amounts to. The account works well, not only for
games, but for all sorts of interaction. Whether I hit you because you hit
me before, or I help you with your harvest because you helped me with
mine yesterday, it makes sense to say that I continue with a response,
commendable or not, the history that you began, and that this is precisely
what it is for your action to be the reason for mine. The account works
well for work. Alfred answers the incoming phone calls for Myers & Myers
because they pay him decently: it makes good sense to explicate this statement as saying that it is in consideration of, that is, in response to, the
likelihood of the company's paying him a certain amount of money at the
end of the month that Alfred answers the phone calls. There are some
cases, however, that do not lend themselves easily to a treatment on these
lines. Two kinds of cases in particular come to mind, things done for some
purpose and things done just for fun.

278   OFTEN we explain what somebody did by indicating the purpose of an
action, as in:

> Reggie opened the window to get [for the purpose of getting] a breath
> of fresh air.[1]

Such teleological explanations, as they are called, are clearly reason explanations. In fact, it would be natural to reinforce the quoted statement against someone who doubted it by saying: "Yes, that was his reason." However, a reason of this sort does not fit into the mold laid out by the present account of reasons. To indicate the purpose of an action is not to indicate a state of affairs to which that action is a response. It is to indicate, rather, what is going to be the result of the action, provided that things work out as intended. Some adjustment is needed, then, either by reinterpreting the proposed account of reasons so that it covers teleological explanations as well, or the other way round, by reinterpreting teleological explanations so that they fit the proposed account of reasons.

A NATURAL adjustment of the latter kind is this. Contrary to appearances,   279
we do not explain what somebody did by reference to the purpose of the action. We explain it by reference, implicit reference that is, to the state of affairs that it was the purpose of the action to change. We explain Reggie's opening the window by reference, not to the fresh air he was going to breathe once the window was open, but to the sticky air he had to breathe as long as it was closed. With this adjustment the proposed account of reasons is back on home ground. The reason for which Reggie opened the window was the sticky air in the office, and to this state of affairs his action is a response. It is true, in other examples the adjustment does not work as smoothly as it does here, where we just have to turn the agent from the fresh air ahead to the sticky air under his nose. To replace

> I ran to catch the train.

by

> On account of the likelihood that, continuing with walking speed, I would miss the train, I ran.

is clumsy, and so is

> Given the probability that, unless I call, I would not know any time soon what Susan thinks about the conference, I called her.

as a substitute for

> I called to ask her what she thinks about the conference.

However, this is only a stylistic difficulty. Materially, there does not seem to be a loss here. Thus there is no reason to suspect that an adjustment of the sort should not work for all examples of explanations by purpose.

280　WHAT if the purpose of an action is not to change a state of affairs, but to prevent it from changing? The air in the office is impeccable, but Reggie sees Dora getting ready to start her old diesel engine right in front of the building, and so he closes the window. We might say here that Reggie closed the window in order to prevent the diesel fumes from entering the room, but this teleological expression can be translated without loss into a phrasing in accordance with the present account: Reggie closed the window, given the probability of bad fumes coming in otherwise. What he did, then, was a response to this danger, and so the danger, not the intended result of what he did, can be considered the reason for which he did it; just as it was the promise of a fine day tomorrow that was the reason for which we got our boots ready (§ 189).

281　IF IT is possible to turn explanations by purpose into explanations by antecedent conditions, it is also preferable to do so. This is because the basic vocabulary of teleological explanations is hard to understand. It is hard to see what "for the purpose of" and "in order to" mean.[2] It is hard to see how Reggie's opening the window and his getting a breath of fresh air are related. Naturally one may suggest that they are related in that Reggie's opening the window took place because there was at some point an idea in his mind of his getting a breath of fresh air. However, this suggestion really takes us outside teleological explanation and back to a traditional explanation in terms of desire and belief. Teleological explanation, after all, was to be explanation by the purpose itself of the action, not by the idea of the purpose. It was not a conception of the end in his mind, but indeed a breath of fresh air, which was supposed to explain Reggie's action. Renouncing that suggestion, however, we seem to be at a loss to say what the relation in question is. We seem to be incapable of explicating the basic teleological locutions.

282　SOME authors think that explanation by purposes is not just one kind of reason explanation among others. Thus for Aristotle it is a commonly accepted starting point that action and deliberate choice are aiming at goals,[3] and for Michael Smith reason explanations *are* teleological explanations[4] (§ 17). These claims, if true, should make one think twice about replacing the teleological conception by a historical one. However, there is little reason to think that these claims *are* true. Smith, for one, just helps himself to his assumption that reason explanations are teleological explanations, an assumption that cannot be deemed obvious. Aristotle, on his part, offers as little reason for the claim that all action is goal-directed. Sarah Broadie considers this a "purely conceptual point,"[5] suggesting that "we could hardly say less."[6] In fact we could very well say less. We could take action to be growing from humans the way rain falls from the sky[7]—naturally, understandably, even predictably within limits, but without purpose; and so argument is necessary to exclude this possibility and to install goal-directedness as a character of all action. Nor will Aristotle invoke here a general teleological conception of nature according to which everything due to nature is for an end, since, contrary to a widespread misunderstanding, he does not hold such a conception. As Charlton insists, "what he maintains is that *some of the things* which are due to nature are for something."[8] Hence the statement that in particular all human action is for an end needs defending, and it appears that no such defense has been produced. Given, then, that teleology is not *the* form of action explanation, but just one kind among others, the present objection against reconstruing teleological as historical explanations falls away, and the conclusion can stand: the reason for which we do something that we do for a purpose is the state of affairs that it is our purpose to change, and the action can be explained as a response to that state of affairs.

MORE difficult to accommodate within the present account of reasons are things done for fun. For instance, what is the reason for which I play the piano? I am not being paid for it, nor do I ordinarily fulfill others' expectations, wishes, let alone needs by playing. The world by and large could not care less whether I play or not. So it seems there is no state of affairs here to which I could be taken to be responding. It is true, sometimes I practice, that is to say, I try to do something about the poor state of my playing, and that poor state, then, is a state of affairs to which my playing can be considered a response. Yet sometimes I do not practice, in this sense. Sometimes I just play, and do it merely for the fun of it, superfluously. It might be suggested here that, when playing in this way, I am not playing for any reason. That is after all what people sometimes seem to indicate in such situations: "Why did you play the piano?" "For no particular reason." And as it is admitted already that people sometimes do things without a reason, witness Henry's asking for shelter in the house on the hill (§ 201), it is all the easier to say the same about my playing the piano.[9] However, in Henry's case something evidently went wrong, and thus it makes sense to claim that the action lacked a reason for which it was done. In the case of my piano playing nothing is, in this sense, going wrong, and so it would be to that extent ad hoc to plead lack of a reason here. As for people's speaking that way, this does not count for much, for they may merely mean that a certain kind of reason was not involved, not that no reason was. Indeed, it would seem a strong argument against a conception of reasons for which people do things, if on this conception it should turn out that things done for fun generally are not done for a reason. One may be inclined to say rather that, on the contrary, if ever we do things for reasons, it is when we innocuously enjoy ourselves doing them.

284   WHAT, then, is the reason for which I play the piano? The standard answer is: my desire to play it. This answer, however, as argued earlier (§ 196), does not do justice to our experience. To be sure, if the answer is meant to be saying only that a cause of my piano playing is a desire of mine to play, then it is not relevant here, the question on the table being what the reason is for which I play; and defenders of the causal statement should clear their case with physiologists, who are the experts on causes of actions. Whether or not, then, my desire is a cause of my playing, a reason it is not. It is not a reason because it is not something on account of which I play (§ 142). If I consider whether to play before I do, I do not normally check what the state of my desire for piano playing is at the moment; and while playing I do not watch the gauge of my piano playing tank go up until it is back to full. I do not do these things because changing the state of my desire is not the point of my playing. Nothing about myself is. Certainly I change through the playing. Thus I may get tired, or excited, and indeed my desire for piano playing may become satisfied, which it was not before. Yet not therefore do I play. Think of masturbation, by contrast: here as well my sexual desire may become satisfied, which it was not before, but in this case that is precisely why I move my fingers the way I do. Playing the piano is not masturbation by other means (or at least normally it is not). Piano players, unlike mastur- bators, need not care about themselves at all; not only in the sense that they need not constantly watch how they are, which will be granted on all sides, but also in the sense that how they are is really immaterial for what they are doing.

285   As THE desire for playing and its satisfaction do not figure in the player's practical landscape, the expression "doing something for fun" is in fact already misleading. It suggests that the fun probably to be gained from playing is the reason for playing, the way the money probably to be gained from answering incoming phone calls for Myers & Myers was Alfred's reason for doing it (§ 277). Actually it is not. While it *is* true that quite likely I shall enjoy myself in playing, the way Alfred quite likely will be getting money in return for answering the phone calls, it is not true that I play on account of the fun I am going to get out of it, by contrast to Alfred who does answer the phone calls on account of the money he is going to get out of it. The argument here is merely phenomenological: except in rare circumstances one just does not milk fun from the activity

of piano playing, the way one does milk money from the activity of answering a company's phone calls.[10] Given, then, that the phrase "done for
fun" is misleading, it should be taken here only in the sense of "what is
commonly called 'done for fun'."

THE TRADITIONAL way of handling things done for fun is an adjusted   286
teleological model. As Reggie opened the window for the purpose of getting a breath of fresh air, so I am said to play the piano for the purpose
of playing the piano. The adjustment needed just consists in allowing that
in the particular case of things done for fun action and purpose coincide,
whereas normally they are different. Aristotle expressly permits an identity
of action and purpose:

> It does not matter whether the activities themselves are the goals of
> actions or something else beyond them.[11]

It does not matter, that is, for the application of the teleological scheme
to all human action, that is stated in the opening sentence of the *Nicomachean Ethics* referred to here (§ 282). In fact, however, it does matter: a
coincidence of action and purpose makes nonsense of the idea of purpose
in the first place. The teleological scheme depends on action and purpose
being different things, for we understand purpose, goal, aim, as what one
is heading for or, as Aristotle's phrase in the first sentence of the *Nicomachean Ethics* may be translated, striving for,[12] and there is no such thing
as a striving for that very striving. We know what we mean by the teleological vocabulary only as long as the comparison with something like
a man shooting for a target is in order,[13] but that comparison is off once
action and aim coincide. Still, could one not, for instance, dance with the
aim of dancing gracefully?[14] Indeed one could not. One can try to dance
gracefully, and one can hope of one's current dancing that it be graceful,
but the aim of one's current dancing cannot be one's dancing gracefully
now, because one's current dancing cannot be, translating again Aristotle's
expression[15] 'toward' one's dancing gracefully now. One's current dancing
can be toward one's dancing gracefully tomorrow, which is to say, one
can practice; or it can be toward such things as the pleasure of the spec-
tators. It cannot be toward itself. That would make nonsense of 'toward'.

STILL, the traditional account of things done for fun has a point, and it is   287
merely misguided to force it into a teleological guise. It does seem right
to say that sometimes people play the piano for the sake of playing. However, this should not be taken to mean that their playing then has a certain
aim, namely, that very playing. It should be taken to mean, rather, that
people then play because of what playing the piano is like. "And what is

it like?" Different things for different people, but here is, as an example, some of what I find in my experience. To play the piano is to be making appear and shaping with one's hands one of these beautiful pieces, that piece with the grand opening theme, or that piece with the subtle harmonic shifts right in the exposition, that piece with its exuberance or that piece with its desolate scarcity. This is what playing the piano is like: for that reason I play, and for that kind of reason people play, the piano. Misleadingly one could even say that I play the piano for Beethoven's sake, or Schubert's, or whoever it is. That would be misleading as it would suggest that I pretend to do these dead composers any good—no such thing, of course. Let "Beethoven" refer, rather, to the character of some of what the person of that name wrote, and the statement makes the right point: a reason for which I play the piano, sometimes, is the fact that playing the piano is like that, that is, that it is of the Beethoven kind. In this way, then, my piano playing does fit into the historical conception of reasons for which people do things. Just as the world met me with threatening bishops, insulting neighbors, and rising barometers, for which reasons I moved my pawn, shouted back, and got my boots ready, respectively, so now the world beckons with Beethoven piano playing, and thus I do play, for that reason.

288 In one way, this reason differs from the other reasons considered so far. Your bishop's threat, my neighbor's insult, and the barometer's rising are novel features of my environment, but it is constantly the case that playing the piano is what it is like. There is no reason, however, why this should affect the reason status of either the former or the latter. The world comes both with standing offers and special sales. True, one may wonder why I am not playing the piano twenty-four hours a day, then, if all the time I have reason to do so. For one thing, I have reason to do other things, too, and most of the time these reasons prevail. For another, while at any time piano playing is what it is like, I still do not always have reason to play. The profile of reasons I have changes, and so at times the fact that playing the piano is what it is like is not a reason I have for playing, for example, when I am too tired. As it is put sometimes, the charms of piano playing are then lost on me. And that is to put it aptly: the charms are still there, only I am no longer receptive to them.

289 What holds for my piano playing holds generally for the things we do for fun: we do them because of what it is like to do them. People dance in ballet, it would seem, because of the control over, and the expressiveness of, one's entire body that dancing involves. People drink wine, normally not because they are lacking fluids, but because drinking wine is to be

experiencing, one mouthful after the other, that rich, fresh, varied taste that wine, and wine alone, gives. To take a rather special taste, I like to dry the wineglasses with a dishcloth after they are rinsed. While I tend to tell others that I do it because, left to dry by themselves, they will not be entirely clear, it may really be because of the sensuous qualities of doing it: holding the glasses carefully, moving with the clean cloth over the frictionless surface, accomplishing perfect transparency. Or to take a contrasting example, I hate to clean the garlic press: that it involves fumbling with these small holes, and that most of the time you still find a bit of garlic left, these are reasons for which I leave the task, if I can, to whoever is my companion in the kitchen. Things are characteristically different where fun or aversion are negligible. Thus I brush my teeth not because this activity has itself a peculiar character. It does have a peculiar character, but that is not a reason for which I do it or refrain from doing it. I do it, and the reason here is the danger of accelerated tooth decay. To be sure, if you find nothing in playing the piano, abhor wine, and are eager to clean any garlic press you can lay your hands on, there is no quarrel here. The argument is not to show that the tastes described are the right ones. It is to show that, whatever you are doing just for fun, playing the piano or drinking wine, or indeed torturing people, you are still doing these things for a reason, and the reason lies in what it is like to be doing them.

You MAY ask now why the fact that, for example, playing the piano is   290
what it is like is a reason I have for playing, and sometimes a reason for which I play, but not perhaps a reason you have for playing. Here the general answer given earlier (§ 225) returns: the range of things that are reasons for somebody to do something, and in particular the range of things that are reasons for which somebody does something, depend on the particular disposition of the person, in the old sense of the term "disposition" (§ 192). If now you want to know why we have these different dispositions, we will have to turn to our respective histories. I have become somebody for whom the fact that playing the piano is the kind of thing it is is a reason to play the piano, and that is due to what I experienced and did so far in my life; and if you press me, I can give you some of the details of how it happened. Also, somebody else can: to explain such things is the art of the biographer. You have not become, let us say, somebody for whom that is a reason: that as well is due to what you experienced and did so far in your life. To explain in this way why something is or is not a reason for somebody is not to give in turn a reason explanation, but it is to give a historical explanation (§ 148). Becoming a person for whom such and such things count or do not count is not

something one did for any reason, but it is something that can be understood through what one did and what happened to one before.

291 IF THE reasons for which we do the things we do for fun lie in what it is like to do them, it is still striking that we rarely present these reasons in explaining what we do. Asked why they play the piano, people are likely to say "Because I enjoy it" or something similar, though this is indeed not normally a reason for which they do it, according to the present argument (§ 285). Actually, it is not hard to understand why we normally answer these questions so evasively. It is because it is difficult to spell out what are the real reasons, in a way that is both close to the phenomena and intelligible for others. These two requirements are not specific for accounts of reasons; they hold generally for any account we give. The point is that it is especially difficult to meet these requirements in the case of the reasons for which we do the things we do for fun. It is difficult to pin down what it is about piano playing exactly that is the reason for which I do it. That I do it because it is to perform one of these beautiful pieces, as suggested earlier (§ 287), is true enough and sufficiently explains my doing it, but one would want to know more precisely what the beauty is to which I am practically sensitive, which this or that piece has. So one would want to know what precisely it is that makes performing this piece attractive. Similarly for drinking wine: the reason for which normally I drink wine is what drinking wine is like, but to spell out, truly, precisely, and illuminatingly, what it *is* like is beyond me and most of us. Some of us are better than others in spelling it out, that is true, but no one is good. Trying to tell a funny incident and finally despairing of getting across what was funny about it, people often say in the end: "It was extremely funny" or "We were roaring with laughter." This is the way we end up saying "I just love it," or "It is such a joy," when we try to explain why we play the piano, drink wine, and do other things of the kind. We are no good at all at describing what it is that we enjoy. The land of joys is certainly not untraveled, but it is largely uncharted territory.

TWELVE

A Rational Agent

292

THE INITIAL question was: what is a reason for which somebody does something, and how is the reason related to the action? The answer explained and defended in the argument so far is: to do something for a reason is to do something that is a response to the state of affairs that is the reason. It remains to consider how this answer affects the idea we have of ourselves, since we are, and understand ourselves to be, creatures who sometimes do things for reasons. Such a creature may be called a rational agent. The question is what, on the present argument, rational agency amounts to.

293

TO CONSIDER this is germane to the present argument. A conception of what it is to do something for a reason will be judged not only on the specific counts discussed so far: whether it can provide for the explanatory role of reasons, whether it can make sense of difficult cases like agents in error and agents doing things for fun, whether it can do justice to related concepts like having a reason for doing something, and so on. It will also, and perhaps primarily, be judged on whether the broad picture of rational agency it offers is acceptable. Writers in philosophy of action are portraying people: in the end the sitters have a say on whether they can recognize themselves. If indeed they cannot, the picture is no good: a theory is for better understanding. What is open to debate is just whether a picture actually is unacceptable, or is in fact only disliked, perhaps because it is unusual, or because it fails to mark distinctions on which people pride themselves. In the past, at any rate, new conceptions of ourselves based on new theories have often been considered unacceptable without good reason. Over the last hundred years or so, for example, it turned out that we can live quite well with theories about the origin of the human species that were widely considered at the time of their appearance to lead to an unacceptable picture of ourselves. It is appropriate, then, to draw at least the rough picture of rational agents emerging from the present account, so as to give a judgment about its acceptability a fair basis.

294   RATIONAL agency, on the present account, requires less mental equipment than was traditionally supposed. To do something for a reason is to do something that is a response to some state of affairs, and for that an agent needs to be aware of the state of affairs in question (§ 130). So rational agents need consciousness, and they need the capacity to act in response to what they are conscious of. They need no more. In particular, they do not need the special faculty called practical reason that in a Platonic tradition broadly construed was deemed necessary for recognizing reasons. They do not need charioteers in the soul, in whatever garb these were clad in the tradition (§ 73). The sort of eyes that horses have, registering what goes on around us, suffices. Nor do rational agents need a desiring part, which in both the Platonic and the Humean tradition was considered necessary for one's doing something for a reason. Certainly rational agents desire things, and certainly it may depend on the agent's desires what is and what is not a reason for which that agent does something (§ 191). Yet the reason and the action themselves need not involve a desire. The fundamental pattern of doing things for reasons is: given this, somebody does that; and in such a story the agent's desire does not figure. It may figure only in an explanation of why the items figuring in a story of somebody's doing something for a reason do figure there. Thus the story of somebody's doing something for a reason is not a psychological one, uncovering the inner springs of the action. It is a historical one, locating the action among things happening (§ 196).

295   SINCE doing things for reasons needs so little mental equipment, it is not a property of humans. Doing things for reasons takes consciousness, and it takes the capacity of doing things in response to things happening: surely these two capacities can be found in other animals as well. In which animals they can be found and in which not is difficult to tell, but that is for those to decide who better know the ways of particular animals. Still, it seems clear that a rabbit chased by a dog is fleeing for a reason, in the sense explained. It is aware of the dog's approach, and its flight is a response to that. Thus its behavior is no different, in the relevant respects, from my protecting my castle from your bishop's attack. On the other hand a piece of wood thrown into the fire clearly does not ignite for a reason. It is not cognizant of the fire, and its igniting is not a response to it, but merely its effect. It does not meet the fire with igniting, the way I

do meet your bishop's attack with protecting my castle and the way the rabbit meets the dog's pursuit with running. Somewhere between the two, between the rabbit and the piece of wood, lies the line separating the creatures that are aware of things and capable of doing things in response to what they are aware of from creatures that are not. Capable only, to be sure: whatever the creature, a lot of the things it does are not done for a reason. Thus when I shiver in the cold, I do not relevantly differ from the piece of wood igniting in the fire.

PRESUMABLY the histories of which human responses form a part are more complex, and in the case of humans both the clues with practical signif- icance and the responses are spread over a wider range of expressions and are more finely differentiated within that range. So what we do for reasons does seem to be a good deal more sophisticated than what, say, ducks do for reasons. Still, there are no grounds a priori for this to be so, and if the experts on ducks tell us otherwise, we must give up this claim as mere arrogance. However this may be, the main point here is that rational agency is not distinctively human. It occurs in a variety of creatures. Titles like "A Theory of Human Action,"[1] while common in the literature, are misguided from the start. Speaking strictly, a theory of human action is philosophically uninteresting. What is interesting about action, in partic- ular what action for reasons involves, has no special connection with the characteristics of our species. "Human action" is an expression like "Phil- adelphia action": just as there is no reason to suppose that what is done in Philadelphia is different in principle from what is done anywhere else, so there is no reason to suppose that what humans do is different in principle from what other animals do.

RATIONAL agents, merely conscious of things going on around them and capable of acting in response to it (§ 294), are no longer bound to be subject to internal opposition. As described in chapter 1, rational agents traditionally first figure out what to do and then, if indeed they are ra- tional, they also do it. Doing things for reasons is always a two-step pro- cedure. Plato's charioteer is gazing at beauty and moderation and therefore he pulls back the horses (§ 73), and Hume's reason, having calculated the suitable means to some end, directs the impulse of desire accordingly (§ 42). As pointed out earlier, this duality brings with it domination within the soul: reason, alone capable of figuring out what to do, becomes master (§ 76). Aristotle gives a memorable image:

> Everybody stops searching how to act once he has traced the beginning of the action back to himself, and here to the leading part, for that is

296

297

the part which decides. This is clear as well from the ancient communities described by Homer: what the kings decided, they announced to the people.[2]

The soul contains kings and people because one part, thanks to its superior knowledge, tells the other what to do. Action is execution. It is to carry out or put into practice the idea of what is to be done conceived by the leading part. On the present conception, by contrast, there is no need for a distinction between leading and inferior parts within the soul. The whole agent follows this or that path the world is offering, and domination within agents ends. Indeed, practical reason is basically sensitivity on this conception. Doing things for reasons is a matter of picking up and continuing threads of histories that the world offers. It is a matter of being receptive to what is coming one's way. Rational agents are animals sniffing their way through the world. They are not in control. They are given to what they encounter.

298 REMOVING the kings within the soul eliminates the traditional problem of 'akrasia' as well. 'Akrasia', commonly translated as 'weakness of will' but translatable also as 'lack of mastery', denotes cases of agents acting against their better judgment; with Aristotle's image, cases of the people not doing what the kings tell them. The problem of akrasia was this: it seemed difficult to understand, but also difficult to deny, that people sometimes knowingly take what at the same time they consider an inferior course of action. However, if the present idea of rational agency is right, the trouble lies, not with 'akrasia', but with 'enkrateia', with 'domination'.[3] We are never master over our actions, so there is no problem about those allegedly special cases in which we are not. One might put it by saying that we are weak-willed all the time, but that would invite the misunderstanding that this shows a human failing, whereas in fact self-mastery is not an ideal, but an illusion.

299 THIS is not to deny that there are those cases that are commonly described as cases of akrasia. It is only to deny that it is helpful so to describe them. Certainly there are people who, while really thinking that it would be best no more to smoke, fall to the temptation of a cigarette, but who told you it had to be otherwise? Falling to temptation is just what, on the present conception, rational agency amounts to. If, notwithstanding your conviction that all in all it would be better not to smoke, you take up the thread of cigarettes' glorious taste and smoke one, you are falling to temptation, but if you take up the thread constituted by the bad effects of smoking on health and refrain from smoking, you are merely falling to

another; and you do for a reason what you do in either case. True, I have a view on which temptation you would do better to fall to, and if I care about you, I shall try to make that reason the more tempting one. As we supposed that you share this view with me, I may well succeed, especially if you are one of those who feel uncomfortable about falling to what they consider themselves a bad temptation. I shall not be as foolish as to try to teach you to stop falling for temptations altogether. To fall for things is the way of practical reason.

ONE MAY object: 300

> This is to deny the phenomena. Sometimes we control ourselves, even if often, regrettably, we do not. Sometimes we check ourselves and pull the hand back from the cigarettes or suppress the malicious witticism we had on our tongue. Moreover, we distinguish between people who are as a matter of habit in control of themselves and others who are not. All these differences vanish if mastering oneself is an illusion.

No, THEY do not vanish, they only need to be redescribed. Of course there   301
is a difference between making the malicious remark and withholding it, but it is not a difference between lacking and having control of oneself. The relevant difference is that between what you pick up in the situation. You may use it as an occasion for a smashing hit, or you may prudently stay silent, on account of what that hit might cost you in the future. And certainly you may find silence difficult with the smashing remark beckoning, but to deny self-control is not to claim that what we do for reasons should always be easy. It cannot be if reasons compete, which normally they do. You do not suppress anything within yourself when you forego making your mean remark. You just take up a different line that suggests itself in the situation. As for those with whom so-called self-control has become a character trait, they may be people who regularly beware of what they might have to pay in the end, or who act the Stoic sage, or who have been frightened to a point where losing one's temper has been extinguished from their action repertoire. In short, what is called self-control, momentary or habitual, can be understood as an agent's being sensitive to one sort of feature of a situation rather than to another. It need not involve any actual domination.

AGAIN, one may object: 302

> Deliberation makes no sense on the account of rational agency proposed here. To deliberate is to consider the reasons for and against a course of action and thereby, if all goes well, to reach a settled judgment on what to do. To go through these considerations makes no sense, however,

if the result is not, at least in principle, put into practice. Yet the idea of putting into practice the result of one's reasoning takes us straight back into the classical framework. We are back with the duality of consideration and execution, the latter subordinated to the former. We are back with Aristotle's kings telling the people what to do. Hence, if you want to eliminate domination within the soul, you need to give up a meaningful notion of deliberation as well. That may be too high a price.

303   No, A meaningful notion of deliberation is not tied to domination in the soul. We do deliberate, but as indicated (§ 234), this just amounts to exposing ourselves to be impressed by relevant features of the situation that otherwise might have gone unnoticed, or might have loomed less large. It amounts to offering oneself to the world's temptations with regard to the matter in question. So we do consider reasons, and in the end one of them may become a reason we act upon. We do not, additionally, determine what to do, given the reasons. We do not, on the basis of the reasons, decide, choose, or conclude what to do. We let ourselves be swayed by what we consider. So we do sometimes change thanks to considering reasons that offer themselves to us in the situation. Thus deliberation is effective and makes sense. But we do not change ourselves, given the reasons. We do not, through deliberation, direct or redirect ourselves. Deliberation is like sunbathing, only with many suns and therefore with results not so easy to predict.

304   IT WILL be objected, finally, that the conception proposed surrenders what is the very core of agency, activity, and turns the agent into a passive object of whatever pulls things may exert. With the idea of self-determination gone, it is not we who shape our doings, it is the world that does; and a conception with that consequence cannot be considered an account of acting for reasons.

305   Two POINTS in reply. First, it is not true that rational agents as envisaged here are bound to be passive. I move my pawn because of, and that is to say, in response to, your bishop's threat. The threat prompts me to move my pawn, and that I move it for this reason reveals my practical sensitivity to the threat. None of this, however, shows me to be passive. There is no idea of the threat making me move my pawn. There is no such idea, not because, with the traditional story, I still have my mental sanctuary where I consider what to do with the threat and then act accordingly (or not), so that it would be the representations in my mind rather than the threat itself, something internal rather than something external, that makes me

move my pawn. (How that expedient should actually save the agent from passivity is not easy to see, but never mind.) There is no idea of the threat making me move the pawn because that just is not the relation between the two things. Here is an example of activity and passivity: my stepping on the plastic bottle made it crack. Nothing of the sort happened when, because of your bishop's threatening my castle, I moved my pawn to protect it. The threat did not make me move my pawn in the sense in which my stepping on it made the plastic bottle crack. I did not suffer a pawn move at your, or your bishop's, hands, the way the plastic bottle did suffer a cracking at the hands of my feet. Given the threat, I moved the pawn, so much is true, but that is a different story from being made to move it by the threat. Nor does "falling for temptation" imply passivity. You are not made to do what things lure you into doing. You do them, given the opportunity.

WHAT leads to the misunderstanding is again the confusion of reasons and   306
causes (§ 142). From the fact that it is because of the threat that I move the pawn, it is concluded that the threat is the cause of my moving it, which leaves me only a passive part—unless, that is, there is the mental switchboard in between, which is supposed somehow to save the agent's active role. As that is discarded on the present account, a passive agent seems to be the consequence. However, this reasoning is based on the assumption that "because of" can always be replaced, with truth preserved, by some phrase like "caused by," and that is not so.[4] The objection is unfounded, then, that the present construal of doing things for reasons leaves to the agent merely a passive role.

SECOND, notwithstanding the words, being active does not lie at the heart   307
of agency. The distinction between active and passive, if it is more than a grammatical distinction, is significant only in a limited area of what we do. Sometimes, it is true, the doer is active and someone or something else is passive, as when I make the plastic bottle crack, or when I hit you. In other cases, though, that distinction does not have a clear grip. When we are dancing together, we are certainly doing something, but who or what has the suffering part? Perhaps your toes, as the joke goes, but other than that? The floor? Our bodies? The dance in itself? None of this makes good sense. Similarly, things like playing the flute, learning a poem by heart, canceling an appointment, giving one's regards to somebody, or paying one's debts are clearly cases of agency, but it is difficult to identify a suitable suffering part. Grammatically, to be sure, there is no problem: if you cancel an appointment, then this appointment is being canceled.

Materially, it does seem contrived to force everything we do under the active-passive mold and to say, for instance, that you inflicted a cancellation on that appointment.

308   IN FACT, the traditional notion that agency involves activity may not be based on the assumption that for any case of agency there is something or someone in the world that is the suffering part. It may be based on the idea that agents are active with respect to their actions: that they are the makers of their actions. This idea, however, seems to be unfounded and implausible. Unfounded: what reason is there to conceive of the relation between ourselves and what we do essentially in terms of the relation between artificer and artifact? Why not allow ourselves to grow actions, the way trees grow leaves?[5] A naturalist, that is, someone who wishes to understand agency in terms derived from our experience of how nature works, should be reluctant to think of actions as something made. Implausible: the experience we have of ourselves as agents is not an experience of ourselves as makers of our doings. We may be making a fence, but we do not make a fence-making. The idea appears as implausible and unfounded in the special case of things we do for reasons. That there is something on account of which we do what we do does not render the idea any more plausible that we are active with respect to our very doing; and the alternative conception on which we grow actions the way trees grow leaves appears as viable in the case of what is done for a reason. MacIntyre wrote that none of us is more than a coauthor of his or her life.[6] The truth is that we are not even coauthors, and the notion of authorship is altogether misplaced here. We do not have a 'poetical', in the literal sense a maker's relationship, to our life. We are the ones living it, no more.

309   THE OTHER (§ 294) characteristic feature of rational agency on the present account is its lack of normative import. Reasons, it is normally assumed, guide us: they recommend courses of action.[7] The reasons there are for or against doing something tell also, so the assumption goes, about whether it is good to do that thing. If the argument above (§§ 246–262) is correct, though, this link between the rational and the good snaps. What reasons there are for doing something and whether it is a good thing to do it are separate issues. Doing things for reasons is, to borrow Heidegger's phrase, a way of being in the world. It need not be a good way. Thus we do not have in our capacity to do things for reasons a built-in compass to what is right and good. We are not built for the good (nor, for that matter, for the bad). Perhaps it is the old tradition of thinking that what there is is basically good that lies behind this idea of a capacity of ours geared to what is right and good to do. Whether or not this is indeed its origin,

the two ideas seem to be equally groundless. What there is is one question, and whether it is good is another, and so how we work is one thing, and whether it is good what we do another. Doing things for reasons is how we sometimes work. What we ought to do is a different matter.

THERE are, then, no imperatives or laws or rules of rationality. Reason   310
does not demand anything. It does not demand that we act morally, as
Kant held[8] and many other writers[9] after him.[10] Neither does it demand
that we act prudently, or wisely, or use the most effective means to our
ends, as Hobbes[11] and as Kant held,[12] along with many other writers[13]
after them.[14] Not even as merely rational agents are we "a law unto ourselves," as Paul memorably and influentially put it.[15] Thomas Hill recently
explicated this idea of autonomy by saying that there is

> some rational standard of conduct, commitment to which is inherent in
> the point of view of agents who try to deliberate and to choose ration-
> ally.[16]

This is precisely the claim that, on the account given, cannot be made
good: there is no standard of conduct to which, just by being rational
agents, we are subject. We are not by authority of reason called upon to
do anything.

To BE sure, if you ask me about some practical problem you have, be it   311
big or small, I shall have to say something, unless it is beyond my ken. I
shall venture to tell you what is recommendable to do in your situation
or what would be a good idea for you to do. I shall speak about what is
good and bad and what you should and should not do. If you challenge
me, I shall offer reasons in support of what I said; considerations, that is
to say, that show, or purport to show, why what I recommended is indeed
recommendable. You may in turn challenge my argument, and I may go
on to defend it. In this way we may continue, and our exchange will come
to an end through fatigue or the like, not through lack of subject matter.
I may even, by saying what I do, succeed in altering your landscape of
reasons for action (§ 229). Yet in all that I shall not invoke the authority
of reason for my recommendations. I shall not tell you that such and such
is the thing, or one thing, that agents capable of acting for reasons ought
to do in the situation. There is no basis for such a claim. To do the thing
in question might be a good idea, a fine thing, an admirable feat: it is not
required by our status as rational agents.

IT MAY be objected that we commonly use the words "rational" and "rea-   312
sonable" as terms of praise, and this suggests that to act well is to act in

accordance with the requirements of reason. It does suggest that, yes, but on the account given, that suggestion must be deemed false, there being no such requirements. And while this conflict with ordinary usage is indeed a point against the account proposed, it does not weigh heavily, for it is easy to understand how that suggestion came to be implied in how we speak. The idea has been dominant in our tradition, or putting it more simply, they kept telling us in school, that in our capacity of acting for reasons we also have a guide for acting well. No wonder that we have learnt to speak accordingly and to praise things by calling them "reasonable" or "rational." If for you these words have become *merely* terms of praise, general ones perhaps that are applicable instead of a wide range of more specific expressions, like "to do this would be a good idea" or "it would make sense" or "it would be wise,"[17] then there is no quarrel with you: the words are free. The issue is not whether we may or may not praise actions by calling them rational or reasonable. The issue is whether, given that we do, we should therefore think that actions worth praising are actions that people are by reason required to do. Yet what they told us in school turns out to be false, and we should not think that.

313 RATIONAL agents, then, are characterized on the present account by the absence of inner domination and of normativity. Rational agents are, in this sense, free: not subject to master or law within. The ducks, though presumably they sometimes do for reasons what they do (§ 296), do not govern themselves, nor are they called upon to heed laws implicit in their kind of agency. We are like them, the idea is, going about our business unbroken. No doubt the business is different: in being unsubordinated within ourselves we resemble them. The inner state of rational agents is anarchy.

314 THE PICTURE of rational agents emerging here may be summed up by saying that they are worldly creatures through and through. Taking their clue from what they encounter and unguided by an authority or law of independent standing, they simply continue the threads of the world. This is not to say that what they do is always more of the same as went on before. On the contrary, turning things upside down may well be a rational agent's response to how things stand. The point is rather that what they do is to be understood only in terms of the histories to which their doings belong. Rational agents as such do not come with a mission to the world, they are not bound to a prior rule. They do what they do merely in response to some state of affairs. The world is their element, and they do not raise their heads above it.

As REGARDS the acceptability of this picture, some will reject it because it   315
leaves no basis for a notion of human dignity. Kant, the central author in
the specifically modern tradition of this idea, declares that the ground of
human dignity is the autonomy of rational agents, autonomy being the
property of these agents to be subject, and only to be subject, to laws of
conduct arising from their rational nature.[18] On the account of rational
agency proposed here, however, there is no such thing as autonomy
(§ 310), and so human dignity falls, too. Even disregarding the philosophical pedigree of the idea, though, and sticking to what people ordinarily
have in mind when talking of human dignity, it is evident that nothing
of the sort remains once doing things for reasons is not a privilege of
humans (and, possibly, higher beings), but shared with all sorts of lowly
animals. If we are not doing better in principle than the ducks, then we
may as well forget about human dignity. And we may be hard put to
forget about it, seeing that important political documents of our time, like
the Universal Declaration of Human Rights of 1948, give that notion
fundamental importance.

THERE is no way but to plead guilty to the charge that on the account of   316
rational agency proposed here the notion of human dignity loses its basis.
Since the members of our species do not, as rational agents, have a special
task or duty, but simply keep going with their worldly histories like other
animals, there is nothing particularly dignified about them. "Humanity"
is a term lacking all honorific overtones and moral significance; it is a
term like "anthood." As for the fundamental role of the idea of human
dignity for our political self-understanding, that point may have been
overstated. The Universal Declaration opens its preamble with the assertion:

> recognizing the inherent dignity of all members of the human family
> and their equal and inalienable rights is the fundament of freedom,
> justice and peace in the world.

That may just be false. It would seem that humans can live together in
freedom, justice, and peace without thinking of themselves as enjoying a
special moral status as rational agents. The question, to be sure, needs
more argument than it can receive at this point. Yet neither is there an
evident case for rejecting the proposed account of rational agency on the
grounds that it surrenders the notion of human dignity. Surrender it it
does, but we may well be able to do without it.

ON THE other hand, the picture of rational agents sketched here should   317
be attractive, too. It shows a life basically in peace. In peace within: since

reason is not a guiding part within us, there is not a subordinate part, either, and we are living, in principle, at one with ourselves. In peace without: there being no mission or duty incumbent on rational agents by their nature, the world is not an alien material for them in which to realize their higher aspirations, it is what in acting for reasons they take up and continue, it is their element. To be sure, this is, within or without, only peace in principle. Rational agents may certainly be unhappy with themselves, and may be struggling with people and fighting states of things. The point is that constitutionally they are not at odds with themselves and their world.[19] Yet what good, it may be asked, can such philosophical peace do us, if it does not alleviate any actual conflict within or without and any suffering caused thereby? This: we need not think of the rational agents we are as set to be at war with ourselves or with things. It happens, like the weather, that we are at war with us or with them, but it is not part of the deal. So basically we can disarm. We need not think of ourselves as forcing rationality onto ourselves and onto things. There is no cursed spite that ever we were born to set the world right.[20] And this may be a helpful, indeed a liberating thought.

318 CONSIDERED from this angle, it may even be an attraction of this picture of rational agents that it does away with the notion of a special dignity they carry. Dignity is something one has to live up to. Thus it is based on pressure, and one has to be in arms, at least against oneself, to protect it. There is, by contrast, relief in thinking that nothing particular is expected from us by virtue of our rational nature. There is relief in being undignified, in shedding any higher calling, in being unreservedly worldly.

319 IN THE end, what may seem to count most heavily against accepting the picture is the fact that it leaves us without guidance in ourselves. Nothing in what we are tells us where to go. To be sure, it is still true, on the picture proposed, that doing this is better than doing that, in the situation at hand or generally, but it is not better in virtue of being recommended by our capacity to do things for reasons. Material considerations alone decide about what should be done. Kant held that reason is something in us that would always lead us to do what is right and good, if only it held exclusive sway over our actions.[21] It might seem that without such a reliable guide within ourselves we must be at sea in our doings. This assumption, however, appears unfounded. No reason is visible why we should not be able to find out what is good to do, in particular and in general, and also to do it without such an organ in us that tells us the path to follow. Our rational nature does not set us a task. Yet we can live without one.

Notes

CHAPTER ONE

1. The general idea is shared by Carl G. Hempel, *Studies in the Logic of Explanation*, part 1, sect. 4; Donald Davidson, "Actions, Reasons, and Causes"; Paul Churchland, "The Logical Character of Action-Explanations"; Alvin Goldman, *A Theory of Human Action*, chap. 3; Robert Audi, "Acting for Reasons"; Michael Smith, *The Moral Problem*, chap. 4; and many others.

2. For a forceful statement of the point see Schueler, *Desire*.

3. P. H. Nowell-Smith, *Ethics*, p. 112.

4. Davidson, "Actions, Reasons, and Causes," p. 4.

5. Audi argues for that claim in "Intending." Nowell-Smith considered using "wanting" in lieu of "pro-attitude," but he decided that this word is too weak "to cover the more violent passions or the most permanent and deep-seated desires," *Ethics*, p. 112.

6. Davidson thinks that it is not unnatural "to treat wanting as a genus including all pro attitudes as species," "Actions, Reasons, and Causes," p. 6. (Note, though, the remark on p. 11 of the same essay, which seems to be saying the opposite.) See also Schueler, *Desire*.

7. Thomas Nagel, *The Possibility of Altruism*, chap. 5; Don Locke, *Beliefs, Desires and Reasons for Action*, p. 243; similarly Mark Platts, *Ways of Meaning*, p. 256, with respect to a corresponding extension of the term 'desire'.

8. A. Baier's example, "Rhyme and Reason," p. 125.

9. Wilson's example, *The Intentionality of Human Action*, p. 171. Examples like this one, involving teleological locutions, are discussed in chapter 11.

10. Davidson, "Actions, Reasons, and Causes," p. 4.

11. Ibid., p. 7.

12. Ibid., p. 4.

13. Melden, for instance, *Free Action*.

14. "Actions, Reasons, and Causes," p. 4. See also Michael Smith, *The Moral Problem*, 103–4.

15. Davidson, "Actions, Reasons, and Causes," p. 4.

16. Ibid., p. 6.

17. Ibid., p. 3.

18. McGinn, "Action and Its Explanation," p. 23.

19. Martha Nussbaum, *Aristotle's* De Motu Animalium, p. 188.

20. Jaegwon Kim, *Philosophy of Mind*, p. 8.

21. Michael Smith, *The Moral Problem*, chap. 4: "The Humean Theory of Motivation"; here in particular pp. 92, 93.

22. Smith, *The Moral Problem*, p. 96.

23. Ibid., p. 116.

24. Davidson's term, "Actions, Reasons, and Causes," p. 4.

25. Thomas Nagel, *The Possibilty of Altruism*, and John McDowell, "Are Moral Requirements Hypothetical Imperatives?" opened this line of thought. Mark Platts, *Ways of Meaning*, chap. 10, and David McNaughton, *Moral Vision*, chap. 3, advocated a similar view.

26. In fact, the 1994 version of his argument, which is being discussed here, differs from its 1987 predecessor, "The Humean Theory of Motivation," mainly in extending the attack against views that admit beliefs that are, or entail, desires.

27. Smith, *The Moral Problem*, p. 117.

28. Margaret O. Little, "Virtue as Knowledge."

29. Ibid., p. 60 and n. 3.

30. The relevant chapter of Smith's book *The Moral Problem* is entitled "The Humean Theory of Motivation."

31. Jay Wallace, "How to Argue about Practical Reason," p. 355.

32. Thomas Nagel, *The Possibility of Altruism*, p. 29. Stephen Schiffer has a similar distinction between reason-following and reason-providing desires, *A Paradox of Desire*, p. 197.

33. Jay Wallace, "How to Argue about Practical Reason," in particular p. 366.

34. Barry Stroud, *Hume*, p. 157, makes a similar point.

35. Smith, *The Moral Problem*, p. 116.

36. G. E. M. Anscombe, *Intention*, sects. 2, 32.

37. Smith, *The Moral Problem*, p. 115.

38. Smith, "The Humean Theory of Motivation."

39. I. L. Humberstone, "Direction of Fit," p. 63.

40. Ibid., p. 64.

41. David Velleman makes a similar point, "The Guise of the Good," p. 11.

42. Smith, *The Moral Problem*, p. 113.

43. Ibid., p. 105.

44. G. E. M. Anscombe, *Intention*, sect. 36.

45. Sarah Buss's objection, in correspondence.

46. GMS 421–422.

47. David Lewis, "Desire as Belief"; John Collins, "Belief, Desire, and Revision."

48. See the critique of Lewis and Collins by Huw Price, "Defending Desire-as-belief," and Jay Wallace's discussion, "How to Argue about Practical Reason," pp. 371–372.

49. See Lewis, "Desire as Belief," p. 325.

50. Ibid., p. 325.

51. Robert Audi, "Acting for Reasons," p. 158; similarly pp. 147, 151.

52. Georg Henrik von Wright, "Practical Inference," p. 166. Many other authors use similar language, for example John Collins, "Belief, Desire, and Revision," p. 333; Jonathan Dancy, *Moral Reasons*, p. 2; and in a different vein Charles Ripley, "A Theory of Volition," p. 143. Hobbes may be expressing the same idea by saying that "the Thoughts, are to the Desires, as Scouts, and Spies, to range abroad, and find the way to the things Desired" (*Leviathan*, chap. 8, para. 16).

53. Audi, "Acting for Reasons," p. 147, makes the connection explicit: "Intuitively, the want—or intention, judgment, or whatever plays the motivational role in our account—*moves* one to act."

54. Kant, GMS 427.

55. Audi, "Acting for Reasons," p. 151; Davidson, "Psychology as Philosophy," p. 231.

56. For instance Davidson, "Intending," pp. 100, 102.

57. The argument here is closely related to David Velleman's in "The Guise of the Good," which points out an incompatibility between the story of motivation and the story of rational guidance that we typically tell about actions.

58. Audi, "Acting for Reasons," p. 151.

59. Plato, *Republic* 439c.

60. Alfred Mele, *Springs of Action*, p. 71.

61. Jacob and Wilhelm Grimm, "Von dem Machandelboom."

62. An account on these lines is ascribed to Aristotle by Jonathan Lear, *Aristotle: The Desire to Understand*, pp. 145–146.

CHAPTER TWO

1. David Hume, *A Treatise of Human Nature*, p. 413. Until § 48, page references to this work will be inserted in the main text.

2. *Treatise*, p. 459, provides further support for this interpretation.

3. The same argument appears p. 415 and is hinted at p. 413.

4. For a similar critique of Hume's argument see Barry Stroud, *Hume*, pp. 159–63, and Rachel Cohon, "Hume and Humeanism in Ethics," pp. 103–7.

5. On Hume's relation to his rationalist predecessors in theory of action and moral philosophy see Stanley Tweyman, *Reason and Conduct in Hume and His Predecessors*, chaps. 4–6.

6. Heitsch, in his translation of Plato's *Phaidros*, p. 30, 93, reads the text as saying that the charioteer has wings, too, but the 'te kai' of 246a7, on which he bases his case, gives that reading too little support.

7. Similarly Jacqueline de Romilly, "Les conflits de l'âme," p. 105.

8. That there is basic agreement between *Republic* and *Phaedrus* is the common opinion of scholars, see for instance Giovanni Ferrari, "The Struggle in the Soul," p. 1. People disagree on the question of priority.

9. Hume, *Treatise*, p. 458.

10. Ibid.

11. The point of the preceding argument is closely related to one Jean Hamp-

ton was concerned to make in a number of her last writings: that, contrary to what is widely assumed, instrumental rationality cannot be understood merely in terms of desires plus knowledge of causal connections. See "On Instrumental Rationality"; "Rethinking Reason"; and chap. 4 of *The Authority of Reason*, posthumously edited.

12. Jon Moline, "Plato on the Complexity of the Psyche"; Julia Annas, *An Introduction to Plato's* Republic; John Cooper, "Plato's Theory of Human Motivation"; Ferrari, "The Struggle in the Soul"; Charles Kahn, "Plato's Theory of Desire."

13. Ferrari, "The Struggle in the Soul," p. 1.

14. Kahn, "Plato's Theory of Desire," p. 80.

15. This is argued in detail by Moline, *Plato's Theory of Understanding*, pp. 60–66.

16. Cooper, "Plato's Theory of Human Motivation," p. 5.

17. For more evidence on this point see Ferrari, "The Struggle in the Soul," part 1.

18. There is similar evidence in *Republic* 440a–e.

19. See for instance Moline, *Plato's Theory of Understanding*, p. 57f.

20. Annas, *An Introduction to Plato's* Republic, p. 131.

21. Cooper, "Plato's Theory of Human Motivation," p. 5; similar expressions appear pp. 6 and 8.

22. Jonathan Lear, *Aristotle: The Desire to Understand,* shows the central importance of this line for Aristotle's thought.

23. This is the line taken by Annas, *An Introduction to Plato's* Republic, p. 131, and Moline, *Plato's Theory of Understanding*, pp. 57–62. Similar language appears in Kahn, "Plato's Theory of Desire," pp. 81–86.

24. Annas, *An Introduction to Plato's* Republic, pp. 142–46; here p. 144.

25. Daniel Dennett, "Artificial Intelligence as Philosophy and as Psychology," p. 123.

26. The link between the loss of traditional moral certainties and the need for founding moral notions on true knowledge is evident also in Plato's *Seventh Letter* (325d3–326b4).

27. Plato, *Republic* 473c–e.

28. See for instance Susan Wolf, *Freedom within Reason*, chap. 4 especially, or Jay Wallace, *Responsibility and the Moral Sentiments*, chap. 6.

29. Condorcet, *Esquisse d'un tableau historique des progrès de l'esprit humain*, p. 259.

CHAPTER THREE

1. Thomas Hill, "Kant's Theory of Practical Reason," p. 129n7.

2. GMS 421, KpV 30. See also GMS 432, 434.

3. Similarly Onora O'Neill: "Kant holds that (mere reflex action apart) we always act on some maxim," "Kant after Virtue," p. 151.

4. For instance GMS 421, KpV 30.

5. See O'Neill, "Universal Laws and Ends-in-themselves," pp. 129. Willaschek, *Praktische Vernunft*, pp. 298–299, denies that for every action there is just

one maxim, whereas Allison, *Kant's Theory of Freedom*, p. 94, distinguishes between the one maxim on which an agent acts and other maxims implicit in the operative maxim as background conditions.

6. GMS 420n; similarly GMS 400n.

7. Blaise Pascal, *Pensées* 418.

8. The same distinction appears in KpV 19–20.

9. That was the title of O'Neill's earlier study of the Kantian conception of agency.

10. Thomas Hill writes, similarly: "in saying we have *wills* we are saying that we can 'make things happen' for reasons, or according to policies or principles," "The Kantian Conception of Autonomy," p. 84. The first "or" in this quotation is to be read as "*sive*." (See also Hill, "Kant's Argument for the Rationality of Moral Conduct," p. 106, "Kant's Theory of Practical Reason," p. 125, "Autonomy and Benevolent Lies," p. 29.) That is to say, doing something for a reason is, for Hill, the same thing as acting according to a policy or principle.

11. Andrews Reath, "Kant's Theory of Moral Sensibility"; Henry Allison, "Kant's Theory of Freedom," sect. 2.2.

12. Allison, "Kant on Freedom," p. 119; similarly Reath, "Kant's Theory of Moral Sensibility," p. 297.

13. *Religion*, p. 24.

14. Reath, "Kant's Theory of Moral Sensibility," p. 300; Allison, "Kant's Theory of Freedom," p. 60; Allison, "Kant on Freedom," p. 111.

15. "Agreement" ("Übereinstimmung") is the phrase Kant uses in the third example in GMS to characterize the relation between maxim and inclination, GMS 423.

16. Ralf Meerbote, "Wille and Willkür in Kant's Theory of Action," pp. 70–71; Hud Hudson, *Kant's Compatibilism*, pp. 42, 155.

17. Meerbote, "Kant on Freedom and the Rational and Morally Good Will," p. 63.

18. Hudson, *Kant's Compatibilism*, p. 155.

19. Otfried Höffe, "Universalist Ethics and the Faculty of Judgment," p. 56, makes a similar point.

20. Marcus Willaschek, *Praktische Vernunft*, p. 49.

21. GMS 400n., 420n., 412; KpV 20.

22. For this phrase see Peter Geach, *Mental Acts*, sect. 18; Anthony Kenny, *Action, Emotion and Will*, sects. 10–11; Kenny, *Will, Freedom and Power*, chap. 3. Kenny, it is true, explicitly rejects the idea that "sayings in one's heart" are silent inner speeches.

23. Ludwig Wittgenstein, *Philosophische Untersuchungen*, sects. 258, 263.

24. Davidson, "Intending," p. 92.

25. See Audi, "Intending," p. 71. A useful clarification of 'doing something intentionally', 'doing something with a further intention', and 'intending to do something in the future' is offered by H. L. A. Hart, "Intention and Punishment," sect. 2.

26. Michael Bratman, *Intention, Plans, and Practical Reason*, sect. 8.7, is attracted by this way of describing cases of intentional, but, apparently, unintended actions.

27. Similarly, KpV 19 tells us that the agent takes a maxim to be valid only for his own will; so presumably for his own will he does take it as valid, hence as imposing an obligation on him. GMS 412 and 427, on an admittedly controversial interpretation, use the term "law" to refer to maxims, and in Mrongovius's notes from Kant's lecture course on moral philosophy, p. 1427, maxims are explicitly called "subjective laws."

28. Romans 2:14. The importance of this passage for modern moral philosophy is demonstrated in J. B. Schneewind, *The Invention of Autonomy*.

29. Bratman, *Intention, Plans, and Practical Reason*, sects 2.2, 7.

30. *Religion*, p. 31.

31. It did so appear to Hegel; see *Phänomenologie des Geistes*, pp. 431–432, 433–434, which is in A. V. Miller's translation *Phenomenology of Spirit*, sects. 609–610, 615.

32. *Religion*, pp. 47–48.

33. Willaschek takes a similar line when he writes that it is action on maxims that enables one "to stay true to oneself," *Praktische Vernunft*, p. 280.

34. Nancy Schauber, "Integrity, Commitment, and the Concept of a Person," p. 120.

35. Harry Frankfurt, *The Importance of What We Care About*; "On caring."

36. See J. L. Mackie, *Ethics*, pp. 38–42.

37. I have discussed this passage in detail in my articles "Maximen" and "Handlungen und Wirkungen," and what follows draws on these papers. However, my interpretation is controversial. Pierre Laberge, "La définition de la volonté comme faculté d'agir selon la représentation des lois (GMS 412)," is an excellent guide to the discussion. See also Allison, *Kant's Theory of Freedom*, pp. 86–94.

38. *De Motu Animalium*, chap. 7.

39. See GMS 403, 404, 411, and KpV 35, 36. This conviction also underlies the doctrine of the fact of reason; see KpV 31: the consciousness of this fundamental law "forces itself upon us." A similar phrase occurs in *Religion*, p. 36.

40. *Religion*, p. 44.

41. Onora O'Neill, "Kant's virtues," pp. 90, 95.

42. *Religion*, p. 24n.

43. *De Motu Animalium* 701a11–13, 19–23. See among many others Anscombe, *Intention*, sect. 33; Cooper, *Reason and Human Good in Aristotle*, pp. 24–26, 33; Kenny, *Aristotle's Theory of the Will*, pp. 142–143; Nussbaum, *Aristotle's* De Motu Animalium, pp. 185–89; Sarah Broadie, *Ethics with Aristotle*, sect. 5.6.

44. *Nicomachean Ethics* 1113a1–2, also 1143b4–5.

45. O'Neill, "The Power of Example," p. 167. See also the more detailed account in her book *Towards Justice and Virtue*, sects. 3.4 and 6.7. A similar line seems to be taken by Höffe, "Universalist Ethics and the Faculty of Judgment," pp. 60–61.

46. Aristotle, *De Motu Animalium* 701a7–25.

47. See, besides GMS 412, GMS 427, whereas GMS 389, it is true, calls for "judgment sharpened by experience" to give the a priori laws access to the human will. As for the second *Critique*, the frequent references to reason's capacity to determine the will directly (for instance KpV 23–25) seem to rely on the account

of agency given in GMS 412, and the explanation of will in KpV 32 as the faculty of rational beings to determine their causality through the conception of a rule comes straight out of that theory.

48. GMS 389, 407; KrV A134/B173.

49. See the "Profession de foi du Vicaire savoyard" in the fourth book of Jean-Jacques Rousseau's *Emile, ou de l'éducation*.

50. Alasdair MacIntyre, *After Virtue*, p. 145.

51. O'Neill, "Kant after Virtue," especially p. 160.

52. O'Neill, "The Power of Example," p. 167.

53. KrV A133/B172. See also KdU 169 and the essay "Über den Gemein-spruch," p. 275.

54. Similarly O'Neill, "Towards Justice and Virtue," p. 180.

55. O'Neill, "The Power of Example," p. 181. William James, *The Principles of Psychology*, vol. 2, p. 1139, makes a similar point.

56. KrV A133–134/B 172–173; "Über den Gemeinspruch," p. 275.

CHAPTER FOUR

1. Adopting Ranke's famous phrase that the point of history is to show "wie es eigentlich gewesen."

2. Zeno Vendler, *Linguistics in Philosophy*, p. 144.

3. Jonathan Bennett, *Events and Their Names*, sect. 60.

4. See for instance P. M. S. Hacker, "Events and the Exemplification of Properties."

5. By contrast to Davidson's peculiar usage, "Actions, Reasons, and Causes," p. 3.

6. Annette Baier makes the same point, "Rhyme and Reason," p. 125.

7. For instance Arthur Danto, *Analytical Philosophy of History*, chap. 7.

8. Walsh, *An Introduction to Philosophy of History*, p. 33, contrasting, as he calls them, 'plain' and 'significant' narratives, distinguishes the former from the latter by their saying "wie es eigentlich gewesen" (what really happened). He thus implies that the significant narratives do not say "wie es eigentlich gewesen."

9. Danto, *Analytical Philosophy of History*, p. 140, makes a similar point.

10. A. Baier, *Rhyme and Reason*, p. 125, Marco Iorio, *Echte Gründe, Echte Vernunft*, p. 144.

11. Norman Malcolm, " 'I Believe That p'," argues that in a vast number of cases to say things like "I think there will be frost tonight" is not even to refer to one's own state of mind, but is only to qualify one's assertion.

12. G. E. M. Anscombe, *Intention*, sect. 35.

13. Derek Parfit, "Reasons and Motivation," n. 28, suggests, strangely, that it is both acceptable to say that reasons are desires and beliefs and to say that reasons are the things desired or believed.

14. Anscombe, too, argues that the farmer's practical reasoning "should just be given in the form 'They have Jersey cows in the Hereford market, so I'll go there,' " and that adding the premise "I want a good Jersey cow" is misconceived, *Intention*, sect. 35.

15. Robert Audi, "Acting for Reasons," p. 148.

16. Thomas Hobbes, *Leviathan*, chap. 36, final para.

17. George Wilson, *The Intentionality of Human Action*, p. 13.

18. KrV A 809/B 837.

19. Annette Baier, *Rhyme and Reason*, p. 125.

20. Alasdair MacIntyre, "The Intelligibility of Action."

21. Robert Audi, "Acting for Reasons," p. 146. Note also the statement referred to earlier (§ 139) that a reason "is that for the sake of which, and on account of which, one acts," p. 148.

22. Audi, "Acting for Reasons," p. 146.

23. "Explanation and Understanding of Action," p. 54.

24. Ibid., p. 55.

25. Ibid., pp. 54, 59. It should be noted, though, that a slightly later essay of von Wright, "Probleme des Erklärens und Verstehens von Handlungen," evidently a close relative of the essay under discussion, does not contain the suggestion that an external reason needs to be internalized through acknowledgment to count as a reason for which the agent does something.

26. Stoutland, "The Real Reasons," p. 47.

CHAPTER FIVE

1. Danto, *Analytical Philosophy of History*, p. 247.

2. Weiser-Aall, "Weihnacht," in *Handwörterbuch des deutschen Aberglaubens*, ed. H. Bächtold-Stäubli, vol. 10, *Nachträge*, cols. 910–915.

3. Hempel's example, "The Function of General Laws in History," p. 232.

4. See for instance R. F. Atkinson, *Knowledge and Explanation in History*, pp. 95, 101–102.

5. See J. Passmore, "Explanation in Everyday Life, in Science, and in History," p. 122.

6. Morton White, "Historical Explanation," p. 216.

7. Ibid., p. 212.

8. White raises this suspicion, ibid., p. 215 n. 2.

9. For the varieties of explaining see Passmore, "Explanation in Everyday Life, in Science, and in History," pp. 106–107.

10. Hempel, "Aspects of Scientific Explanation," pp. 412–15.

11. Hempel, "Aspects of Scientific Explanation," p. 412. See also David-Hillel Ruben, *Explaining Explanation*, pp. 16–19.

12. Hempel, "The Function of General Laws in History"; *Studies in the Logic of Explanation*.

13. David Lewis, "Causal Explanation," p. 217.

14. William Dray, *Laws and Explanation in History*, chap. 5, and "The Historical Explanation of Actions Reconsidered." Dray in turn acknowledges, *Laws and Explanations in History*, pp. 121–122, his debt to R. G. Collingwood; see the latter's *The Idea of History*.

15. Hayden White, "The Historical Text as Literary Artifact," pp. 85–92, here p. 86.

16. Paul Roth, "How Narratives Explain," p. 468.

17. Hempel, "The Function of General Laws in History," p. 237.

18. Ibid., p. 236.

19. Hempel and Oppenheim, *Studies in the Logic of Explanation*, p. 264.

20. Ibid., p. 251, n. 7. A case in point is Stegmüller's confident statement: "Historical explanations, too, need to be based on laws." ("Wissenschaft und Erkelärung," p. 256.) Further relevant sources are collected by B. Trill and H. Lenk in the article "Erklären, Erklärung" in *Historisches Wörterbuch der Philosophie*.

21. Hume, *Treatise*, p. 105.

22. Hempel, "Aspects of Scientific Explanation," p. 354.

23. See K.-G. Faber, *Theorie der Geschichtswissenschaft;* A. J. Greimas, "Sur l'histoire événementielle et l'histoire fondamentale;" R. Koselleck, "Ereignis und Struktur;" Peter Szondi, "Für eine nicht mehr narrative Historie;" W. Dray, "Narrative versus Analysis in history."

24. Dray defends his conception in this way, *Laws and Explanations in History*, pp. 141–142.

25. Raymond Geuss makes a related point in his critique of Habermas, *The Idea of a Critical Theory*, p. 66.

26. See for instance Weber, *Wirtschaft und Gesellschaft*, pp. 196, 292–293, 504–505; "Die Grenznutzlehre und das 'psychophysische Grundgesetz'," p. 395.

27. Weber, "Der Sinn der 'Wertfreiheit'," p. 534; *Wirtschaft und Gesellschaft*, p. 10.

28. Hayden White, *Metahistory*, part 2.

29. Roth, "How Narratives Explain," p. 469.

30. Davidson, "Actions, Reasons, and Causes," p. 3.

31. See for instance Georg Henrik von Wright, *Explanation and Understanding*, p. 13.

32. David Lewis, "Causal Explanation," p. 228.

33. The classical source is Nelson Goodman, *Fact, Fiction, and Forecast*.

34. See Melden, *Free Action*, pp. 88–90. Melden speaks of explanations by motives, a difference that is immaterial in the present context.

35. Ibid. p. 88.

36. See Davidson, "Actions, Reasons, and Causes," p. 10, and Beckermann, "Intentionale versus kausale Handlungserklärungen," p. 472.

37. Davidson, "Actions, Reasons, and Causes," p. 11.

38. Ibid., p. 10; similarly p. 11.

39. For recent discussions of the distinction see Georg Henrik von Wright, *Explanation and Understanding*; Martin Hollis, *The Philosophy of Social Science*, chap. 7; and Fred Dallmayr and Thomas McCarthy, eds., *Understanding and Social Inquiry*, with useful bibliographies.

40. J. G. Droysen, "Grundriß der Historik," sects. 14, 15, 7.

41. Wilhelm Dilthey, "Der Aufbau der geschichtlichen Welt in den Geisteswissenschaften," pp. 82–88.

CHAPTER SIX

1. The reasoning that follows is not owed to any particular author, but it brings together lines of argument taken from the following texts: Peter Winch, *The Idea of a Social Science*; Charles Taylor, "Interpretation and the Sciences of

Man"; Taylor, "Social Theory as Practice"; Alasdair MacIntyre, *After Virtue*, chap. 15; MacIntyre, "The Intelligibility of Action"; Martin Hollis, *The Philosophy of Social Science*, chap. 7.

2. This is the point MacIntyre makes in saying: "the concept of an intelligible action is a more fundamental concept than that of an action as such," *After Virtue*, p. 195. See also Taylor: "in so far as we are talking about behaviour as action, hence in terms of meaning," "Interpretation and the Sciences of Man," p. 24.

3. Winch, *The Idea of a Social Science*, pp. 51–52.

4. MacIntyre, "The Intelligibility of Action," p. 66.

5. Taylor, "Social Theory as Practice," p. 105.

6. Hollis, *The Philosophy of Social Science*, p. 155. See also Taylor, "Interpretation and the Sciences of Man," p. 32.

7. Aristotle, *De anima* III.8, 431b21.

8. Martin Heidegger, *Über den Humanismus*, p. 53.

9. See for instance Taylor, "Social Theory as Practice."

10. "Gesetzt der Physiognome haschte den Menschen einmal, so käme es nur auf einen braven Entschluß an sich wieder auf Jahrhunderte unbegreiflich zu machen." *Schriften und Briefe* 3, 269.

11. *Philosophische Untersuchungen*, 2, p. 263.

12. Rawls, "Two Concepts of Rules."

13. See for instance John Searle, *Speech Acts*, chap. 2.5; Taylor, "Interpretation and the Sciences of Man," pp. 33–36; Hollis, *The Cunning of Reason*, pp. 137–138.

14. Searle, *Speech Acts*, p. 33; Hollis, *The Cunning of Reason*, p. 138.

15. Hollis, *The Philosophy of Social Science*, p. 153.

16. Taylor, "Interpretation and the Sciences of Man," pp. 34–35. The final clause of the quotation sounds truncated, and perhaps "possible" should be inserted before "without."

17. See Rawls, "Two Concepts of Rules," p. 25; Searle, *Speech Acts*, p. 35.

18. Rawls, "Two Concepts of Rules," p. 25, the emphasis being Rawls's. Similarly Searle, *Speech Acts*, pp. 35–36.

19. Searle, *Speech Acts*, p. 51.

20. Ibid., p. 51.

21. Ibid., chap. 2.7.

22. Winch, *The Idea of a Social Science*, p. 52; Hollis, *The Cunning of Reason*, p. 138.

23. Taylor, "Social Theory as Practice," p. 105.

CHAPTER SEVEN

1. Stephen Darwall, *Impartial Reason*, chap. 1.

2. Ibid., p. 31.

3. Iorio, *Echte Gründe, echte Vernunft*, sect. 6.7, also draws attention to this kind of case.

4. For Jonathan Dancy, *Practical Reality*, sect. 6.1, the fact that these cases are peculiar is evidence against the desire/belief theory, since on that theory they would have to be deemed standard.

5. Darwall, *Impartial Reason*, p. 37, makes a similar point.

6. Dancy disagrees: his solution to the problem of the agent in error rests on allowing "that something that is not the case can explain an action." (*Practical Reality*, sect. 6.3.)

7. Bernard Williams, "Internal and External Reasons," p. 102.

8. Davidson, "Mental Events," p. 221; "Psychology as Philosophy, pp. 236–39; Peter Lanz, *Menschliches Handeln zwischen Kausalität und Rationalität*, pp. 102–5.

9. Bittner, "Verständnis für Unvernünftige."

10. For traditional transcendental arguments this was shown by Barry Stroud, "Transcendental Arguments."

11. As it is taken for granted, for instance, in Davidson, "Psychology as Philosophy," p. 237, and Lanz, "The Explanatory Force of Action Explanations," p. 298, an essay with which Davidson in turn expresses emphatic agreement, "Reply to Peter Lanz," p. 302. Doubts on this head are nourished by the empirical research of Tversky and Kahneman, for instance, "Rational Choice and the Framing of Decisions." Davidson, "Hempel on Explaining Action," pp. 272–73, has a discussion of Tversky's earlier paper, "A Critique of Expected Utility Theory," but it is brief and, with regard to the point at issue here, unsatisfactory.

12. John McDowell, in his 1982 lecture "Criteria, Defeasibility, and Knowledge," has effectively dismantled this traditional line of argument. The disjunctive conception he advocates instead, namely, that an appearance can be either a mere appearance or the fact that such-and-such is the case making itself perceptually manifest to someone (p. 472), is a close parallel in the theoretical field to the solution recommended here for the practical case.

CHAPTER EIGHT

1. With G. F. Schueler, *Desire*, p. 66, and against the suggestion of Williams, "Internal and External Reasons," p. 101, and his usage, as shown in *Ethics and the Limits of Philosophy*, p. 192.

2. Smith uses this expression, *The Moral Problem*, p. 94.

3. Darwall uses this expression, *Impartial Reason*, p. 30.

4. Thus Williams: "If it is true that *A* has a reason to ø, then it must be possible that he should ø for that reason," "Internal Reasons and the Obscurity of Blame," p. 5.

5. Michael Smith, *The Moral Problem*, pp. 94–98.

6. Similarly Williams, "Internal Reasons and the Obscurity of Blame," p. 5.

7. Thomas Pogge's objection, in correspondence.

8. Stampe, "The Authority of Desire," pp. 345–346.

9. Davidson, "Actions, Reasons, and Causes," p. 9.

10. Ibid., pp. 9–12.

CHAPTER NINE

1. Williams's 1980 essay "Internal and External Reasons" opened the current discussion of internalism.

2. I am using here Williams's explanation in his more recent essay "Internal Reasons and the Obscurity of Blame," p. 35.

3. Williams, "Internal and External Reasons," p. 109; *Ethics and the Limits of Philosophy*, p. 192.

4. Christine Korsgaard, "Scepticism about Practical Reason."

5. Jay Wallace, "How to Argue about Practical Reason." Wallace takes himself to be developing ideas of Thomas Nagel, *The Possibility of Altruism*, chap. 5.

6. See in particular Rachel Cohon, "Are External Reasons Impossible?"; Brad Hooker, "Williams' Argument against External Reasons"; Elijah Millgram, "Williams' Argument against External Reasons"; Derek Parfit, "Reasons and Motivation." The interpretation advocated here is closest to Cohon's.

7. Williams, "Internal and External Reasons," p. 106.

8. Ibid., p. 107.

9. Ibid., pp. 102, 106.

10. Williams, "Internal Reasons and the Obscurity of Blame," p. 39.

11. Wilson's suggestion, see in particular his recent essay "Reasons as Causes for Action," p. 68.

12. My suggestion put forward earlier, § 159.

13. Williams, "Internal and External Reasons," p. 107.

14. See for instance Audi, "Acting for Reasons," p. 147; Darwall, *Impartial Reason*, p. 199; Williams, "Internal Reasons and the Obscurity of Blame," p. 5.

15. Dancy, *Practical Reality*, chap. 1.1.

16. Joseph Raz dissents, since he treats the statement that somebody has reason to do something and the statement that he ought to do it as equivalent, *Practical Reason and Norms*, pp. 29–30.

17. This line of argument may be found in Jean Hampton, "Rethinking Reason," sect. 6, and Christine Korsgaard, "The Normativity of Instrumental Reason," p. 229.

18. Kant, GMS 432–433.

19. Korsgaard, "The Normativity of Instrumental Reason," p. 245; see also Korsgaard, *The Sources of Normativity*, pp. 103–105.

20. Korsgaard, "The Normativity of Instrumental Reason," p. 243.

21. GMS 414.

22. See Korsgaard, "The Normativity of Instrumental Reason," pp. 219 and 239 with n. 52, and compare Kant, KpV, p. 32, *Religion*, p. 139.

23. Korsgaard, "The Normativity of Instrumental Reason," p. 254; see also p. 247. Korsgaard prefers elsewhere the language of one's "practical identity" (*The Sources of Normativity*, pp. 100–102), but in substance the idea is the same.

24. See G. A. Cohen, "Reason, Humanity and the Moral Law," p. 185.

25. "The Normativity of Instrumental Reason," pp. 247, 254.

26. For instance ibid., p. 215.

27. John Broome, "Normative Requirements" and "Practical Reasoning."

28. "Normative Requirements," sects. 2–3. Actually he distinguishes four such relations, but the fourth, normative recommending, bears little interest in the present context.

29. Broome, "Normative Requirements," sects. 3, 6.

30. Broome's example in "Practical Reasoning."

31. Ibid., sect. 4; similarly "Normative Requirements," sect. 2.

32. Broome, "Normative Requirements," sects. 5–6, "Practical Reasoning," sect. 4.

33. Broome, "Normative Requirements," sects. 5–6, "Practical Reasoning," sect. 5.

34. Broome, "Normative Requirements," sects. 5–6.

35. Ibid., sect. 6.

36. The point is developed at more length in my essay "On Learning from Experience."

37. Korsgaard, "The Normativity of Instrumental Reason," pp. 228–229.

CHAPTER TEN

1. Broome argues that this holds for "good" and "better" as well; "Goodness Is Reducible to Betterness," pp. 163–164.

2. Joseph Raz, *Practical Reason and Norms*, p. 26. See also Raz, "Reasons for Action, Decisions and Norms," pp. 129–130.

3. Raz, *Practical Reason and Norms*, p. 26n.

4. See in particular Frankfurt, "The Importance of What We Care About," pp. 80–81.

5. Ibid., p. 85.

6. *Necessity, Volition, and Love*, p. 162.

7. "The Importance of What We Care About," pp. 80–82.

8. *Necessity, Volition, and Love*, p. 130.

9. I owe the expression to Martin Hollis.

10. Frankfurt, "The Importance of What We Care About," pp. 86–87; see also *Necessity, Volition, and Love*, p. 80.

11. "The Importance of What We Care About," pp. 80–81.

CHAPTER ELEVEN

1. Wilson, *The Intentionality of Human Action*, p. 171.

2. Sehon, while supporting Wilson's argument for holding reason explanations to be explanations by purpose, admits to "having no *analysis* of the crucial teleological connectives," "Teleology and the Nature of Mental States," p. 65.

3. Aristotle, *Nicomachean Ethics* I.1.

4. Smith, *The Moral Problem*, pp. 116–117.

5. Sarah Broadie, *Ethics with Aristotle*, p. 10.

6. Ibid., pp. 8–9.

7. See Aristotle, *Physics* 198b18–21.

8. Charlton, *Aristotle's* Physics *Books 1 and 2*, p. 120. See also the discussion in Broadie, *Nature, Change, and Agency*, sects. 28–42.

9. This is the line Iorio takes, *Echte Gründe, echte Vernunft*, sect. 7.7.

10. Aristotle makes a similar point, *Nicomachean Ethics* X.4.

11. Ibid., 1094a16–17; see also 1094a4–5, 1140b5–6.

12. *'Ephiesthai'*, *Nicomachean Ethics* 1094a2.

13. See Aristotle, *Nicomachean Ethics* 1094a23–24.

14. David Velleman's objection, in correspondence.

15. 'Pros to telos', for instance *Nicomachean Ethics* 1145a6.

CHAPTER TWELVE

1. This is the title of Alvin Goldman's book of 1976.

2. *Nicomachean Ethics* 1113a5–9.

3. Mele is one of the few authors to insist on the link between the problem of 'akrasia' and a conception of 'enkrateia', that is, self-control (*Irrationality*, p. 50).

4. George Wilson, *The Intentionality of Human Action*, chap. 7. 2.

5. I suggested that line in "Handlungen und Wirkungen," p. 25.

6. MacIntyre, "The Intelligibility of Action," p. 75.

7. A representative statement of the idea is in Darwall, *Impartial Reason*, pp. 35, 80.

8. See GMS 389, 411, KpV 31.

9. For instance Alan Gewirth, *Reason and Morality*; Stephen Darwall, *Impartial Reason*; David Gauthier, *Morals by Agreement*.

10. I have argued that morality is not a demand of reason in *What Reason Demands*.

11. Thomas Hobbes, *Leviathan*, chap. 14.

12. See GMS 413–414. Kant's normative understanding of instrumental rationality was emphasized by Thomas Hill, "The Hypothetical Imperative," and more recently by Jean Hampton, "On Instrumental Rationality."

13. See for instance G. R. Grice, *The Grounds of Moral Judgment*, p. 27, D. A. J. Richards, *A Theory of Reasons for Action*, pp. 27–28; Thomas Hill, "The Hypothetical Imperative," pp. 18, 32.

14. A more elaborate argument for denying even requirements of instrumental rationality is given in my article "On Learning from Experience."

15. Romans 2:14.

16. "The Kantian Conception of Autonomy," p. 87.

17. This is how Allan Gibbard uses the word "rational," *Wise Choices, Apt Feelings*, pp. 6–7.

18. See GMS 436, 440, 432–433, and Thomas Hill's illuminating articles "Humanity as an End in Itself," especially p. 47, and "The Kantian Conception of Autonomy."

19. The basic idea here is Hegelian, see *Phänomenologie des Geistes*, chap. VCa and VIC.

20. Shakespeare, *Hamlet*, end of act 1.

21. GMS 453.

Bibliography

Allison, Henry E. (1990). *Kant's Theory of Freedom*. Cambridge: Cambridge University Press.

———. (1996). "Kant on Freedom: A Reply to My Critics," in Allison, *Idealism and Freedom*. Cambridge: Cambridge University Press.

Annas, Julia (1981). *An Introduction to Plato's* Republic, Oxford: Clarendon Press.

Anscombe, G. E. M. (1972). *Intention*. Oxford: Blackwell.

Apel, Karl-Otto (1972). "The A Priori of Communication and the Foundation of the Humanities." *Man and World 5*, 3–37

Aristotle. *De Anima*.

———. *De Motu Animalium*.

———. *Nicomachean Ethics*.

———. *Physics*.

Atkinson, R. F. (1978). *Knowledge and Explanation in History*. Ithaca: Cornell University Press.

Audi, Robert (1973). "Intending," in Audi, *Action, Intention, and Reason*. Ithaca: Cornell University Press (1993).

———. (1986). "Acting for Reasons," in Audi, *Action, Intention, and Reason*. Ithaca: Cornell University Press (1993).

Ayer, A. J. (1970). *Man as a Subject for Science*. San Francisco: Freeman Cooper.

Bächtold-Stäubli, H., ed. (1938/1941). *Handwörterbuch des deutschen Aberglaubens*. Berlin: de Gruyter.

Baier, Annette C. (1985). "Rhyme and Reason: Reflection on Davidson's Version of Having Reasons," in Ernest LePore and Brian McLaughlin, eds., *Actions and Events*. Oxford: Blackwell.

Beckermann, Ansgar (1977). *Gründe und Ursachen*, Kronberg: Scriptor.

———. (1979). "Intentionale versus kausale Handlungserklärungen," in H. Lenk, ed., *Handlungstheorien: Interdisziplinär*. Munich: Wilhelm Fink.

Bennett, Jonathan (1988). *Events and Their Names*. Oxford: Clarendon Press.

Bittner, Rüdiger (1974). "Maximen," in G. Funke, ed., *Akten des 4. Internationalen Kant-Kongresses*. Berlin: de Gruyter.

————. (1980). *What Reason Demands*. Theodore Talbot, trans. Cambridge: Cambridge University Press.

————. (1986). "Handlungen und Wirkungen," in G. Prauss, ed., *Handlungstheorie und Transzendentalphilosophie*. Frankfurt: Klostermann.

————. (1989). "Verständnis für Unvernünftige." *Zeitschrift für philosophische Forschung 43*, 577–92.

————. (1994). "On Learning from Experience," in Hans Friedrich Fulda and Rolf-Peter Horstmann, eds., *Vernunftbegriffe in der Moderne*. Stuttgart: Klett-Cotta.

Bratman, Michael E. (1987). *Intention, Plans, and Practical Reason*. Cambridge: Harvard University Press.

Broadie, Sarah Waterlow (1982). *Nature, Change, and Agency in Aristotle's Physics*. Oxford: Clarendon Press.

————. (1991). *Ethics with Aristotle*. New York: Oxford University Press.

Broome, John (1999). "Goodness Is Reducible to Betterness: The Evil of Death Is the Value of Life," in Broome, *Ethics out of Economics*. Cambridge: Cambridge University Press.

————. (1999). "Normative Requirements." *Ratio 12*, 398–419.

————. (n.d.). "Practical Reasoning," typescript.

Charlton, William (1970). *Aristotle's* Physics, *Books 1 and 2*. Oxford: Clarendon Press.

Churchland, Paul (1970). "The Logical Character of Action-Explanations." *Philosophical Review 79*, 214–36.

Cohen, G. A. (1996). "Reason, Humanity, and the Moral Law," in Christine M. Korsgaard, *The Sources of Normativity*. Cambridge: Cambridge University Press.

Cohon, Rachel (1986). "Are External Reasons Possible?" Ethics 96, 545–556.

————. (1988). "Hume and Humeanism in Ethics." *Pacific Philosophical Quarterly 69*, 99–116.

Collingwood, R. G. (1946). *The Idea of History*. Oxford: Oxford University Press.

Collins, John (1988). "Belief, Desire, and Revision." *Mind 92*, 333–342.

Condorcet, M. A. N., marquis de (1971). *Esquisse d'un tableau historique des progrès de l'esprit humain*. Paris: Editions Sociales.

Cooper, John M. (1975). *Reason and Human Good in Aristotle*. Cambridge: Harvard University Press.

————. (1984). "Plato's Theory of Human Motivation." *History of Philosophy Quarterly 1*, 3–21.

Dallmayr, Fred, and Thomas McCarthy, eds. (1977). *Understanding and Social Inquiry*. Notre Dame, Ind.: Notre Dame University Press.

Danto, Arthur (1965). *Analytical Philosophy of History*. Cambridge: Cambridge University Press.

Dancy, Jonathan (1993). *Moral Reasons*. Oxford: Blackwell.

————. (2000). *Practical Reality*. Oxford: Oxford University Press.

Darwall, Stephen (1983). *Impartial Reason*. Ithaca: Cornell University Press.

Davidson, Donald (1963). "Actions, Reasons, and Causes," in Davidson, *Essays on Actions and Events*. Oxford: Clarendon Press (1980).

———. (1970). "Mental Events," in: Davidson, *Essays on Actions and Events*. Oxford: Clarendon Press (1980).

———. (1974). "Psychology as Philosophy," in Davidson, *Essays on Actions and Events*. Oxford: Clarendon Press (1980).

———. (1976). "Hempel on Explaining Action," in Davidson, *Essays on Actions and Events*. Oxford: Clarendon Press (1980).

———. (1978). "Intending," in Davidson, *Essays on Actions and Events*. Oxford: Clarendon Press (1980).

———. (1993). "Reply to Peter Lanz," in Ralf Stoecker, ed., *Reflecting Davidson*. Berlin: de Gruyter.

Dennett, Daniel C. (1981). "Artificial Intelligence as Philosophy and as Psychology," in Daniel C. Dennett, *Brainstorms*. Cambridge, Mass.: MIT Press.

Dilthey, Wilhelm (1910). "Der Aufbau der geschichtlichen Welt in den Geisteswissenschaften," quoted by page numbers in vol. 7 of Dilthey, *Gesammelte Schriften*. Stuttgart: Teubner (1958).

Dray, William (1957). *Laws and Explanation in History*. Oxford: Oxford University Press.

———. (1963). "The Historical Explanation of Actions Reconsidered," in S. Hook, ed., *Philosophy and History*. New York: New York University Press (1963).

———. (1985). "Narrative versus Analysis in History," in Joseph Margolis et al., eds., *Rationality, Relativism and the Human Sciences*. Doordrecht: Nijhoff (1986).

Droysen, Johann G. (1882). "Grundriß der Historik," in Droysen, ed. Rudolf Hübner. *Historik* Munich: Oldenbourg (1974).

Faber, Karl-Georg (1971). *Theorie der Geschichtswissenschaft*. Munich: Beck.

Ferrari, G. R. F. (1985). "The Struggle in the Soul: Plato, *Phaedrus* 253c7–255a1." *Ancient Philosophy 5*, 1–10.

Frankfurt, Harry G. (1988). "The Importance of What We Care About," in Frankfurt, *The Importance of What We Care About*. Cambridge: Cambridge University Press.

———. (1999). "On Caring," in Frankfurt, *Necessity, Volition, and Love*. Cambridge: Cambridge University Press.

Gauthier, David (1986). *Morals by Agreement*. Oxford: Clarendon Press.

Geach, Peter (1957). *Mental Acts*. London: Routledge.

Geuss, Raymond (1981). *The Idea of a Critical Theory*. Cambridge: Cambridge University Press.

Gewirth, Alan (1978). *Reason and Morality*. Chicago: University of Chicago Press.

Gibbard, Allan (1990). *Wise Choices, Apt Feelings: A Theory of Normative Judgment*. Cambridge, Mass.: Harvard University Press.

Goldman, Alvin I. (1976). *A Theory of Human Action*. Princeton, N.J.: Princeton University Press.

Goodman, Nelson (1965). *Fact, Fiction, and Forecast*. Indianapolis: Bobbs-Merrill.

Greimas, Algirdas J. (1973). "Sur l'histoire événementielle et l'histoire fondamentale," in Reinhart Koselleck and Wolf-Dieter Stempel, eds., *Geschichte—Ereignis und Erzählung, Poetik und Hermeneutik* 5, Munich: Fink.

Grice, Geoffrey Russell (1967). *The Grounds of Moral Judgment*. Cambridge: Cambridge University Press.

Grimm, Jacob, and Wilhelm Grimm (1996). "Von dem Machandelboom," in *Grimms Kinder- und Hausmärchen*. Darmstadt: Wissenschaftliche Buchgesellschaft.

Hacker, P. M. S. (1981). "Events and the Exemplification of Properties." *Philosophical Quarterly 31*, 242–47.

Hampton, Jean E. (1992). "Rethinking Reason." *American Philosophical Quarterly 29*, 219–36.

———. (1996). "On Instrumental Rationality," in J. B. Schneewind, ed., *Reason, Ethics and Society: Themes from Kurt Baier, with His Responses*. Chicago: Open Court.

———. (1998). *The Authority of Reason*. Cambridge: Cambridge University Press.

Hart, Herbert L. A. (1968). "Intention and Punishment," in Hart, *Punishment and Responsibility*. Oxford: Clarendon Press.

Hegel, G. W. F. (1952). *Phänomenologie des Geistes*. Hamburg: Meiner. (In English: *Phenomenology of Spirit*, trans. A. V. Miller. Oxford: Oxford University Press [1977]).

Heidegger, Martin (1968). *Über den Humanismus*. Frankfurt: Klostermann.

Hempel, Carl G. (1942). "The Function of General Laws in History," in Hempel. *Aspects of Scientific Explanation: And Other Essays in the Philosophy of Science*. New York: Free Press (1965).

———. (1963). "Reason and Covering Laws in Historical Explanation," in S. Hook, ed., *Philosophy and History*. New York: New York University Press.

———. (1965). "Aspects of Scientific Explanation," in Hempel, *Aspects of Scientific Explanation: And Other Essays in the Philosophy of Science*. New York: Free Press.

Hempel, Carl G., and P. Oppenheim (1948). *Studies in the Logic of Explanation*, in Hempel, *Aspects of Scientific Explanation: And Other Essays in the Philosophy of Science*. New York: Free Press (1965).

Hill, Thomas E., Jr. (1973). "The Hypothetical Imperative." *Philosophical Review 82*, 429–450.

———. (1980). "Humanity as an End in Itself." *Ethics 91*, 84–99.

———. (1991). "Autonomy and Benevolent Lies," in Hill, *Autonomy and Self-respect*. Cambridge: Cambridge University Press.

———. (1992). "The Kantian Conception of Autonomy," in Hill, *Dignity and Practical Reason in Kant's Theory*. Ithaca: Cornell University Press.

———. (1992). "Kant's Argument for the Rationality of Moral Conduct," in Hill, *Dignity and Practical Reason in Kant's Theory*. Ithaca: Cornell University Press.

———. (1992). "Kant's Theory of Practical Reason," in Hill, *Dignity and Practical Reason in Kant's Theory*. Ithaca: Cornell University Press.

Hobbes, Thomas (1651). *Leviathan*.

Höffe, Otfried (1993). "Universalist Ethics and the Faculty of Judgment: An Aristotelian Look at Kant." *Philosophical Forum 25*, 55–71.

Hollis, Martin (1987). *The Cunning of Reason*. Cambridge: Cambridge University Press.

————. (1991). "Penny Pinching and Backward Induction." *Journal of Philosophy* *88*, 473–88.

————. (1994). *The Philosophy of Social Science: An Introduction.* Cambridge: Cambridge University Press.

Hooker, Brad (1987). "Williams' Argument against External Reasons." *Analysis* *47*, 42–44.

Hudson, Hud (1994). *Kant's Compatibilism.* Ithaca: Cornell University Press.

Humberstone, I. L. (1992). "Direction of Fit." *Mind 101*, 59–83.

Hume, David (1978). *A Treatise of Human Nature*, ed. P. H. Nidditch. Oxford: Clarendon Press.

Iorio, Marco (1998). *Echte Gründe, echte Vernunft.* Dresden: Dresden University Press.

James, William (1981). *The Principles of Psychology*, ed. Burkhardt et al. 3 vols. Cambridge, Mass.: Harvard University Press.

Kahn, Charles H. (1987). "Plato's Theory of Desire." *Review of Metaphysics 41*, 77–103.

Kant, Immanuel (1781 and 1787). *Kritik der reinen Vernunft* (abbrev.: KrV), in Königlich preußische Akademie der Wissenschaften, ed., *Kant's Gesammelte Schriften*, vols. 3 and 4. Berlin (1911); quoted by page numbers of the two original editions.

————. (1785). *Grundlegung zur Metaphysik der Sitten* (abbrev. GMS), quoted by page numbers in vol. 4 of the Academy edition.

————. (1788). *Kritik der praktischen Vernunft* (abbrev.: KpV), quoted by page numbers in vol. 5 of the Academy edition.

————. (1790). *Kritik der Urteilskraft* (abbrev.: KdU), quoted by page numbers in vol. 5 of the Academy edition.

————. (1793). *Die Religion innerhalb der Grenzen der bloßen Vernunft* (abbrev.: *Religion*), quoted by page numbers in vol. 6 of the Academy edition.

————. (1793). "Über den Gemeinspruch: Das mag in der Theorie richtig sein, taugt aber nicht für die Praxis," quoted by page numbers in vol. 8 of the Academy edition.

————. (1979). "Moralphilosophie Mrongovius" (notes from Kant's lectures) in *Kant's gesammelte Schriften*, vol. 27.2.2. Berlin: de Gruyter.

Kenny, Anthony (1963). *Action, Emotion and Will.* London: Routledge and Kegan Paul.

————. (1975). *Will, Freedom and Power.* Oxford: Blackwell.

————. (1979). *Aristotle's Theory of the Will.* New Haven: Yale University Press.

Kim, Jaegwon (1996). *Philosophy of Mind.* Boulder, Colo.: Westview Press.

Korsgaard, Christine 1986, "Scepticism about Practical Reason," *Journal of Philosophy 83*, 5–25.

————. (1996). *The Sources of Normativity.* Cambridge: Cambridge University Press.

————. (1997). "The Normativity of Instrumental Reason," in Garrett Cullity and Berys Gaut, eds., *Ethics and Practical Reason.* Oxford: Clarendon Press.

Koselleck, Reinhart (1973). "Ereignis und Struktur," in Reinhart Koselleck and

Wolf-Dieter Stempel, eds., *Geschichte—Ereignis und Erzählung*. Poetik und Hermeneutik 5. Munich: Fink.

Laberge, Pierre (1989). "La définition de la volonté comme faculté d'agir selon la représentation des lois," in Otfried Höffe, ed., *Grundlegung zur Metaphysik der Sitten*. Frankfurt: Klostermann.

Lanz, Peter (1987). *Menschliches Handeln zwischen Kausalität und Rationalität*. Frankfurt: Athenäum.

———. (1993). "The Explanatory Force of Action Explanations," in Ralf Stoecker, ed., *Reflecting Davidson*. Berlin: de Gruyter.

Lear, Jonathan (1988). *Aristotle: The Desire to Understand*. Cambridge: Cambridge University Press.

Lewis, David (1986). "Causal Explanation," in Lewis, *Philosophical Papers*, vol. 2. New York: Oxford University Press.

———. (1988). "Desire as Belief." *Mind* 97, 323–32.

Lichtenberg, Georg Christoph (1972). *Schriften und Briefe 3*. Wolfgang Promies, ed. Munich: Hanser.

Little, Margaret O. (1997). "Virtue as Knowledge: Objections from the Philosophy of Mind." *Nous 31*, 59–79.

Locke, Don (1982). "Beliefs, Desires and Reasons for Action." *American Philosophical Quarterly 19*, 241–49.

MacIntyre, Alasdair (1981). *After Virtue*. London: Duckworth.

———. (1986). "The Intelligibility of Action," in Joseph Margolis et al., eds., *Rationality, Relativism and the Human Sciences*. Dordrecht: Nijhoff.

Mackie, J. L. (1977). *Ethics*. New York: Penguin Books.

Malcolm, Norman (1991). " 'I Believe That p'," in Ernest Lepore and Robert van Gulick, eds., *John Searle and His Critics*. Oxford: Blackwell.

McDowell, John (1978). "Are Moral Requirements Hypothetical Imperatives?" *Proceedings of the Aristotelian Society,* suppl. vol., 13–29.

———. 1982. "Criteria, Defeasibility and Knowledge". *Proceedings of the British Academy 68*, 455–479.

McGinn, Colin (1979). "Action and its Explanation," in Neil Bolton, ed., *Philosophical Problems in Psychology*. London: Methuen.

McNaughton, David (1988). *Moral Vision*. Oxford: Blackwell.

Meerbote, Ralf (1982). "Wille and Willkür in Kant's Theory of Action," in Moltke S. Gram, ed., *Interpreting Kant*. Iowa City: University of Iowa Press.

———. (1984). "Commentary: Kant on Freedom and the Rational and Morally Good Will," in Allen W. Wood, ed., *Self and Nature in Kant's Philosophy*. Ithaca: Cornell University Press.

Melden, A. I. (1961). *Free Action*. London: Routledge and Kegan Paul.

———. (1977). *Rights and Persons*. Oxford: Blackwell.

Mele, Alfred (1987). *Irrationality*. New York: Oxford University Press.

———. (1992). *Springs of Action*. New York: Oxford University Press.

Millgram, Elijah (1996). "Williams' Argument against External Reasons." *Nous 30*, 197–220.

Moline, Jon (1978). "Plato on the Complexity of the Psyche." *Archiv für Geschichte der Philosophie 60*, 1–26.

————. (1981). *Plato's Theory of Understanding*. Madison: University of Wisconsin Press.

Morton, Adam (1991). *Disasters and Dilemmas*. Oxford: Blackwell.

Nagel, Thomas (1970). *The Possibility of Altruism*. Oxford: Clarendon Press.

Nowell-Smith, P. H. (1954). *Ethics*. Harmondsworth: Pelican.

Nussbaum, Martha (1978). *Aristotle's* De motu animalium. Princeton, N.J.: Princeton University Press.

O'Neill, Onora (1989). "Kant after Virtue," in O'Neill, *Constructions of Reason*. Cambridge: Cambridge University Press.

————. (1989). "The Power of Example," in O'Neill, *Constructions of Reason*. Cambridge: Cambridge University Press.

————. (1989). "Universal Laws and Ends-in-themselves," in O'Neill, *Constructions of Reason*. Cambridge: Cambridge University Press.

————. (1996). "Kant's Virtues," in Roger Crisp, ed., *How Should One Live?* Oxford: Clarendon Press.

————. (1996). *Towards Justice and Virtue. A Constructive Account of Practical Reasoning*. Cambridge: Cambridge University Press.

Parfit, Derek (1997). "Reasons and Motivation." *Proceedings of the Aristotelian Society*, suppl. vol. 71, 99–130.

Pascal, Blaise (1963). Pensées, in *Oeuvres complètes*, Louis Lafuma, ed. Paris: Éditions du Seuil.

Passmore, John (1962). "Explanation in Everyday Life, in Science, and in History." *History and Theory 2*, 105–23.

Plato. *Phaidros*.

————. *Politeia*.

————. (1993). *Werke. Vol. 3, 4 Phaidros*. Translation and commentary by Ernst Heitsch. Göttingen: Vandenhoeck and Ruprecht.

Platts, Mark (1979). *Ways of Meaning*. London: Routledge and Kegan Paul.

Price, Huw (1989). "Defending Desire-as-Belief." *Mind 98*, 119–27.

Rawls, John (1955). "Two Concepts of Rules." *Philosophical Review 64*, 3–32.

Raz, Joseph (1975). *Practical Reason and Norms*. London: Hutchinson.

————. (1978). "Reasons for Action, Decisions and Norms," in Raz, ed., *Practical Reasoning*. Oxford: Oxford University Press.

Reath, Andrews (1989). "Kant's Theory of Moral Sensibility." *Kant-Studien 80*, 284–302.

Ripley, Charles (1974). "A Theory of Volition." *American Philosophical Quarterly 11*, 141–7.

Romilly, Jacqueline de (1982). "Les conflits de l'âme dans le Phèdre de Platon." *Wiener Studien 16*, 100–13.

Roth, Paul (1988). "Narrative Explanations: The Case of History." *History and Theory 27*, 1–13.

————. (1989). "How Narratives Explain." *Social Research 56*, 449–478.

————. (1991). "Interpretation as Explanation," in David R. Hiley, ed., *The Interpretative Turn*. Ithaca: Cornell University Press.

Rousseau, Jean-Jacques (1964). *Emile, ou de l'éducation*. Paris: Garnier.

Ruben, David-Hillel (1990). *Explaining Explanation*. London: Routledge.

Schauber, Nancy (1996). "Integrity, Commitment, and the Concept of a Person." *American Philosophical Quarterly 33*, 119–29.

Schiffer, Stephen (1976). "A Paradox of Desire." *American Philosophical Quarterly 13*, 195–203.

Schneewind, J. B. (1998). *The Invention of Autonomy*. Cambridge: Cambridge University Press.

Schueler, G. F. (1995). *Desire*. Cambridge, Mass.: MIT Press.

Searle, John (1969). *Speech Acts: An Essay in the Philosophy of Language*. Cambridge: Cambridge University Press.

Sehon, Scott (1994). "Teleology and the Nature of Mental States." *American Philosophical Quarterly 31*, 63–72.

Shakespeare. *Hamlet*

Smith, Michael (1987). "The Humean Theory of Motivation." *Mind 96*, 36–61.

———. (1994). *The Moral Problem*. Oxford: Blackwell.

Stampe, Dennis W. (1987). "The Authority of Desire." *Philosophical Review 96*, 335–81.

Stegmüller, Wolfgang (1970). "Wissenschaft und Erklärung." *Zeitschrift für allgemeine Wissenschaftstheorie 1*, 252–63.

Stoutland, Frederick (1998). "The Real Reasons," in J. Bransen and S. E. Cuypers, eds., *Human Action, Deliberation and Causation*. Dordrecht: Kluwer Academic Publishers.

Strawson, P. F. (1959). *Individuals: An Essay in Descriptive Metaphysics*. London: Methuen.

———. (1966). *The Bounds of Sense: An Essay on Kant's Critique of Pure Reason*. London: Methuen.

Stroud, Barry (1968). "Transcendental Arguments." *Journal of Philosophy 65*, 241–56.

———. (1977). *Hume*. London: Routledge and Kegan Paul.

Szondi, Peter (1973). "Für eine nicht mehr narrative Historie," in Reinhart Koselleck and Wolf-Dieter Stempel, eds., *Geschichte—Ereignis und Erzählung, Poetik und Hermeneutik 5*. Munich: Fink.

Taylor, Charles (1971). "Interpretation and the Sciences of Man," in Taylor, *Philosophy and the Human Sciences*. Philosophical Papers 2. Cambridge: Cambridge University Press (1985).

———. (1985). "Social Theory as Practice," in Taylor, *Philosophy and the Human Sciences*. Philosophical Papers 2. Cambridge: Cambridge University Press.

Thomson, James, and Judith Thomson (1969). "How Not to Derive 'Ought' from 'Is'," in W. D. Hudson, ed., *The Is-ought Question*. London: Macmillan.

Trill, B., and H. Lenk (1972). "Erklären, Erklärung," in J. Ritter, ed., *Historisches Wörterbuch der Philosophie*, vol. 2. Darmstadt: Wissenschaftliche Buchgesellschaft.

Tversky, Amos (1975). "A Critique of Expected Utility Theory: Descriptive and Normative Considerations." *Erkenntnis 9*, 163–73.

Tversky, Amos, and Daniel Kahnemann (1986). "Rational Choice and the Framing of Decisions." *Journal of Business 59*, 251–78.

Tweyman, Stanley (1974). *Reason and Conduct in Hume and His Predecessors*. The Hague: Nijhoff.

Velleman, J. David (1992). "The Guise of the Good." *Nous 26*, 3–26.

Vendler, Zeno (1967). *Linguistics in Philosophy*. Ithaca: Cornell University Press.

Wallace, R. Jay (1990). "How to Argue about Practical Reason." *Mind 99*, 355–385.

———. (1994). *Responsibility and the Moral Sentiments*. Cambridge: Harvard University Press.

Walsh, W. H. (1951). *An Introduction to Philosophy of History*. London: Hutchinson.

von Wright, Georg Henrik (1963). "Practical Inference." *Philosophical Review 72*, 159–79.

———. (1971). *Explanation and Understanding*. Ithaca: Cornell University Press.

———. (1981). "Explanation and Understanding of Action," in von Wright, *Practical Reasons*. Philosophical Papers, vol. 1. London: Blackwell (1983).

———. "Probleme des Erklärens und Verstehens von Handlungen." *Conceptus 19*, Nr. 47, 3–19.

Weber, Max (1972). *Wirtschaft und Gesellschaft*. Tübingen: Mohr.

———. (1982). "Die Grenznutzlehre und das 'psychophysische Grundgesetz'," in Weber, *Gesammelte Aufsätze zur Wissenschaftslehre*. Tübingen: Mohr.

———. (1982). "Der Sinn der 'Wertfreiheit' der soziologischen und ökonomischen Wissenschaften," in Weber, *Gesammelte Aufsätze zur Wissenschaftslehre*. Tübingen: Mohr.

White, Hayden (1973). *Metahistory: The Historical Imagination in Nineteenth-Century Europe*. Baltimore: Johns Hopkins University Press.

———. (1974). "The Historical Text as Literary Artifact." *Clio 3*, 277–303.

White, Morton G. (1943). "Historical Explanation." *Mind 52*, 212–29.

Willaschek, Marcus (1992). *Praktische Vernunft*. Stuttgart: Metzler.

Williams, Bernard (1981). "Internal and External Reasons," in Williams, *Moral Luck*. Cambridge: Cambridge University Press.

———. (1985). *Ethics and the Limits of Philosophy*. Cambridge, Mass.: Harvard University Press.

———. (1989). "Internal Reasons and the Obscurity of Blame." *Logos* (USA) *10*, 1–11.

Wilson, George (1980). *The Intentionality of Human Action*. Stanford: Stanford University Press.

———. (1997). "Reasons as Causes for Action," in Ghita Holmström-Hintikka and Raimo Tuomela, eds., *Contemporary Action Theory*, vol. 1, *Individual Action*. Dordrecht: Kluwer.

Winch, Peter (1958). *The Idea of a Social Science*. London: Routledge and Kegan Paul.

Wittgenstein, Ludwig (1967). *Philosophische Untersuchungen*. Frankfurt: Suhrkamp.

Wolf, Susan (1990). *Freedom within Reason*. New York: Oxford University Press.

Index of Names

N.B.: Numbers denote paragraphs. A name appearing in a note only, not in the accompanying main text, is indicated by the relevant paragraph number and, after "n.," the number of the note.

Index of Subjects

N.B.: Numbers denote paragraphs.

DATE DUE

DATE DUE			
SEP 0 9 2003			
SEP 0 6 2005			
GAYLORD			PRINTED IN U.S.A.